GOOD MEN STILL LIVE!

The Odyssey of a Professional Prisoner

GOOD MEN STILL LIVE!
("I AM THE OTHER KAREL ČAPEK")

by Alan Levy

A Howard Greenfeld Book
J. PHILIP O'HARA, INC.
Chicago

J. Philip O'Hara, Inc. 20 East Huron, Chicago, 60611.
Published simultaneously in Canada by Van Nostrand
Reinhold Ltd., Scarborough, Ontario.

LC Number: 73-4746

ISBN: 0-87955-308-1

First Printing D

"Bohemia is nothing more than the little
country in which you do not live."

—William Sydney Porter (1862–1910),
"The Country of Elusion"

Contents

DEDICATION

Mé Vlastě a mé vlasti,
kde dobří lidé ještě žijí.

    —Karel Čapek (1930—)

One Man's Life

I am Alan Levy and, being an American, I speak to you always in italics and seldom in the past tense. It is the twelfth day of 1971 and I am being interrogated at police headquarters in Prague, Czechoslovakia. I am not saying more than I have to, for I know I am guilty. I have been caught in crimes of truth-telling that—under the "socialist legality" of this Soviet-occupied Republic—carry penalties of 5,615 years in jail. With time off for good behavior, I might see my family again in twenty or thirty centuries—but where?

I must hold my tongue as much as I can, for I have committed manifold crimes that my inquisitors have not discovered yet. A month and a day ago, they seized sixty-five pages of a manuscript I've written. In those pages, describing recent history I've witnessed, I use such punishable words as "invasion" and "occupation" to describe what began in 1968, instead of the approved euphemisms: "timely arrival of troops" and "friendly assistance." I tell of murders and mayhem I saw or verified. I even refer to Comrade Leonid Brezhnev, the Soviet Union's first-among-equals, in the Cosa Nostra terms that befit his crimes against Czechoslovakia.

All this my interrogators know—and they seem remarkably satisfied that simply by relieving me of those sixty-five pages, they have stopped the threat I represent. They refer to the pages as "this book full of lies and slanders against our Republic and our allies, which we cannot allow to be published."

11

Can it be that they don't recognize that every one of the pages they've had in custody for thirty-two days is a Xeroxed photocopy? Don't they realize that sixty-five pages do not a whole book make? Sixty-five pages are barely one-tenth of it. The original manuscript, intact, has been smuggled safely into the West and is right now being processed for publication.* I know better than to tell this to my inquisitors.

Three hours into today's interrogation, I am asked, "Do you know the name Karel Čapek?"

I try the easy answer first, though I know it will do no good: "The Prague science-fiction writer [1890–1938] who introduced the word 'robot' into the English language. Did you know he did that?" My interrogators look at me blankly. "It was in R.U.R. [Rossum's Universal Robots]," I go on. "That play of Čapek's was required reading in the New York City high schools when I was a boy." My interrogators couldn't care less. I meditate on whether R.U.R. is still part of the New York State Regents' requirements—probably not. I meditate very hard, because I am trying to obliterate every hint of another Karel Čapek. . . .

To no avail, for they know I know—after four years of living in Prague and now speaking fluent Czech—that Karel Čapek is an everyday name, meaning Charles Stork; in the Prague phone book, the number of Čapeks must lag only slightly behind Nováks and Novotnýs. My chief interrogator says, "We are talking about the confessed former U.S. Counterintelligence agent, not the playwright."

"I used to know a Karel Čapek," I reply, "who drove a taxi."

"That is the man."

I think back to Friday, August 16, 1968, five days before the "timely arrival" of half a million Soviet troops, put overnight into a land of fourteen million people who merely wanted to travel, to read, and to hope. It is noon in the Firehouse Square and the Number 22 tram's conductors and motormen must be

---

* *Rowboat to Prague*, by Alan Levy; New York, Grossman Publishers, 1972, 531 pp.

*having a picnic lunch together out at White Mountain, where
the line begins, because nothing comes and nothing goes. Reluctantly, I hail a taxi and I notice, even as I board, that it is
not the usual shiny black Volga, but a battered gray Warszawa
with white dotted lines and a chrome headband that says
"Taxi."*

*The driver says in Czech, "Get in, sir, and make yourself
comfortable. Where would you like to go?"*

*I have a lunch date in the upstairs restaurant of the House
of Food department store at the top of the broad boulevard
that is Wenceslas Square. In my halting 1968-model Czech, I
communicate these three broad concepts: "Dům potravin,
Václavské náměstí, nahoru."*

*The driver slams his 1964-model Polish shift into gear; it
takes two tries before it catches. Then he switches into excellent American-accented English: "Do you want me to take
the long, fast way that will cost you the most on the meter but
get you there quickest—or do you want me to take the short,
slow way that will cost you less?"*

*I am dumbfounded, for this is a terribly complex comparison
for a Slav to communicate in our language. I am deep enough
into my language lessons to appreciate what it means for a
Czech, with his seven precise cases, to express this so exactly
in the permissive blur that is English grammar. So, when I
recover my speech, I say, "I have a little time. Let's take the
short, slow way." I want the extra time to know my driver
better. I ask this man—whose cab registration compartment
identifies him as "Čapek, Karel"—the usual question that
opens such a conversation: "Where did you learn your
English?"*

*In the rearview mirror, I perceive two eyes and some gold
teeth twinkling out of a round, unshaven face. "The prisons
of our country in the nineteen-fifties," Čapek answers, "were
the best education for everything in this world. We taught
ourselves English. We taught ourselves Spanish. And I learned
much more about life in those study halls for eleven years than
my fellowmen seem to have learned on the outside."*

He tells me a little of his story. By the time we bid each other adiós *on Wenceslas Square twenty-five minutes later, I am believing him—and I have taken his address in case I have some future need. I think I may need him in September. Without a car of my own, and with both of my daughters ready to start in the French kindergarten (for ages four to six) across town, I will need wheels plus a kindly driver to transport them.*

Čapek has shown me snapshots of his own little boy and girl. Nevertheless, I hesitate to entrust my children to a stranger who has been in prison. What if he is a sex criminal masquerading as a political prisoner? On Monday—the nineteenth of August—I call up an official of K-231, the organization founded that spring by former political prisoners to fight for their own rehabilitation and compensation as well as to weed out the Nazis, perverts, thieves, and murderers from the 62,000 innocents who were jailed by the State for political offenses between 1948 and 1967. The official of K-231 knows of Čapek's case the minute I mention him, but he digs out his file anyway and reads it to me. It verifies most of the details Karel has told me, does nothing to contradict any of the others, and adds a few new ones to my store of knowledge. I thank K-231, ring off, and transfer Čapek's name and address from a slip of paper to my permanent address book.

I'm lucky I've called K-231 on Monday, for on Tuesday night the Red Army comes—and K-231 is no more.

"You were extremely close with Čapek," my interrogators ask.

"He drove my children to school five mornings a week for a year."

"And was that all?"

"Sometimes we'd ask him to bring them home in the afternoon."

"And he came into your house?"

"He always brought Monica and Erika to the door, and we usually invited him to stay and have lunch with them and us."

"And he always stayed?"

"Not always, but often."

"What was he after?"

"*He liked American cooking.*"

"*But you knew about his past in prison?*"

"*Yes. I'd checked him out quite thoroughly.*" I don't say where.

"*Your wife knew, too?*"

"*Yes.*"

"*And your children, too?*"

"*Yes, they found out.*"

"*Do you mean you told your children they were being driven to school by one of your colleagues in U.S. Espionage!!?*"

"*I never told them such a thing! One day, my wife made BCTs—*"

"*BCT? What code is that?*"

"*Bacon, cabbage, and tomato sandwiches—on toast. In America, we call them BLTs, but there was no lettuce on the market here that week.*"

"*Are you criticizing our economy?*"

"*No,*" I say, hastening to forestall another five or ten years in jail being tacked onto my menu of 5,615. "*I'm just saying that because the sandwiches were thick and on toast, Karel said he couldn't eat them. He said his teeth had been neglected in prison.*"

"*So you let him criticize our State dental system to your children?*"

"*Oh, no, there was no dental system in your prisons, so there was nothing to criticize. But Čapek didn't even criticize your prison system. He was just apologizing in a matter-of-fact way for not eating my wife's BCT sandwiches.*"

"*How did your children react to this revelation?*"

"*Later, in private, they asked me why Karel had been in prison and I told them what I knew. And they felt sorry for him.*"

"*Is that why you helped Čapek to emigrate?*"

"*I didn't!*" I protest. "*In fact, when I heard he'd escaped, I was a little angry and disappointed because now I had to find a new taxi driver.*" And it is easy to refrain from telling them what Karel Čapek told me, in September of 1969, just before he became a refugee: "*My son will soon be starting school in*

Prague, and now what kind of education will he get? The new minister of education says they'll be teaching Marxism-Leninism in the first grade. It would be like another fourteen-year sentence to hear my son bringing home this garbage to me."

For my sins of truth-telling—that is, for "spreading great lies"—I am to be parted from my sixty-five page book. My "book" will stay in custody in Prague—for the full 5,615-year term, one can imagine—while I must leave the country within forty-eight hours. The expulsion order also applies to my wife and daughters, who "made friendships for the purpose of gathering information for the notorious" me. We go sadly, reluctantly, but almost gratefully because, even in the frenzy of packing and good-byes, all four of us know a little of how lucky we are still to be together.

In January of 1972, I am a visitor from Vienna—a haven for refugees, among whom the American Family Levy has made a new home—when I work my way west to Cicero, Illinois, not far from a Western Electric factory that looks like a toy Central European castle or town hall. (Perhaps this is why so many Slavic refugees settled in Cicero, starting in the 1930s, after the gangsters who gave Cicero its bad name were run out of town.) My host, who is bringing me from the airport, turns off the secondhand miracle mile of used car lots that bears the proud, martyred Slavic name of Cermak Road.* The 2100 block of South Forty-ninth Avenue is, after Cermak, balm to the eye: an array of turn-of-the-century, two-family, red-brick row houses built by Western Electric for company housing and now privately owned. Only the house numbers distinguish one building from the other, but Number 2106 is a landmark because it has an old rocking chair ("which does not rock, but must not break," my host explains) on its porch. In fact, a landmark is what that chair is supposed to be. "I found it around and put it out there with the landlady's permission,"

* Mayor Anton J. Cermak of Chicago was shot to death in Miami in 1933 by an assassin trying to kill the newly elected President Franklin D. Roosevelt.

my host, the upstairs tenant at 2106, explains to me, "after I came home to the wrong address late one night and all the lights in the neighborhood went on when the lady started screaming. Now everybody else depends on our chair, too. The other night, I took it upstairs for further repairs, and five people on the block got lost and two of them came around to complain. Still, we are lucky to live here. In how many American cities would a chair stay on a porch without being stolen?"

We do not stand around to ponder the question, for it is the coldest Friday night in many a year and the Greater Chicago mercury has dropped to a frostbiting, tooth-numbing, 15-below-zero (Fahrenheit, not Siberian centigrade!). Karel Čapek of Cicero and Alan Levy of Vienna climb the creaky stairs, remove our shoes in the vestibule, and don the slippers ("house shoes") that any thoughtful Central European host provides out of consideration for his floors and his guests. (Thoughtful guests carry their own fold-up "house shoes" around with them when they go visiting.) I am ushered into a cozy, $125-a-month furnished apartment; "American five rooms or European three rooms," I am informed.

I am fed a Cognac, and soon we are exchanging memories and redistributing old friends. Past midnight, we switch to beer and I back into what I must tell my host. I say, "I don't think I told you how long I'd like to stay with you, if I can."

"You can stay as long as you like, as long as you can, as long as your wife doesn't want you back in Vienna," Karel tells me expansively.

His wife wonders, "Can you stay the whole weekend?"

Now it must come out. I will stay much longer in their apartment and in their life. But first I must tell the Čapeks how, having been just young enough to miss out on World War II, I'd read all the blockbuster books and followed the epic war crimes trials and absorbed the cumulative statistics before stumbling across a slender 237-page paperback called Anne Frank: The Diary of a Young Girl. And nothing I'd learned had reached me the way the voice of that fifteen-year-old girl did, right up to her last words to me: ". . . and finally I twist my heart round again, so that the bad is on the outside and the good is on the

*inside and keep on trying to find a way of becoming what I
would so like to be, and what I could be, if . . . there weren't
any other people living in the world." With the shattering
realization that, in the process of eradicating six million, the
Nazis had destroyed this one beautiful soul, I had begun to
comprehend the incomprehensible.*

*Having said this and having presented the Čapeks with an
autographed copy of my own documentary history of years we
shared in Prague, I explain that I need to know and want to
relate how the history whose climax we lived through came
about. And what it was like and how it felt to be caught up,
changed, and shaped in its evolution. For I know, after my
experience with Anne Frank, that such a tale must be told
from inside the essence of all history: one human being.*

*Even in Prague, I had known who he would be: a man my
age (or, rather, less than two years older than myself) whose
life was lived on the other side of the coin simply because he
was born in Prague in 1930 instead of New York City in 1932.
I had never spoken to him about it in Prague, but whenever I
thought about this ambition I saw this dark, sometimes scowl-
ing, other Karel Čapek of whom the world knows naught—a
man an American can start out pitying, find himself laughing
with, and wind up almost envying. His story must be told in
his words, both Czech and English assimilated through the
American consciousness by my typewriter, where I find truth
every day. For purposes of storytelling and protection against
reprisals, some names, events, and even dates may have to be
changed, simplified, disguised, or juggled. But not by tamper-
ing with the essence of the two truths that must prevail:* What
It's Like *and* How It Feels *to be Karel Čapek at any given moment in his life that we see fit to transmit. On the printed page,
I will speak in a slanted typeface and Čapek will speak in
straightforward Roman—and he will do most of the talking, to
me, just as Anne Frank addressed her diary until Hitler spoke
back.*

*Karel Čapek, however, is not the Anne Frank of Communist
Czechoslovakia. To begin with (and we must learn how he did
it), Čapek is a survivor. Or, as a visitor to our home in Prague*

*once asked him point-blank, "What are you anyway, Čapek?
A cabdriver or a linguist or an agitator or what?" Karel had
thought this over for a long minute and then answered rather
ponderously: "I guess . . . you might say . . . that what I am
. . . is . . . a professional prisoner!"*

*Like the whole Czech nation, I'd thought at the time—and I
think it again, sitting in the Midwestern home of a man who
still believes, perhaps more realistically than we know, that
there are three kinds of people in this world: those who have
been in prison, those who are in prison, and those who are going to prison. It is his skin that I must penetrate and his soul
that I must turn inside out, much as Anne Frank did to herself
before she died.*

*I have to admit that, as I reveal myself to my unsuspecting
hosts in Cicero, I feel at least as noble as a male Eleanor Roosevelt dictating a preface to Anne Frank's unearthed diary. I
have come to tell my unique émigré Everyman that his twenties, the best years of his life, were not in vain—no, they were
the raw material of a document to enlighten future generations. I have come to tell him that I have an agent, an editor, a
publisher—and, in my left hand, a contract for me to tell his
story in a book. Performing my magic errand of redemption on
the coldest night in Cicero's memory, I am put in my place
with these words: "Život lidský je tak složitý, že život jednoho
človeka je proti tomu úplný hovno."*

I will recognize it as a quote from Jaroslav Hašek's The Good
Soldier Schweik, *but my Czech and my Schweik are now too
rusty to translate it accurately. And my English is too demanding to settle for the kind of literal rendition that has made
Schweik almost incomprehensible (not to mention unenjoy-
able) in English. After a Saturday of arguing about it, however,
we will agree upon this version of the Cicero Čapek's instinc-
tive reaction to beckoning immortality: "People's lives are so
complicated that one man's life is every bit as meaningful as a
piece of shit."*

*Whereupon, with punctured pomp and an end to all cere-
mony, I plug in my tape recorder and my host goes on
talking. . . .*

Part 1

"I Am the Other Karel Čapek"

I wasn't named after Karel Čapek, the writer, when I was born on Wednesday, April 23, 1930, to Tony and Rose Čapek of Prague. I was named after my uncle and godfather, Karel Vaníček and nobody even thought twice about the combination of an ordinary first name and an ordinary last name giving me one of the most famous names in Czechoslovakia. I was an only child. Sometimes, when I had nobody to play with, I used to wonder how I'd managed to set such a bad example that I stayed brotherless and sisterless. Only much later did I realize that I owed my status first to the hard times of the 1930s and then to years of Nazi occupation. In neither time was the world I lived in ripe for bringing children into it.

My father was a locksmith. When I say that nowadays, Czechs laugh—because, ever since 1948, the official biographies of most Communist big shots say "he began as a locksmith" and worked his way, through steadfast diligence and loyalty, up to *aparatchik*. Actually, on his way through the party college, he may have spent a day or two following a locksmith around. But even the ones who really started up through the ranks as mechanics or ironworkers like to say they were locksmiths. It doesn't carry the *Lumpenproletariat* tone of "factory worker"; no, "locksmith" sounds the right ring of craftsmanship while hewing to the key signal: "working class origins." These career Communists can be the most status-conscious people in the world, which may be why they might

21

just as well call their club the Locksmiths Society as the Workers & Peasants Party. Anyway, locksmithing used to be a respected profession back when my father was practicing it. I'm not boasting, but I *am* proud when I tell you he was a genuine locksmith and a good one—not some bureaucrat who qualified for the title of ex-locksmith by fitting his key into his office door all by himself.

My father was always somebody else's locksmith; he never lasted long working for himself, though he was highly independent, very much his own man. His trouble, like many experts, was that he had a bad head for business: he was too naïve, too believing, too trusting that people were just as open and shut as locks. Every time he ventured out on his own, he got hurt financially. Once, he was inventing a special motor for motorcycles when some friends warned him he ought to patent his idea. They went partners with him and rigged everything so that they would get the patent and the money and even the credit. They were after something for nothing, but the idea stayed locked up in my father's head and hands— so, when he realized what they were trying to do to him, he simply didn't invent his invention and thus did nothing come of something. My father wasn't bitter. He had a mind for mechanics, so for him the joy could be all mental and manual, not glory or riches. And he always tried to be around engines.

He liked to hang around politics, too. He was a National Socialist—which doesn't mean the Nazis, but a liberal centrist party that pretty well embraced the philosophies of the first two presidents of Czechoslovakia as well as my Prague boyhood: Thomas Garrigue Masaryk (1850–1937), who founded the Czechoslovak State at the end of World War I, and Eduard Beneš (1884–1948), who was actually the party leader of the National Socialists. My father read all the party journals, and it was in this press that one of the first names I ever saw in print was my own: my father brought home the journal *Tomorrow,* and one if its contributors was the famous Karel Čapek.

I was born into what is called the First Republic, or the T. G.

Masaryk era. Masaryk was held up to us kids as a "perfect person," as our ideal, but he was not just a statue on horseback, not just a "Founding Father"—he was *Tatíček* (Daddy!). Can you imagine living in America in the time of George Washington?

Just as you know the story of George Washington and the cherry tree, we knew the story of Masaryk and the "manuscripts"—and ours was no legend. It began as a fake, though, early in the nineteenth century, when a scholar named Hanka "unearthed" some "thirteenth-century Slavic texts" that "proved"—at a time when the Czech people, under Hapsburg oppression, wanted very badly to believe it—that we had nourished a body of literature back when our occupiers were still subsisting on acorns. Hanka's "manuscripts" chronicled the wanderings, many centuries earlier, of the princess Libuše, who had built her empire on a high rock called Vyšehrad, from where she prophesied the grandeur and glory of the city that became Prague.

Hanka's "revelations" helped ignite the nationalist revival that forced the Hapsburgs to legalize the Czech language in 1848 and inspired Smetana to compose his opera *Libuše* and his symphonic poem *Má Vlast (My Country)*, both of which take root from the legend of the princess and the rock. Thus, in the late nineteenth century, when more scientific investigators determined that the Hanka "manuscripts" were forgeries, a number of influential professors and politicians wanted the unmasking kept secret. It was by now, they said, a foundation stone of Czech culture. To reveal that it was unsound, they said, would topple the whole structure.

It was Masaryk, then a professor of philosophy, who fought back and proclaimed publicly that the foundation was false. And he didn't wreck Czech culture. On the contrary, because he let our myths stand the test of daylight, they were discussed and argued and they stayed alive as literature and art, if not as fact. In Masaryk's time, part of which was part of my time, our culture for once had an honest base in a land whose motto has been, for more than five centuries, "Truth Prevails."

The Hanka argument launched Masaryk as a politician, too. And we learned the morals of this success story many times over in school.

When Masaryk died in 1937, barely a year before his Republic died the first of several deaths, I was seven and my parents took me across the river, the Vltava, to view his body lying in state at the Prague Castle. But the procession of people paying their respects to him was so many miles long that I fell asleep standing up and my mother had to take me home.

Of all the epitaphs and eulogies of Masaryk, his own words proved the most prophetic: *"No matter what stand you take, I shall not leave you in peace."* And I credit the advice he gave often to young people with saving my life: the gist of it was that if you make your way from A to B and then go from B to C and keep on going, eventually you will go the impossible distance from A to Z. As a man now in his forties, on my way from XL to L, I recognize that if I had not actively practiced this philosophy, I would not have lived through prison.

Back in school in 1937, our teachers were already teaching us beginners the Masaryk lessons that they usually didn't take up until high school—such as how he handled a ritual murder in which the accused was Jewish and the dead girl's body had been bled and drained as in kosher slaughter. Masaryk could have unleashed a pogrom against the Jews, and he could almost *not* have prevented one, but he insisted that it be tried as an ordinary murder. By teaching this to six- and seven-year-olds, our teachers were indoctrinating us with as much decency as they could before Hitler came. They didn't know how much indecency even *they* had to learn.

Despite Masaryk's debunking of the princess Libuše and the enchanted rock of Vyšehrad, both were very real in my life. I grew up on a street called Libušina in the Vyšehrad quarter of Prague. We lived there comfortably because my father, for all his business failings, was an adequate provider who never let his misfortunes alter our way of life. Sometimes my mother had to take work as a saleslady, and then my grandmother would look after me a little, but my father's ups and downs never affected my childhood more than that. And so I played through the 1930s in Vyšehrad Park with the same crowd of boys and girls. There was an ancient pool there. It had no water, but it must have been the baths of Libuše and her maidens! We used it as our amphitheater to act out and embroider upon the legend of Libuše and the plowman Přemysl, with whom she fell in love. We played these romances with respect and even restraint in this mystic place. We ran a little slower and shouted a little softer. And, when grown-ups felt obliged to remind us that these were man-made fairy tales, we nodded— but went on believing. It is the way my son behaves now toward Santa Claus. He no longer believes in Santa. But, at Christmastime, he wants to believe; maybe it's to his advantage to believe; and so he does believe!

When just the boys got together in Vyšehrad Park, we played a game that you might call "League of Nations." One boy, holding a ball, was the referee or League of Nations, while each of us was a different country. The League of Nations boy would chant an eeny-meeny-miney-mo sort of rhyme in Czech (*"Soup is ready/Meat's on table/Whoever comes next/Must hit who he's able!"*), ending with the name of the country, and throw the ball in the air. All of us, who'd formed a circle around him, would now scatter—except the boy whose country had been named. As soon as he caught the ball, he'd shout "Stop!" and we'd have to freeze wherever we were. Then he'd throw the ball, trying to hit one of us. If he missed, he became the League of Nations for the next round. If he hit somebody, that target became the League of Nations. To be the League of Nations was to lose. Nobody wanted to be the League of Nations.

Everybody wanted to be Czechoslovakia, which shows how wrong kids can be. Nobody wanted to be Germany, which I like to think says something good. When I was eight years old, most of us stopped wanting to be Czechoslovakia. We wanted to be Russia or America or, if necessary, England or France. Our parents weren't talking politics with us, but we were hearing them and feeling what was in the air. Betrayal at Munich was coming—and even the children playing in Vyšehrad Park were forming alliances and seeking powerful friends. We no longer were proud or even willing to be who we were.

There were one or two German Czechs in our group and, at first, we all had to bully them into playing Germany in our game. In 1938, though, they began to play the role more willingly—so much so that, every now and then, one of us would repeat (making sure they heard) a wishful slogan of the times: "If ever the Germans should attack us with their helmets, the Russians will come and beat them with their caps." But our Czech parents were more than willing to defend themselves— and, on May 21, 1938, soon after Hitler annexed neighboring Austria and the Germans in our Sudetenland made Nazi noises, there was a mobilization. I remember my father putting on a uniform that didn't fit him very well and marching off to war with a plaid suitcase in his hand. My mother cried, but I was happy for my father. While we were playing League of Nations, he could play soldier, too.

My father returned home after a few days of driving a tank around Milovice.* The mobilization had impressed Hitler, for he decided to win at the bargaining table what he might have trouble taking by naked aggression. Suddenly, English names like Chamberlain and Lord Runciman† were spoken as curse words in our kitchens—and nobody wanted to play England or France in our children's game anymore. In September, 1938, our powerful friends betrayed us in Munich at a four-power conference (Britain, France, Germany, Italy) on the Czechoslovak problem to which Czechoslovakia was not invited. The partitioning of Czechoslovakia was sanctioned at Munich. Then, while Prime Minister Neville Chamberlain spoke of "peace in our time" and a "quarrel in a faraway country, between people of whom we know nothing," those of us at the faraway end of Sir Neville's nearsighted looking glass were say-

---

* A garrison town in central Bohemia now evacuated to serve as the main Soviet Army of Occupation base.

† Head of a British mission sent to Prague to pressure the Beneš leadership into appeasing Hitler.

ing, "We were robbed of our country." In school, we were told to black out the word "Československo" on our maps and in all our books. The teacher who gave that order added softly, "But not indelibly, not forever."

The Nazis entered the Sudetenland and parts of our country were acquired by Poland and Hungary, but Prague wasn't occupied until the night of March 16, 1939.

The next morning, my father and I walked over to the Square of Charles IV—where the New Town Hall* stands— "to see the Germans." In sleet and snow laced with rain, the pavements were lined with people like us feeling very Czech and very sad. I could see hate and fear woven on their faces. And tears! I'd never seen anyone weeping on the streets of Prague. Now almost everyone was. Some were shaking their fists and others were spitting. There were no Germans in sight.

Then there was a noise like hornets and, because it was a new sound to me, I knew it was the Germans. Swarms of motorcycles with sidecars buzzed through the square. The drivers—and the officers in the sidecars—wore green uniforms, steel helmets, and rifles. The crowd stopped spitting and shaking fists, but the weeping grew stronger and louder. For better or worse, this was the kind of lame but eloquent protest at which we Czechs had become adept over the centuries.

The first German I saw was a man of about thirty, driving a motorcycle. All I could really see of him was his face. He had a square chin and, for a moment, I thought that he, too, was weeping. Then I realized his eyes were watering from driving a motorcycle in winter weather. He and all the others looked straight ahead. They never saw us. My father said they must have been strictly told to mind their own business. Now that I think of it, they might have been afraid of us, too. Many of them had come, but they were, after all, outnumbered by the people on the streets.

A few days after that, the Germans were hardly to be seen. It was a semi-invisible occupation. Life went on, but the to-

---

* Prague's *New* Town Hall was started in 1367. The *Old* Town Hall, not far away, was begun two centuries earlier.

talitarian presence was felt. For example, I lost my stamp collection. My father had promised me a stamp album, but hadn't bought me one yet. Late one night, when he didn't come home, my mother—panicking because he might be in trouble with the Germans, who would then certainly come and search our house—ran around destroying all the taboo literature on the premises. One of the first books to go was the volume by T. G. Masaryk in whose pages I'd kept my stamps dried and neatly sorted. My father came home a few hours later, but when I awoke next morning, I was no longer a stamp collector.

There were bigger changes. Proclamations were now in German and Czech. One of them said that dancing in public places was *verboten*. Goods began to disappear from the shops —and then there was rationing. German became the compulsory second language in the schools. And the Germans switched our traffic from the left-hand side of the road (the way the English still drive) to the right. In the last two years of Czechoslovakia (we were now in "The Third Reich Protectorate of Bohemia and Moravia"), this reform had been debated, and the big question had been: How long would it take to make the conversion? The Germans did it overnight— by decree.

My father was working as a taxi driver at the time. I remember that after the announcement that right-hand driving would begin the next morning, he had a sleepless night. When he went off to work, my mother said farewell to him at least as emotionally as she had a year earlier, when he'd marched off to be mobilized. He came home that night, unscarred, and was greeted like a returning hero.

He was no longer a locksmith. That vocation would have meant his being put to work right away in German industry. Driving a taxi (which I learned early to respect as a flexible trade) kept him out of direct German control for a while longer. But when taxis were abolished by the Nazis because of the gas shortage on the home front, he was made a factory hand—for a while in Germany and later back in Prague.

All these changes that the "invisible occupation" wrought in the fabric of everyday life were felt by a child. In the third or fourth grade, I remember one of my favorite teachers telling us, "This will be a hard time. I will not be able to talk to you openly after a while, so please listen closely and learn to read between the lines." A little later, she was gone.

My two closest chums in school were also named Karel—Karel Svoboda and Karel Blažek. Together, we were known as "The Three Karels," but the times swiftly drove us apart. Karel Svoboda (the word *"svoboda"* means "freedom") happened to be Jewish, so he and his family escaped to Switzerland soon after the Nazis came; I was a bit hurt that he never said goodbye, though later I understood. Karel Blažek said right away that he was "glad the Svobodas packed up and left in a hurry"—which was interesting because, while his father was Czech, his mother was German. Karel Blažek was less infected with racism than anybody I knew with German blood in him. But his mother saw the advantages of applying for German citizenship for her whole family: bigger and better ration cards; more educational opportunities in the German schools of Prague; and all the healthy outdoor activities of the Hitler Youth. She wanted the best for her son—and soon Karel Blažek was no longer a classmate of mine. Now he was in the German school and renamed Karl Blaschek. He was having trouble there, though, "because I don't speak any German." We stayed friends—but after school.

You may well imagine how little enthusiasm was expended on the obligatory teaching of German in our schools. Our teachers gave us just enough for us to pass the exams, but they made it so boring that they taught us to hate the German language. Which is why I was at first stunned when my mother told me she'd arranged for me to get private tutoring after school in German!

This shock came right on the heels of another shock that had everybody buzzing. On the streets and in the trams, we'd started to meet people wearing yellow stars on the left side of their clothes—and inside each star, in black letters, was the word *"Jude."* I asked one of them—a youngish man who looked no different from anybody else, except for that one thing—what it was about and he whispered, "We are Jewish

and you are not allowed to talk to us and we are not allowed
to talk to you." Even in a whisper, he spoke proudly. And it
was I, nine years old, who felt ashamed.

I kept asking my relatives and friends, "Why can't we talk
to the people with the yellow stars that say '*Jude?*'" I never
got an answer while the Jews were there—but, even after they
disappeared, the question lingered.

Every single person in Prague was aware of this, and what
it represented. Whenever I hear Germans—or, for that matter,
Czechs—saying they had no idea what was going on, I know
they are concealing something. *You couldn't help knowing!*
The Germans didn't tell us Czechs anything because we were
an inferior people, but if I—a nine-year-old Czech!—knew,
surely any member of the Master Race had to know at least
as much as I knew.

And it was because of this outrage that I was to be given
German lessons. My parents knew hardly any Jews, but a
friend of my mother's knew one who needed help. He was a
bent-over but distinguished-looking scholar in his sixties who
lived all by himself in another neighborhood. My mother's
friend guessed (and then ascertained from neighbors) that he
was too proud and dignified to go out at all wearing a yellow
star. "I'm living too close," she said, "and if people who know
me see me helping him, then I'm in trouble. But if someone
from another district came for some good reason . . ."

Bearing salami, bread, and butter, my mother went to see
the old Jew. He asked, almost belligerently, why she had
come—and she sensed that he would be too proud to accept
her sympathy or her charity if she offered it directly. So she
said her son wasn't doing well in German at school, and it was
because of the way it was taught there. Would he do her the
favor of teaching me German the right way? She couldn't
afford to pay much, but here was some food.

Maybe he saw through her, but he didn't say so. As soon as
my parents told me that studying German while delivering
food would be my contribution to fighting the Nazis and keeping a Jew alive a little longer, I started going to his house
three times a week. With him, as with nobody else, I was

obedient and studious. I didn't play any of my usual tricks—and from him I learned German!

One day in 1940, with a hunk of salami wrapped in a bag, I knocked on my tutor's door—and a Sudeten German *Hausfrau* with a pig's-knuckle face answered. She said, "The professor doesn't live here anymore. We do."

"He didn't tell me he was moving," I remarked.

"He's gone to the hospital for a special treatment, but he won't be coming back here to live. What do you have to do with him?" she asked, sniffing suspiciously at my salami.

"He taught me to speak good German," I said in my best German.

"Ah, well, there's some good in all of us," she said. I left as quickly as I could. Even under rationing, nobody in the Čapek household could eat the professor's meat that night—or our own.

A few weeks later, I saw the pig's-knuckle-faced *Hausfrau* on the street. She didn't recognize me, but I asked her if she happened to have the professor's new address. She flinched and then, placing me in her neat little mind, said, "You'd better get yourself a new teacher. The professor died of pneumonia."

When I told this to my parents, my father snorted and said, "German pneumonia! They put Jews in cold concrete cells with no clothes on and then they die of pneumonia. It's something terrible, I tell you." Even *we* didn't know much, but we *did* know about the concentration camps. And we thought we could guess the limits to which they went. We were putting two and two together, but we didn't have the imagination to think it would add up to six million.

Once, my mother and I were riding in a tram in our district when a man started shouting for the police in bad German. He was a Czech with a swastika pin in his lapel. The motorman clanged his bell and a Czech policeman came running. The passenger pointed with horror to a yellow-starred Jew huddling in a corner. Technically, Jews weren't even allowed to ride public transportation, but everybody felt so sorry for their fate that nobody enforced this rule. The policeman, more embarrassed than anybody, dragged the Jew off the tram. With that, the other passengers in that car disembarked. Nobody wanted to ride with that collaborator-informer. "Take him away!" we shouted and, with a happy clang, the trolley moved forward happily with only the motorman and the conductor and that one hateful passenger aboard the front car.

As soon as the tram was safely out of sight, the policeman let go of the Jew, apologized to him, and to everybody present. "I haven't heard the last of this," the policeman said, "because I know that chap and he knows me. He's a Czech married to a German. Some of them are worse Nazis than the Nazis. He probably has some Jew's apartment now, but his time will come."

"You must tell me about it," said the Jewish passenger, "in the next world."

Every now and then, homesick German enlisted men on patrol would pull up and watch us play. They wanted friendship, liked children, and liked chocolate, but weren't allowed to fraternize or shop in the stores. One of the Germans would hold out some marks and say, "Buy us some candy in the store and keep a little for yourselves."

Occasionally, one of the younger children would do so. Most of us, including myself, would just run away in a flock. Once, three older boys said yes, took the money, and disappeared with it. When the Germans realized what had happened, they simply took away the next three children who came up that street—and those three, two boys and a girl, were never seen again.

During Prague's six years and seven weeks of Nazi occupation, we lived in a numbed state of shock. But, even so, people had to work, people had to live, people even had to laugh, and people liked to listen—to the British, American, and Russian shortwave broadcasts in Czech. All of us knew people who'd fled the country and people who'd been persecuted because their relatives had escaped. Now we started hearing some of these voices that were no longer among us, including President Beneš from London and T. G. Masaryk's son, Jan, who was foreign minister in Beneš's exile government.

They told us what we vaguely knew would come to pass, but could scarcely believe: that the Nazis could not and would not last. Life changed so little—and rarely for the better—from day to day that this hardly seemed possible. The broadcasts told us, too, of Czechoslovak Legions that were forming abroad. Perhaps they raised our hopes higher than was justified. When we talked about the length of the war, we talked in terms of months. Anyone who spoke in terms of years was looked upon as a cynic or worse.

The Germans, of course, were listening, too. They tried to jam the broadcasts—particularly the British ones, which were the most thorough and reliable. When the jamming didn't work, the Germans ordered everybody's set to be taken to the nearest radio shop for surgery. One little part was amputated to short out the shortwave. But Czechs are great hoarders of spare parts, and, before long, we and everybody else had possession of a tiny coil that we called "Little Churchill" *(Čůrčilek)* because, strategically inserted within the radio, it brought in the BBC.

On every radio I saw during the war, there was a dark pink card that said: YOU ARE REMINDED THAT LISTENING TO BROADCASTS FROM ABROAD IS FORBIDDEN AND PUNISHABLE BY DEATH. Not having that card on your radio was also punishable, so my father made a point of keeping it on even as he turned the radio upside down to insert or remove Little Churchill.

Friends made a point of never paying visits during the half-hour broadcasts. If they did, they had to be prepared to wait outside the door while their hosts removed and hid their Little Churchills before responding. My father, an expert mechanic, had it down to two minutes, but most people took longer. Hosts seldom entertained visitors with the BBC. Listening to it was something almost holy that you did in private.

The ambush of the German Protector, Reinhard Heydrich, in May of 1942, brought the first real terror into the everyday life of occupied Prague. The assassins, Czech parachutists from London, were trapped right near our home, inside the Church of Saints Cyril and Methodius, where they killed themselves. But the reprisals were fierce. Only later did we hear that the whole village of Lidice, just outside Prague, had been massacred in retaliation. We already knew, however, that hundreds of random hostages were being taken, tortured, and executed in Prague. In the house-to-house searches, the slightest hesitation or linguistic misunderstanding led to death on the spot. When husbands went off to work, their wives said good-bye to them as though it was the last time they'd ever kiss.

The prevailing Czech attitude went: "Heydrich deserved to die, but he wasn't worth so many lives." This was particularly true in our district, where the Gestapo was searching high and low for weapons. They didn't find many—but that summer I did. I was swimming in the Vltava just under Vyšehrad when I came upon a sealed wooden crate. I rounded up several other boys and we pulled it out. Inside were forty different pistols and rifles of various ages that must have been stashed there during the Heydrich searches. We dried them, oiled them, and buried them under some rocks near the Baths of Libuše— for future use.

It was prospecting for hidden weapons the following summer that cost me my virtue at the age of thirteen. Bathing in the Vltava one day, I spotted a woman on the riverbank. She was washing her underwear and gazing straight at me. She was wearing a two-piece green bathing suit. I didn't know why, at the time, but I stopped my searching and just paddled back and forth in her view.

Her eyes never left me. Though she went on washing absent-mindedly, she seemed to be making calculations that definitely involved me. She was twenty-three or twenty-five and very attractive—I know now, even better than ever, even better than I knew then, but I knew then, too, how attractive she was. She smiled at me several times and I smiled back. Then, when she was certain she had my undivided attention (which didn't take much calculating) and that nobody else was around, she began stroking her well-washed bras and panties in a way that would do nothing to dry them or me up. I stopped swimming altogether and floated on my back, watching intently until I could hardly see over my erection, so I trod water instead. Smiling at this, she beckoned me toward her.

I swam ashore, trying not to pant. After a few words (she spoke very proper, educated Czech) about the weather and the water, she handed me her laundry and I followed her back to a cabin she was using. Outside it, we hung her lingerie together in silence. When we went inside the cabin, she took off her bathing suit and, while I stared with mixed fright and interest, she handed it to me and asked me to go outside and hang it on the line.

I hated to leave, but I did so, stumbling and fumbling all the way, fearing that this was some kind of tease and that she would lock the door while I was out. But she was there waiting, with a towel wrapped around her, to take my bathing suit out, hang it on the line, survey the scene to make sure nobody was watching this complicated washday, and then come back and lock us both inside.

When I emerged two hours later, I was no longer a virgin and my swimsuit was dry. I went back many times, but I never saw her there again. Most of the time, there was nobody there. Four or five times that summer, the cabin looked locked and there were men's bathing suits or clothes hanging primly on the line beside hers. Once, there was a German SS man's shirt on the line, and I suddenly remembered that, in our few words of conversation, she had referred to the Vltava as the Moldau. I took this revelation—that she was Czech, but willing to sleep with the Nazis as well as thirteen-year-old boys—as my cue to stay away, though I thought if I should ever meet her again, I'd want to say thank you to her.

In 1943, the year I said hello to women, I said good-bye to my German-Czech frend Karl Blaschek, alias Karel Blažek. We'd kept in touch, though I'd seen less of him once he started wearing the Hitler Youth uniform. Still, I envied him the dagger that went with his costume. Now he was going off to a camp for the deeper indoctrination that they gave to German boys at thirteen.

"I still have trouble with the German language," Blažek told me, "but I must learn to defend my Fatherland to death."

"Your father is Czech," I reminded him.

"You're right," he said ruefully. "Make it my Motherland."

The end of the war was nearing, and people kept maps, in their own codes, of the advancing Allies and retreating Axis. Then we began seeing the Allied planes flying over Prague. I can remember only two air raids, though. One was on a factory clear across the city from us, but it must have been quite heavy because my father, who stood on a table to see the bombers better, was knocked to the floor by the impact of the explosions. "You wanted to see them fly," my mother told him, "but instead we saw you fly." The other air raid must have been improperly addressed because they dropped a small load of bombs on some homes along Vinohradská (Wine-Castle Boulevard) and wrecked a monastery near where we lived.

Let me interrupt, as I will every now and then. It is a quiet Sunday night in Cicero, Illinois. The children are asleep. In the dining area, Čapek and I are talking into the tape recorder on the table. At the other end of the living room is a turret that juts out over Forty-ninth Avenue. This small turret houses the Čapeks' TV, which is showing John Wayne in True Grit *tonight. Halfway between the table and the turret sits Mrs. Karel Čapek, watching John Wayne, mending the kids' clothes for school in the morning, and eavesdropping a little. As Karel Čapek describes the location of the bombed monastery, I have trouble placing it on my mental map of Prague. "You start,"* Karel says, *"on the lower part of Karlovo náměstí [the Square of Charles IV], the corner of which is Faust House. . . ."*

"Faust House?" I say, totally mystified.

"You should know Faust House," says Karel. "It's almost next door to where your daughter had her operation."

"I suppose I know the building," I admit, "but why the name?"

"You know the story of how Faust's soul flew through the ceiling after he made his deal with the devil?"

"*And that took place in Prague, too?*"

"*Of course it did! Right there in Faust House! At least, that's what we were told all our lives. And we had to believe it because we could see for ourselves that the Faust House had a hole in the ceiling.*"

"*It should have been in the floor,*" I observe.

"*Well, Alan, one man's ceiling is another man's floor,*" says Karel. "*But now you know where it is, right?*"

"*On the corner of the square and Vyšehrad Street,*" I say.

While Karel is positioning me precisely, I glance over at his wife. She has stopped sewing. Her needle is poised in the air. Our eyes meet. She says in her emphatic, if limited, English, "*We will show it to you.*"

I laugh and say, "*When we all go back to Prague together?*"

And Mrs. Karel Čapek of Cicero, Illinois, says, "*I do not want to die in this place.*"

Later we learned that we'd guessed right: the Allied planes hadn't meant to bomb the homes and monastery. They simply had to drop their load before going home. I suppose that explains everything, but nobody I knew thought so. We rejoiced, though, that the war would be ending. More and more of the German soldiers we saw were injured, crippled, or wounded. I suppose that was good; at least, I was told so.

When I finished elementary school at fourteen, it was 1944. I passed the entrance exam for academic high school (*Realgymnasium*), but this was just a pretense: no Czechs were allowed to enter *Realgymnasium* anymore. The Germans needed all the teen-aged manpower they could lay hands on for cannon fodder and forced labor. Fortunately, my parents very carefully "neglected" to register me with the various youth organizations, so I was on a minimum of lists—and able to pass unnoticed from school into work as an apprentice in book publishing.

Publishing in Czechoslovakia was a traditional and respected profession and my employer was one of the best: Václav Linhart, a publisher and seller of law books, with printing

plant and shop on the Opletal Street across a park from the
Woodrow Wilson Railroad Station.* An apprentice, even in
those times, was treated as a student and future publisher, not
just an odd-jobs man or errand boy or extra body. I was handed
a three-year program, which was adhered to strictly as I moved
from department to department and job to job. I learned bind-
ing, selling, negotiating, invoicing, editing, typesetting, contract writing, cataloging, and (what I enjoyed the most) proof-
reading. There was supposed to be a night school for apprentices, too, but it wasn't in existence when I began; I took the
course after the war, passed an examination, and was awarded
a license that entitled me to publish books or music scores and
sell not only them, but antiques, vases, and paintings. I remember old Mr. Linhart congratulating me on my license and telling me, "It entitles you to do anything in books except write
one."

On Friday, May 4, 1945, I left work at noon for lunch and
saw everybody tearing down the German billboards and pla-
cards and store signs that had been mandatory since 1939. And
suddenly I, too, didn't want to see any of that heavy German
lettering; it had always offended my eye, but now I couldn't
live with it, so I fetched a ladder and took down the word
"Buchhandlung" (bookstore) from Linhart's. When nobody

* It is indicative of the Czech mentality and its ability to think the best
thoughts that Čapek refers to the street where he worked as "Opletal,"
the postwar name it was given in honor of a student martyr whose
tumultuous funeral of November 17, 1939, "provoked" the Nazis into
closing all Czech universities. At the time Čapek apprenticed there, it
was the Lützow Street, named after the Prussian commander of the Black
Rifles who fought against Napoleon in 1813 and 1814. Similarly, Čapek
calls the railroad depot near where he worked "Woodrow Wilson Station," the name it had been given in the First Republic out of gratitude
to the friendship and hospitality another scholar-statesman had extended
to T. G. Masaryk during his World War I exile in America. (The Czechoslovak Constitution, in fact, like our own, was drawn up in Philadelphia.)
The Nazis renamed Wilson Station as just plain *Hauptbahnhof* (Main
Railroad Station). Later, the Communists, following the Nazis' example,
called it *Hlavní nádraží* (Main Railroad Station, in Czech). Prague's
other principal railroad depot suffered a similar fate: it was Masaryk
Station in good times and Central Station most of the time.

shot me, I took down the word *"Verlag"* (publisher), too. I heard a staccato noise from below. It was Mr. Linhart and some of my fellow employees applauding.

This was how the Prague Uprising against the Nazis began for me. There had been many false alarms and a few almost-true ones about the Russians coming or the Americans coming. Some boys I knew had actually been disarming German soldiers by jumping them in the side streets of Prague and taking away their weapons. The Germans had put up very little resistance. Either they were the aging, maimed warriors we were getting used to or else very young boys, barely my age and very frightened. Now, when I saw the matter-of-fact way in which people were going about committing the capital offense of tearing down German signs and even swastikas on Wenceslas Square, I knew this was it.

Some German soldiers passed by while we were at work dismantling more of their signs. A couple of them watched us with interest, but did nothing to harm us or stop us. A little later, the German high command posted sentries with light machine guns to defend their few remaining signs to the death. But these troops looked sheepish and, in fact, looked the other way when one daring young man tore down a sign anyway. No shots were fired and nobody was hurt in my vicinity that afternoon. Exploring Wenceslas Square, I stopped eyeing the Germans warily. Instead, I started studying Czech faces; people were beginning to smile at each other.

After our lunch hour was up and none of us had eaten, we went back to work. But not for long. For Mr. Linhart said something which was so unlike him that, right there and then. the date of May 4, 1945, became a memorable one. He said, "The weather may become a little hot this afternoon, so why don't we all take the afternoon off and go home?" Which is what I did: listening to the BBC and learned that the U.S. Army was approaching Pilsen and the Red Army was still quite far from Prague, but on its way. That night, I slept lightly. I kept listening for shooting, but there wasn't any.

On Saturday morning, I decided not to go to work. I guessed that Linhart's wouldn't open up as usual. Everything sounded very quiet, so I decided to get a haircut. The barber shop was more crowded than usual—indicating that I was not the only one staying home from work. A slightly drunk man was in there selling little swatches of ribbon: the Czechoslovak tricolor—the white-red-and-blue. He tried to sell me one, but I didn't like the idea of someone cashing in on our poor flag, so I said, "No, I can't afford it. I have just enough for a haircut." The drunken salesman leaned closer and gave it to me anyway, saying, "So have it free!" Then the barber did the same—and May 5, 1945, started out as a day of days.

With my tricolor in my lapel, I headed back toward my house when the loudspeakers—which the Germans had put on every street for air-raid warnings, proclamations, and other major events—suddenly started talking Czech, asking "all good Czechoslovak patriots to come to the aid of our country. The revolution has begun! The German enemy is retreating on all fronts, but we need help to rid Prague of them." The voice on the loudspeakers was very eloquent and very recognizable. It belonged to a prominent Czech broadcaster who'd been silenced by the Nazis and whom I later had the honor to meet— in prison.

I wondered where to join up, but I was distracted by a tram that came clanging right past its stand and through a red light. It had no passengers, but a Prague policeman was hanging out of the *wrong* side of the trolley car (out the left-hand door, which was customarily sealed, ever since the Nazis reversed the rules of the road). The policeman was calling something out to me, but I couldn't hear what he was saying, so I cupped a hand over one ear. With that, he leaped off the moving tram and barely landed on his feet right in front of me. The tram kept on going.

He was a big, strong, ruddy man in his forties. He repeated what he'd been shouting: "Hey, boy! Do you know where there are some weapons?"

You had to be suspicious of a Czech policeman in Nazi times, so I hesitated for a second. But just for a second. Then I decided that any man who'd been riding on the wrong side of a tram had to be on my side.

"I know a school where there are lots of weapons," I told him, "but I think there are still German soldiers there—a dozen or so." I knew this school particularly well because it was the one from which I'd graduated a year earlier; now the Germans were billeted there. I could savor the irony with which I told him, "I've looked the place over many times. I know how to get in there."

He said, "Show me!"

I led him there and made myself useful by reaching between the bars and opening the school's gate from within. His hands would have been too large, but mine were still small enough. And then he strode across the school yard, with me just behind him, as though we were ten men strong; one could never feel outnumbered on this cop's side.

All in the same motion, he flung open the door of the school building with one hand while pulling out his pistol with the other. Then he looked up and down the passages. There was nobody to be seen.

"The soldiers," I told him, "are all in two rooms near the center of the building."

"Follow me!" he said. We came to one of the two rooms and he flung open the door. This time, we were confronted by a dozen German soldiers. Only they didn't look like soldiers because they were in their underwear. Some were lying in bed; some were sitting on the edges of their double-decker bunks. On the right side of the room was a rifle rack with boxes of ammunition underneath.

"*ACH-TUNG!*" the policeman called. All the Germans jumped to attention. Even those who'd been sleeping leaped out of bed and landed on their feet, straight as ramrods. "HANDS—UP!" he said, and they obeyed. Then he started counting cadence and he marched them to the far left side of the room—away from the rifle rack.

At this moment, five or six Czech men appeared out of nowhere, behind me, pushing me aside and grabbing for guns. "Help yourselves, men!" the policeman told them. They must have been following us all the time, though I hadn't seen hide nor hair of them until this very moment. I grabbed a gun and some ammunition, but I was lost in the shuffle. When I saw them leaving, I rushed to catch up with them; otherwise, I'd have been left alone with the Germans. On the street, the policeman called "Thanks, kid!" to me—and he and his band of men disappeared toward Wenceslas Square.

Enriched by a rifle and some shells that seemed hot in my hands, I headed home through Vyšehrad Park. Walking down Libušina Street, which had known me since I was a baby, I saw (and still remember) the surprised and admiring faces that looked out at Karel Čapek with a rifle. And I stopped feeling afraid. I felt like—like Somebody! I came home much older than when I'd gone out a couple of hours earlier for a haircut.

My mother put me in my place real fast. "Take that Thing out of your hand!" she said, lunging for it as if to take a toy shovel away from an infant. I yanked it out of her reach and held it behind my back. "There's a revolution going on!" I reminded her.

"Revolution or no revolution," she said, "no son of mine carries a Thing like that. I'm calling the police!"

And she did! She brought in a policeman who lived in our building—a man not unlike the one with whom I'd just stormed my old school. He told me in a fatherly way, "Well, son, you've got a rifle, all right, but you don't have much experience. So hand it over." I stared at him blankly—stunned with outrage, but trying to look cold and impassive—until he said, "Besides, your shells don't fit in this rifle." I blushed and he encountered no resistance when he wrested it away from me.

There are very few people in this world that I hate, but that cop remains one of them to this very day—through no fault of his own. If I think about it with detachment, I would say he handled the teen-age desperado Karel Čapek quite well. But who can think detachedly about being shamed by and before his own mother? I almost think that, in the next few days, if I'd met him with the right rifle and the right ammunition in hand, he might have met with a fatal accident.

I went away sulking—but not for more than fifteen minutes. I headed straight toward the Baths of Libuše, where the other boys and I had buried the weapons I'd found in the river three years earlier.

The first parcel I dug up was in perfect order—two Czech-made 765 handguns wrapped in a kind of waxed paper, greased with vasoline, and packaged (by my chums and me) with the *right* ammunition. The loudspeakers were still calling for help in Czech, and I was determined to fight, though I didn't know where to begin. Leaving our arms cache, I was discovered—by a pal who was headed for the same buried treasure. When he'd armed himself, we agreed that, inasmuch as the Radio was inciting us to rebel, we would go to the studio and help defend it.

It was now 11:30 A.M. and we started to hear shooting from all directions. A German jet fighter—the first nonpropeller plane we'd ever seen and therefore doubly terrifying—was making low, swooping passes over all of Prague. Men and women were hurrying this way and that. All the people on the streets wore Czechoslovak tricolors and they'd warn you if there was a German sniper on the next block; otherwise, it was hard to tell. So many Czechs were at their windows with rifles, but all you saw first was the rifle barrel, and it was fool-ish to try to peer at whoever was behind the trigger. The snipers, people said, were mostly Hitler Youth. I thought of my half-German classmate and friend, Blažek, and wondered whether he was right now defending his Motherland or his Fatherland to the death.

We reached the Radio by a circuitous route, and it was still a combat zone. The German defenders had barricaded them-selves in two offices and some washrooms. While the trans-mitters and studios were already in Czech hands, Czechs who tried to storm the Germans' last fortress were being shot down like flies.

The Radio was the first place where I saw blood being shed. A young man in his twenties lay gasping with pain in the first passage we took. He had been wounded in several places and the white stretcher beneath him was almost totally red; his face grew whiter and whiter as the life drained out of him.

Seeing him dying, my friend and I didn't argue much when everybody told us we were "too young to fight." Instead, we became stretcher-bearers. We were told not to carry any wounded men since we weren't medics, but we made ourselves useful bringing empty stretchers to the medics, who wasted no time filling them with casualties.

Somewhere between 4:00 and 5:00 P.M., the Prague Fire Department rode to our rescue. They arrived with fire engines screaming. Hearing the noise, a handful of frightened Germans came out and surrendered. The firemen ordered us all out of the building. Then, with hoses turned on full blast, they marched in and literally flushed most of the remaining Germans out into abject, soaking captivity. The last holdouts retreated to the cellar like trapped rats, but still biting with bullets. The firemen methodically pumped water into the cellar and, after ten minutes of this, a white flag appeared.

The first man to emerge from the Radio building with his hands up was a middle-aged, sleek-looking Czech fat man. Everybody within reach slapped his face with open hands and he began to cry. He was one of the two most infamous collaborationist broadcasters. Then, when nothing but Germans started coming out and the Czech rebel broadcasters moved in safely, I headed for home. I was afraid to be out when it would be *too* dark, but I wanted to get home when it was just dark enough for me to quickly conceal my weapon from my mother in a safe place—my old schoolbag!

That night, just as I was going to bed early, I heard a roar outside my window and peered out to see a convoy of German artillery—ten or twelve trucks with cannon—whizzing past. Both the equipment and the men were in the most spick-and-span condition that I'd seen anything German in for some time, so I knew Prague wasn't free yet. And these troops worried me. Even their camouflaged uniforms looked as if they'd been customed-tailored in the best greenhouse. They were some sort of elite corps, and only later did I learn that they were racing for Pilsen to surrender to the Americans rather than to the Russians. That night, though, they seemed so unreal that

I dismissed them as a bad dream and, putting it behind me, slept ten hours.

On Sunday morning, there was work to be done. The neighborhood Sokol Hall* had been turned into a temporary jail for captured German soldiers and civilians (some of whom turned out to be fleeing soldiers and Gestapo). Nobody objected to my carrying a weapon this time. In fact, it was yet another Prague policeman who took two of us boys on patrol. Our job was to bring in a German family living high on a nearby hill in a villa that had been taken away from some Czechs who'd disappeared.

Arriving on foot, we walked up the driveway. Instinctively, we checked that our clothes were neat; less naturally, we made certain our weapons were ready. Then the cop rang the doorbell. A well-dressed German man of about fifty answered the door right away—and, all of a sudden, none of us knew what to say.

He looked at us, we looked at him, and finally the policeman said, "You see, there is a revolution and we would like you to come with us."

Somebody else was peeping from behind a door, and so the policeman added, "And, if you don't mind, everybody else here, too."

"There is only my wife," the man said sadly. "Both our sons are dead in Russia."

A woman stepped forth and took his arm. They stood there comforting each other with dignity and love I had to admire. We didn't know how to tell them that we'd have to search the house for other Germans, but the man made it easier for us: "Would you help me lock up everything first?"

We did—and that way we were able to ascertain that nobody else was in the villa. We would have missed a couple of rooms if our host hadn't called them to our attention. Of course, if anybody armed *had* been hiding there, he'd have been able

* Sokol was the Czech gymnastic organization that first the Nazis and later the Communists outlawed.

to kill us with no real difficulty. We were so embarrassed that we took no security precautions at all—and, even while I knew it wasn't so, I couldn't help feeling like a Nazi rounding up Jews. When we had closed up the whole house, the German handed the policeman the keys. While we locked the front door, the German couple took a long last look at the place and held hands tightly. I could tell that they loved each other and the house very much.

Along the way, we met other Czech patrols leading German civilians to the Sokol Hall. The Czechs looked sheepish, their captives looked resigned. We delivered our couple to our neighborhood commander, who was a Czech military man. He asked them a few questions while a clerk made out a receipt for their house keys. Then they were taken away, still together when I last saw them.

Two or three days later, I passed by their villa, which we had so scrupulously locked up with the help of our host. It had been burgled, looted, and stripped of all its furnishings. I wondered if its pre-German owners would ever reappear and I shuddered, partly, perhaps, because I felt like a vulture myself. It was the same feeling I'd had at the time we locked it up, which is why that Sunday, I begged off any further "patrols." Hoping to learn more about weapons, I worked at the Sokol Hall trying to match up some spare parts with some missing cogs in the weapons on hand. It was like doing a defective jigsaw puzzle. I didn't qualify as an armorer by the end of that day, but at least I didn't have to evict any more Germans from places they called home.

The next morning, we awoke to cannon fire. The Germans were counterattacking from high atop the seven hills of Prague. I learned that their shells had demolished one wall of the Old Town Hall and set fire to the railway bridge over the Vltava, which already was more war damage in one day than had been done to Prague in more than six years of occupation: architecturally, that is.

On our side, the first atrocities had begun to appear. I only *heard* that two SS men had been hanged and set afire in Wenceslas Square. But I actually *saw* two killings of informers.

On my way to the Sokol Hall in the morning, a mob of forty Czechs came toward me. They were folk I knew from the neighborhood, but now I hardly knew them, for they were inflamed, writhing, dragonlike, the way people grow when a crowd becomes a mob. As this dragon of a mob neared, it parted—as if opening its mouth to swallow—so I could see what it was digesting: a man, more dead than alive, but still moving or being kept in motion by the momentum of the mob. A woman I knew, who was always telling me to remember her to my mom, was tearing the man's hair. Someone else kicked out his few remaining teeth before my eyes. A woman stuck a tin pail over his head and everyone who could started beating on it.

I had a gun, but I did nothing to stop it. I simply jumped out of the way for fear that I, too, would be enveloped by this terror and become just another spike on this vicious dragon's tail. The mob kept moving forward for about a block—and then it stopped to disband. I knew the man's body must be not only dead but broken, so I didn't look back.

The Sokol Hall offered no sanctuary for my sensibilities that morning. As I arrived, even before I could tell anyone the horror I'd seen, another Czech informer was brought in on a stretcher. This one had been beaten even worse than the first man when I'd seen him last, but this one was still breathing. He was under a bloody sheet, so I never saw his face. But the man directing the stretcher-bearers had a gleam in his eye that I can see to this day. He said, "This is a terrible man who deserved to die long ago." Then those gleaming eyes lit on me and he said, "You have a gun. Shoot him!"

I shook my head no. I hadn't spoken a word all morning and now I couldn't speak. But I shook my head no.

"That's an order!" the fanatic said. "Shoot him!"

I must not have been a very capable liberator of Prague, if this was what liberation was about. But I was a pretty fair defender. When this man, who was small and wiry, said, "All right. Then *I'll* finish him off," and lunged for my gun, I fought him off much harder than I'd battled my mother.

He stormed out, but I saw him coming back a minute or two

later with a gun. I was afraid he was coming to get even with me, but he didn't even see me. He went to the stretcher, stood over the wreckage of a man, who could be heard breathing hard under the sheet, and fired one shot into where his face must have been once.

The heavy breathing noise had stopped by the time the explosion died down. I couldn't bring myself to look at the mess on the stretcher. Instead, I found myself staring at the fanatic—a hitherto rare species of Czech who suddenly became quite numerous in those days. I suspect he hadn't suffered much at Nazi hands. People who've suffered seldom wish to perpetuate suffering.

I'm sorry I didn't save or prolong a life, but I'm relieved I didn't participate. Nothing I've done in my forty-three years or been jailed for has ever made me ashamed for long—sorry, yes; ashamed, seldom—but this would have scarred me inside for life.

Outside our neighborhood, but not far away, people were building barricades to slow down German reinforcements that were reportedly heading into Prague from the south. And so those of us in the Sokol Hall found ourselves suddenly handling a good many responsibilities: looking for German invaders, looking around for stray German snipers, and looking after our German prisoners. I was kept busy, so I didn't think much then about the atrocities in which I'd almost participated. Killing a half-dead man was considered a moral, even brave, deed by the standards that were beginning to prevail among us in those days, even as the German evil receded. And I remembered hearing my father, after listening to the BBC, talking with other men who said that after the Germans were gone and the informers and collaborators, it would be a far better world, with opportunity and liberty and justice for all. "Even better than it was before the war," one man had said.

And my father had disagreed: "The war may be over, but people won't change."

Now, on Monday, May 7, 1945, I was dispatched on another patrol—to see what, if anything, the Germans were up to in the neighborhoods surrounding Vyšehrad. In Pankrác, German tanks were rampaging up and down the streets and firing at random—at no particular targets, but just to keep Prague partisans from besieging them. Pankrác's chief claim to historical fame is that it houses Prague's most notorious prison. As a parting gesture, the Nazis had released some of the worst criminal elements from custody in the prison—but these misfits were still inside the walled compound battling among themselves.

"The firemen will come soon and flush them out," our patrol leader said as we skirted the turbulence.

"Who wants them out?" another member of our ten-man— or, rather, ten-boy—patrol wondered.

People coming from Smíchov, across the river, were smiling. The first—and, alas, last—Americans had been sighted just outside the city limits of Prague: a reconnaissance jeep from Pilsen that went back there to report, but not to summon help.*

Late that afternoon, our patrol climbed the hill on which the Žižkov district lies. People coming downhill kept giving us two reports: "The SS are putting out eyes, locking the blinded people into cellars, and flooding them," and "Those creepy kids from the Hitler Youth are trapped in the trolley barn."

It sounded safer to look into the latter—and, besides, we were curious about what kids our age could be doing on the other side.

Hearing a brief volley of shots, we crept around the walls of the Žižkov trolley garage and met a patrol of middle-aged men, one of whom was waving a German weapon while another was proclaiming, "Well, there's one German beast who won't be shooting this anymore. Now let's go and get the rest of them in there!"

* General George S. Patton's Third Army had liberated Pilsen on Sunday, May 6, but halted there. A. U.S. commander had even forbidden a force of seven thousand Pilsener volunteers to march on Prague, sixty miles away. A Soviet-American agreement, made in early April, had defined Pilsen as a "line of demarcation." The Russian high command had already mapped "Operation Prague" and asked the Americans to let them liberate the capital. It was neither the first nor last time that the big powers "played spheres" (of influence) with Czechoslovakia.

We wanted to see the face of the "beast" and his proud killers told us, "He's in the second backyard over there—a Hitler Youth. He was trying to escape from the garage and we shot him off a wall. He was dead when he hit the ground."

Another man added, "Funny thing was that his Hitler Youth friends were also shooting at him."

"But it's us who got him!" the first man insisted.

"Yes," said the other, "but maybe he was running away from them, too."

The "beast" was lying face down. An ex-schoolmate named Ota and I pried it onto its side. The "beast"'s face was intact— and it belonged to our former school chum, Karel Blažek, alias Karl Blaschek.

His face was unscarred. His brown hair, even in violent death, was more neatly parted than I'd ever seen it in life. And, while Blažek was about my size, he looked so small in death that, for the only time in *my* life, I almost wanted to kiss him. But I didn't. Only four of us in the patrol had known Blažek. We just looked and looked until our leader said, "Stop staring at it. You enjoy seeing dead Germans too much."

So we went away. We didn't see any combat at the trolley garage—the Žižkov commandos had also decided to wait for the firemen—and we made our way back to Vyšehrad. All the way home and through much of that night, I thought about poor Blažek, and how, three times that day, I'd come to know that even if there would be a glorious, victorious outcome, the revolution was not all fine.

Tuesday, May 8, 1945, began as a day of fear—with many rumors: of German reprisals, of Russian rapes, of American cowardice (because they hadn't fought past Pilsen). Not knowing what the day would hold, our Sokol Hall command put us to work building barricades and fortifying Vyšehrad Park with trenches and ammunition caches. Then, supervised by our neighborhood's World War I veterans in their vintage uniforms, we were staked out in battle positions, ten yards apart, on a firing line. My own sniper's nest was near the railway viaduct, just a few steps from where I'd first been accosted and enlisted by the ruddy Prague policeman seventy-two hours ago.

In the afternoon, the first foreign troops were spotted from a rooftop through our militia's only pair of binoculars. It was one grayish body of men, flecked with brown horses, approaching swiftly along the riverbank from the south. The horses told us it certainly wasn't the Americans, and it didn't seem likely to be the Germans, but it was the wrong direction for the Russians to be coming from. So we adjusted our sights and our battle positions for combat as we waited anxiously for these unknown soldiers to draw into range.

As the army drew closer, its uniforms grew blacker. And this puzzled us because we expected either greens from the Germans and Americans or browns from the Russians. We knew, though, that certain SS liquidation and extermination units sometimes wore black. And so it was a cry of relief when someone shouted, "Those aren't Germans! Those are Vlasov's Men."

Vlasov's Men were an army of Russians, mostly Ukranians, formed under Hitler's auspices by a Russian general, A. A. Vlasov. They were recruited and trained in Germany, where they'd wound up as prisoners of war or Red Army deserters or (thanks to the various changes of ownership that parts of the Ukraine have experienced) as forced labor or concentration-camp inmates. General Vlasov himself was a peasant's son and Communist hero who had risen through the ranks until he was close enough to power to conclude that Stalin was almost as insane as Hitler. Taken prisoner by the Germans after his Soviet Second Shock Army was decimated at the Volkhov River, he had cast his lot with his captors in the belief that he could then offer his own people a Russian alternative to Stalin.

The Germans had given Vlasov's two divisions captured Russian and Polish horses and carts and cannons—and Vlasov's Men had fought in vain against their own people at Frankfurt-an-der-Oder. They had fought fiercely, but the Germans had never quite trusted them—and Hitler had, in fact, complained about Vlasov's own charisma. So nobody knew, on May 8, 1945, whether Vlasov's Men were coming to help the Germans or us.

Apparently, with the Third Reich in shambles, they were trying to redeem themselves. Even from the distance, we could see that they were waving to and embracing and behaving in a friendly manner toward any Czechs they encountered. They had heard our radio calling for help, and so, having nowhere to hide from the Red Army, they had come to help us. It was as simple as that to them—and, on that day, to us. They came as brothers and we greeted them as brothers.

Vlasov's Men were small, dirty, and mostly very young: very Russian-looking in the boatlike caps we called *lodičky* (canoes) and very menacing with grenades (looking more like eggs than pineapples) on their belts. They were tired, but like many Ukranians, wiry, quick, and in a hurry. Their first question was: "We're thirsty. Have you water to drink?" They accepted our water and sometimes a little food, but right after the first or second sip, they would ask the invariable second question: "Now where are those Germans you're afraid of?"

It was easy to communicate with them. Part of the Ukraine was once part of Slovakia (or maybe it was the other way around; it is hard for even a native Czechoslovak to keep track), and so an ordinary Czech, if he takes pains to speak slowly and simply, can make a Ukranian understand him, and vice versa.

Vlasov's Men had come with fight in their eyes. When we told them that the Germans were still making trouble in the neighboring Pankrác district, they left as quickly as they had come, with a few Czechs showing them the way. There were a couple of hours of heavy firing and then the Germans were gone from Pankrác and gone from Prague. The scouts we'd sent with Vlasov's Men came back happy. We would not see the Germans again. Nor did we ever see Vlasov's Men again. They had headed for Benešov, where the last major German garrison near Prague was. Soon we heard that the Germans were gone from Benešov, too.

The fact that Prague had been liberated by Vlasov's Men was never mentioned—not right after the war and certainly not after 1948—until 1968. Even then, it was alluded to rather hesitantly. People who'd seen what I'd seen and heard what I'd heard had trouble admitting that Prague had been liberated by an army of Soviet traitors—an army whose heroism in this particular instance was obliterated by history. Vlasov's Men were forcibly repatriated and liquidated in the Soviet Union; Vlasov himself was captured in Czechoslovakia and executed as a traitor. But the fact remains that the brief battles in Pankrác and Benešov and a couple of other spots were the only times during the liberation of Prague that the German Army was confronted in direct battle by experienced soldiers rather than civilian volunteers—and it was Vlasov's Men who chased the Germans away. May 9 is now celebrated in Czechoslovakia as Soviet Liberation Day, but, as far as I'm concerned, Prague was liberated on May 8 by Vlasov's Men.

The next day, Wednesday, May 9, was therefore relatively dull and anticlimactic. The Red Army arrived from the north after freeing the few survivors of the concentration camp at Terezín (Theresienstadt). They entered Prague from the other end of town, so our neighborhood was one of the last to see them.

I had been doing routine sentry duty at the viaduct, but there had been no action at all—thanks to Vlasov's Men. Late in the afternoon, I spotted three Russian soldiers, surrounded by a dozen Czechs who were assaulting them with flowers and kisses. Two of the Russians tried to play with some neighborhood kids, who were too shy—until one of the soldiers produced an accordion. I liked what I saw. It felt good and warm to hear music in the streets and watch people singing and dancing. I yawned—and it felt good to yawn. Then I asked myself what on earth I was doing up there above the viaduct with a weapon. I decided I must look more like a sniper than a sentry. Now I felt endangered for the first time that day. I descended quietly and made my way home, hiding my weapon in the umbrella rack for the last time. (Later there was door-to-door disarmament and my father turned in my arsenal for me.) Peace in our time was upon me.

It took us less than a month to be sorry we had the Russians

while Pilsen had the Americans. A good many of Prague's
"liberators" had no notion that we were on their side. At least,
they seemed to think that they had fought the Germans and
conquered the Czechs. They drank heavily. They would pay
anything for a shot of hard liquor, but they would rather not
pay anything.

Very soon after these conquering heroes arrived belatedly
from the east, I saw, in an arcade off Wenceslas Square, a
happy and slightly drunken middle-aged Czech wave a bottle
of slivovice (plum brandy) at a Russian officer and offer him
a drink. The officer accepted and the Czech held the bottle
for him. Then the Russian asked for the whole bottle. The
Czech said, "What will you pay for it?" The Russian named a
price. The two men bargained and a price was agreed upon.
The Russian counted out the money, held it out with his right
hand, took the bottle with his left hand, withdrew his right
hand before the Czech could collect his payment, started
gulping from the bottle in his left hand, and, when the Czech
had the audacity to argue, hit him in the face with the bottle
fairly hard (hard enough to mess up his face without breaking
the bottle), hit him in the stomach with his right fist, and
kneed him in the groin, too. It was one bloody Bolshoi ballet.

Similarly, we learned not to wear our watches on our wrists
in the streets of Prague. If a Russian asked, "Do you have the
time?" he meant "Give me your watch!" Some boys I knew
had occasional fist fights with the Russians, but it was our girl
friends and mothers who had the most to fear. There were
numerous reports of rapes from the rural areas, but even these
would have been much greater if the Russians didn't have a
good supply of German women prisoners upon whom to practice their manly art of lady-killing.

Although Prague was perhaps the most undamaged—
physically and materially—Central European city after World
War II and we therefore had the least to rebuild, we suffered
from shortages after the war ended. The quality of what was
available was poor; our shoes had wooden bottoms and I felt
like a little Dutch boy whenever I walked on them. Rationing
went on—with the main difference being that, under Czech

management, you didn't always get what your ration card entitled you to. (The Germans had been stingy, but scrupulous.) The penalties for profiteering were less severe than in wartime, and many goods therefore found their way onto the black market. If you didn't have relatives or friends in the farm country, you had to throw yourself upon the dubious mercies of strangers and shopkeepers or else take whatever you could get from UNRRA (United Nations Relief and Rehabilitation Administration), which did a good job of providing basic subsistence. But this meant a family's living for three days on a pot of groats.

We had relatives who farmed near Nymburk, about forty miles from Prague. Even during the war, I used to pedal out there periodically on my bicycle and stay the weekend. Now I did so every second weekend—going with spare parts furnished by my father for the farm equipment and returning with my bike loaded like a grocery delivery boy's. The main differences now were that I didn't have to risk being searched at German roadblocks—and that this trip, which used to be an adventure, was now a necessity.

People grumbled, but there was really very little to complain about, for 1945 was a year of returns and reunions. Already, though, politics got into the act. We wondered why President Beneš, who'd been in London, had to return in triumph via Moscow. The answer was: at Stalin's insistence. When our fighting exiles returned, first came our infantrymen from the east and, only a quite a bit later, our airmen and tankmen fighting with American and British forces in the west. Relatives of our western exiles chafed—and meanwhile the returnees from Russia (of whom a heavy proportion were now Communists) got first crack at the best housing and best jobs. They also took the lion's share of the glory; the exuberance was a bit dimmed by the time the heroes from the west straggled home. Call it psychological conditioning or Communist evangelizing if you will, but rest assured that none of it was accidental.

There was, however, another piece of psychological conditioning working against the Communists. It was Nazi propa-

ganda—in the form of a placard that had been posted everywhere during the occupation. It showed a red hand grabbing
a city. Beneath it was the slogan: IF IT EVER GRABS YOU, YOU
WILL DIE. Even during the war, some people would tear it
down when nobody was looking, but others would disagree
with it or argue about it in private—and still others would
wonder. We already knew Stalin as a man who had imprisoned
or liquidated many good people and who had liberated all
kinds of criminals, some of whom were among the soldiers
who had liberated us. Now, when hammers and sickles were
sprouting everywhere, that red-hand poster remained vividly
and effectively etched in our minds. And, in the end, it proved
more true than untrue.

The Red Army went away when enough good Communists
had come home early enough to gain a firm grip in the postwar
coalition rule under President Beneš. And now we began to
receive another group of returnees: the concentration-camp
survivors. They came last—because many of them had to be
hospitalized or just beefed up to survive the trip home. A good
many didn't live long after their return, but "see Prague and
die" had been the dream that carried them through their
ordeals. The scenes at bus stations—of families barely recog-
nizing their emaciated survivors—were sights I would walk
several blocks out of my way to avoid.

The birth of the political animal that is Karel Čapek began
around 1945. The German past was over and an awful lot of
people were saying (sometimes prefaced by "Like it or not . . .")
that "the Russians are the coming people: the people of tomorrow." Judging by what I'd seen, though, in their few months
among us, I doubted this. On the contrary, they looked like a
throwback to some uncivilized past.

Still, being a young man with a personal stake in the future,
I looked into the domestic brand of Communism as soon as I
could. The Communists were holding an outdoor People's
Congress in a park in the nearby (and unpronounceable for
you) suburb of Krč. It was a balmy night, so I went—but I
didn't hear or see anything new under the stars. No, let me
retract that. For the first time since the war ended, I heard

people speaking about and for *one part* of the whole nation. This *part* they were extolling was "the working class."

If I thought about it, I was a member of the working class, but what they were saying had nothing to do with me or for me. When they ranted about who'd "betrayed the working class" before the war, during the war, and now after the war, I didn't feel betrayed; I felt bored. They pointed fingers often and said, "Let's talk about this" and "Now let's talk about that," but I noticed that they didn't talk, they agitated. They were noisy, but the noises they made didn't have the sound of reason. And, knowing nothing more of them than what I saw and heard, at least half the speakers impressed me as fanatics of no character. If I closed my eyes, their rhythms and vibrations (though not their words) were the same as the pro-Nazi Czechs one occasionally heard in wartime.

Once, working for Linhart's, I was given a package to deliver to "one of the leading Communist lady lawyers in Prague; if you want a real treat, insist that the Comrade sign for it herself, in person." The law office was busy and hectic, but I persisted. And I was glad I did, for the woman who scrawled her well-known name on the receipt was indeed a beauty: the same one who'd deflowered me (and defoliated at least one SS man) along the Vltava (alias Moldau) in 1943. I recognized her, even with clothes on, but she didn't recognize me, even when I said, emphatically, "Thank you, thank you, many times over." By then, I had a notion of what nymphomania was. I rejoiced in having partaken of its better fruit, without wishing to pledge allegiance to either nymphomania or Communism.

(Two years after this second and last meeting of ours, my ambitious seductress became a judge. A year later, she resigned. A week later, she was arrested. Five years later, she died in jail, poor woman. All I ever gave her was my first seed and a law book—and I might have liked her less if I'd known her better—but, oh, how I would have wished her a better fate!)

I kept my eyes open and read the papers. In contrast with the rest of the press—which preached unity in the new coalition, called the "National Front"—the Communist daily,

Rudé Právo (*Red Justice*), was divisive. For example, the film industry and some heavy industry were nationalized right after the war ended. These measures might have been justified. At least, nobody protested them very loudly and the press either quibbled with or explained them. Not *Rudé Právo*, however. It hailed these nationalizations as "decisive victories for the working class in the struggle against capitalist exploitation."

What's worse: for all its scapegoating and scandalmongering, *Rudé Právo* was just about the dullest paper in Prague.

I preferred to read a magazine called *Argus*, which first introduced me to Walter Lippmann in Czech. And it was through reading, rather than heredity, that I developed the liberal centrist political tendencies of my father. I was too young to become a member of his party, the National Socialists, but I joined its youth group. Thanks to Walter Lippmann, I also joined the Prague Friends of the U.S.A. Club. My long-range goal was to learn English and eventually read Walter Lippmann in his original tongue. (I managed this only long after the club was no more and, when I did, I found that Lippmann had been much more comprehensible in Czech than in English.) My short-range goal as a Friend of the U.S.A. was to meet girls at the club's dances.

When I did find a steady girl, it was 1947 and I was seventeen. Her name was Božena and I met her not at a dance, but swimming in the Vltava. My friend Karel Štěpán and I were paddling a canoe and, when it filled with water, we needed a place to empty it. The nearest "island" was the "Blue Pool"— a floating public country club moored on the water with a swimming pool emptying into the river and a kiddie pool sealed in by strips of natural grass: plus lockers, refreshments, and an officious lifeguard. In those days when the water was clean enough for swimming, the Vltava was speckled with several such oases for instant escape from the city heat. Štěpán and I usually hung out at the "Yellow Pool," a little closer to home, but we'd been to the Blue Pool many times, too. It was sometimes called "Honza's Blue Pool" because it was frequented by T. G. Masaryk's son Honza, which is the affection-

ate diminutive for Jan. I'd seen Foreign Minister Jan Masaryk
there twice—a fat friendly man (easy to talk to, though I never
talked to him) who could look suave and at home wearing a
bathing suit or tails. Unlike most fat men, he could probably
look just as comfortable in nothing—but never, never in pre-
mature death.

Masaryk wasn't there the morning we paddled our water-
logged canoe into the Blue Pool. It was so early in the day
that the only swimmer there—and she wasn't swimming, but
reading a book at poolside—was a well-built brunette, wearing
an auburn bathing suit and a suntan that combined with the
other colors to breathe a cool breeze of autumn into our summer
flounderings and horseplay. She turned out to be our age, but
she seemed older, yet attainable, as our clowning around—
largely to keep her attention—also caught the attention of the
lifeguard.

"No boats in the Blue Pool!" he screamed.

"It's not a boat, it's a canoe," Štěpán told him.

"I don't care what it is. Get it out of the Blue Pool."

"It's a public pool," I reminded him.

"For people, not for boats. And, if you come in here, you
come in from the land, not from the water."

We teased him by hiding underwater, standing under the
canoe, lifting it up like a hat whenever we needed to breathe—
all the time trying to draw a laugh out of the girl. She didn't
laugh, but she didn't go back to her book. Instead, she watched
us. And I must have been watching her because I didn't watch
my step and, all of a sudden, my finger was caught between
our canoe and a stone.

Now it was the lifeguard's turn to laugh. "Serves you right,"
he said between chortles that turned to a scream when he saw
that the little accident had wrenched off my fingernail: "No
bleeding in the Blue Pool! Get out of here with your bloody
canoe!"

The girl gave a gasp, too, and found the lifeguard's first-aid
kit. Expertly, she bandaged me, while the lifeguard, who
seemed to know her quite well, said, "They don't belong here,

Božena. And look what that blood is doing to the Blue Pool!"

"What will Honza think?" she murmured, more to me than to him.

"Want a ride?" I asked her when my finger was patched up.

She didn't ask where but simply joined Štěpán and me in our canoe without a word or a wave of farewell to the lifeguard. We took her to an old houseboat that used to belong to the Boy Scouts before Štěpán and I "bought" it from the Scoutmaster in exchange for an old but working motorbike. We fished our small "arms cache" of beer out of the cool water below and, for the summers of 1947 and 1948, our houseboat had a housekeeper. Božena, though, was an old-fashioned girl with such good control of her own libido that she was able to keep ours within bounds for even those puritanical times. She was a sister to Štěpán and a girl friend to me. While daytime teasing and nighttime petting (on the stairs to her widowed mother's apartment) could have gone that big step further, it didn't. In the normal course of events, our romance would have led to marriage. But events were not on a normal course in our land.

I went on working at Linhart's and started attending the night-school program for apprentices that I'd missed out on during the war. There were thirty of us in the course—all youths my age who'd been deprived of this one phase of learning the trade. Our teacher was a pallid, grayish, middle-aged man who was always dressed in gray and spoke very slowly. His name was Cibulka, which means "Little Onion."

Professor Cibulka had served in our army in the east, but the Russians had seen special merit in him and sent him to a special training camp for secret policemen. Now he was just biding his time in book publishing until the country went Communist. He'd say "when" and we'd say "if" and then he'd say, "You'll see, all of you, that no matter how you try to stop the inevitable, your efforts will be in vain. A Red Czechoslovakia will inevitably happen. It is not possible to stop it. You will see. Just wait."

This is the way a good many Communists talked—and this certainty was their most imposing (and most frightening) argument. When you tried to debate with Professor Cibulka, he would either stop abruptly or pull rank, saying, "Remember your place. I'm the teacher and you're the pupil." Or: "This is a school for publishing, not politics." And then, having silenced us, he would resume the droning litany of "You'll see. Just wait."

We were waiting, too. In the 1946 elections, the Communists had polled the largest share of the vote—38 percent—but this was mostly because the liberal, center, and rightist parties were fragmented (not to mention infiltrated) and just beginning to feel their way, while the Communists had the momentum of monolithic certainty, plus Mother Russia's public support. The next free elections would be in 1948, and they were what we were waiting for. It was clear to every observer that the Communists' popularity had peaked in 1946. They would certainly not gain in 1948 and would almost certainly lose many deputies in Parliament. It didn't occur to anybody but the Communists that, this being the case, there would be no free election.

Probabilities became certainties in 1947, when Czechoslovakia was invited to join the Marshall Plan. It was such a good idea that Jan Masaryk persuaded the whole Cabinet, including Communist premier Klement Gottwald and the other Communist ministers, to accept the invitation to receive American aid. The Cabinet vote was unanimous—and there was dancing in Wenceslas Square that night. But Masaryk and Gottwald were summoned to Moscow, where they were treated to one of Stalin's rages and warned that involvement with the Marshall Plan would be construed as an unfriendly act. By another unanimous vote, Czechoslovakia withdrew from the Marshall Plan. "I went to Moscow as the foreign minister of a sovereign state," Jan Masaryk said, "and I came back a stooge of Stalin."

Now the polls showed that the Communists would be lucky to win 15 or 20 percent of the vote. Whereupon strange events began to happen: two months later, Masaryk and two other prominent non-Communists—the minister of justice and the leader of our National Socialist party—received bombs through the mails, in wood boxes labeled "Perfume." The bombs were detected and, despite obstruction at every turn from the Communist minister of interior (which means police, not conservation), the minister of justice traced the bombs from the makers to the sender to the instigator: a Communist functionary who also happened to be Gottwald's son-in-law.

The plotters were never brought to trial, for, when Gottwald and his Communist ministers sat on the justice minister's report and the interior minister even fired several of the investigating officers (one of whom I later met in jail), twelve of the non-Communist ministers in the twenty-six-member Cabinet resigned in February of 1948. They were hoping to force Beneš to appoint a new government and maybe even advance the May election to March. Instead, with Soviet deputy foreign minister Valerian Zorin in town to choreograph the spontaneous rallies, general strikes, and insistent demands made upon an ailing President Beneš, the Communist party applied force.

On February 20, 1948, the People's Militia—a postwar Communist creation masquerading as a "workers' defense force" within the bigger factories—proclaimed "a state of battle" in Prague. Thousands of People's Militiamen, all over the country, were issued ammunition and trucked into Prague to seal the president off from the people and vice versa. The national commander of the People's Militia was General Josef Pavel, a Spanish Civil War hero; his deputy, in command of Prague, was Josef Smrkovský, a hero of the 1945 uprising against the Germans.

When the students of Charles University marched on the Prague Castle to show Beneš their solidarity with his ministers who'd quit, the People's Militia repelled them with clubs and bullets. (Young people had been the first to see through the Red illusion. In the preceding year, the Communist youth organization's membership had plummeted from 600,000 to less than half that figure.) But, isolated from the real public opinion and still recuperating from a stroke, Beneš was a virtual prisoner in his Castle. Nevertheless, he managed to summon the "nonpartisan" minister of defense, General Ludvík Svoboda, a warrior whose exploits on the eastern front had made him a Hero of the Soviet Union, and asked him whether the armed forces would defend the State if the police and the People's Militia tried to seize it. Svoboda made it clear that "the Army goes with the nation" and proceeded to confine to quarters all high-level anti-Communist officers.*

On February 25, 1948, a sick and tired Beneš capitulated. Gottwald proclaimed a new Cabinet, and his voice broke with joy when he named his own son-in-law, the perfume-bomb instigator, as the new minister of justice. The next night, the son-in-law's predecessor defenestrated himself by jumping out of a third-story window—and lived to spend the next twelve years in jail for "false accusation of attempted assassination." And, a fortnight after the democracy his father had founded went Communist, Jan Masaryk lay dead in the courtyard of his foreign ministry—officially a suicide by defenestration. My girl friend Božena and her mother went to see him lying in state. It was early enough in the history of the Czechoslovak Socialist Republic; a few weeks later they would have been afraid to go. As it was, Božena's mother whispered when she told me she'd seen what everybody I knew who went there remarked upon: "The poor man had a sunflower on his temple to cover his wound. I saw it!" I didn't have to go see for myself; I believed what many I knew were saying: "Those swine killed him!" Božena and I could never bring ourselves to revisit Honza's Blue Pool, where our romance had begun.

Where was I when my country was going Communist? Out in Wenceslas Square with all the other young people jeering at the People's Militia—those grim-faced "workers" with red

---

* Ironically, Pavel and Smrkovský were imprisoned for four years apiece by the Communists during the 1950s, and Svoboda was held in the Ruzyně jail for several months. Thus, all three of these clever men could be numbered among the victims of the *coup d'état* they carried out for their masters in Moscow and Prague. And all three of them must have found religion (for a while, at least, in Svoboda's case) somewhere along the line, because they rose to the top of 1968's Prague Spring: Pavel as Alexander Dubček's benign, democratic minister of interior; Smrkovský as the outspoken speaker of Parliament; and Svoboda as president of the Republic. Still, it is small wonder that their fellow ex-prisoners had trouble trusting Pavel, Smrkovský, and Svoboda even as late as 1968.

armbands and all sorts of uniforms. When I heard of how the students had tried and failed to storm the Castle, I first began to think the thought that became my undoing: if just one well-organized group had opposed Smrkovský's and Pavel's militia openly and physically, they would have turned around and run. They were well-disciplined, all right, but gray and weary and not so much afraid as beaten-looking around the eyes. As they marched behind bed sheets painted with slogans, we laughed at them, but we didn't fight them—and I, for one, felt ashamed.

Later, I heard people say many times, "The Communists were arming while the rest of us were just talking."

The Communists took power by the time we finished shaking our heads. They weren't necessarily capable, but always well-organized. In every factory, in every store, in every home, they materialized out of the woodwork. A stranger would walk through the front door, stride directly into the manager's office, and sit down in his chair. The staff would wonder how the manager would cope with this affront, until, after a few hours, it dawned on them that the manager was never coming to work again. Or some long-time sales clerk would show up one day in a suit instead of a smock and take over the boss' office.

If you stood a chance of keeping your job, you found an application to join the Communist party on your desk or workbench. If you didn't apply, your days on the job were numbered.

My father was working at the time as a factory foreman. He was handed a party application. Several of his underlings asked him each day *when*, not if, he was going to sign it. "Maybe tomorrow," he answered. Then he'd come home, poor man, and my mother would start in on him. He should sign, she'd say, because it didn't mean anything and the Communists wouldn't last long. Everyone would know where he stood anyway and everyone who was already making the same pretense he was being asked to make would remember how long and how well he held out. My father said, "Perhaps. Perhaps not." Then one day he was out of his job, out of the factory, and lucky to find work as a chauffeur.

Nobody asked me to apply, but perhaps I was still too young to matter; I was not quite eighteen. Besides, I just wasn't on many dossiers or youth registers, thanks to my parents. I think that if I'd been asked to apply, I might have worried more. My choice certainly would have been *no*. I didn't *feel* Communist.

No, I felt depressed. Less than three years after Hitler and the Nazis, who had decimated so many good people, were driven away, there were suddenly enough Czechs and Slovaks to oppress the Czechoslovak nation. And it was shocking to see people all around me—virtually everybody who had a chance to join, except my father and one or two of his friends—taking advantage of the opportunity, so that suddenly this upstart Communist party was almost everybody.

Just as fast as it was happening, people were growing afraid. Afraid of each other. Afraid of themselves. Afraid that the wrong word for what had happened in February would slip out: "overturn" instead of "turnover," the officially approved word; or "takeover," instead of "turnover." It was easy, in such circumstances, for the tongue to slip. Or to utter taboo words like *puč*, which is how the Czechs spell *Putsch*.

Nobody officially closed the frontier. You just couldn't get a passport or a visa. Or, if you had a valid one, you were turned away and told to get a new one; meanwhile, the frontier police kept the old one. It was all very shadowy. You had difficulty or you knew you'd have difficulty or you thought you'd have difficulty or you feared you'd have difficulty or you knew that *if* you had difficulty you'd be in real trouble—so you didn't apply, you didn't try. Some people were called in and asked to turn in their passports; "We're going to issue new ones" they were told but they never got them and most of these people knew better than to ask for them. If your passport expired, why bother to apply for a new one? There was too much at stake to risk a "no" answer.

Nobody came to your job or your home to arrest you—at first. It was much more shadowy. You'd leave your house or your office and two men would be waiting, saying, "Will you please come along and tell us a few things?" If several people lived in a building, they'd look out the windows and see the two men and a Škoda auto (later, the secret police used other vehicles, too—fancier cars confiscated from people they'd arrested) and wonder for whom they waited. A tenant would go out and come back. Then another. Then another. Eventually, you knew it was for you. . . .

The Russians were the most shadowy of all. We *knew* they were there, but we never saw them. We heard they were in the ministries, but now the ministries were like fortresses—nobody who worked there dared tell; nobody who didn't work there dared ask. Nobody knew where they lived, where they ate, where they shopped. But we knew they were there.

Beneš resigned in June and died in September—a broken man who'd worked with Masaryk to make a dream come true in 1918 with the founding of the First Czechoslovak Republic, and who had presided over its two greatest tragedies: dismemberment in 1938 at Munich, where, in his words, "they decided about us without us," and betrayal in 1948.

Too bad about Beneš and too bad about Jan Masaryk, we thought. We wished they could have lived to see the end of the aberration, because few of us thought it would last. I was one, though, who felt we would have to hasten its downfall. I told trusted friends like Karel Štěpán, "We have to fight them with arms. They won because they had the weapons; now we need arms to fight them." Perhaps my words sounded too much like the follies of history; in any event, I wasn't yet ready to act upon them. The bandits stood with guns to our heads—and we were still trying to *talk* them out of shooting. I wrote letters to the National Socialist party press, complaining that the Communists were strangling the voters and the system. A couple of my letters were printed and there were no repercussions. Apparently, Karel Čapek was not an easy name to track down.

How people evolve! In late summer of 1968, over a bottle of Dalmatian cherry liqueur, an argument takes place in the American Family Levy's kitchen in Prague. The question, toward midnight, is whether, after the August invasion—with the three other key leaders (Communist party first secretary Alexander Dubček, Prime Minister Oldřich Černík, and Parliament Speaker Smrkovský) abducted by the Russians—the president of Czechoslovakia was right in going to Moscow to negotiate with Brezhnev and the Soviet Politburo. The alternative would have been continued passive resistance that might have forced the Russians to set up a military occupation government.

The kitchen debaters in 1968 are a DOVE, a HAWK, and an AMERICAN.

HAWK: *With a visible enemy, the Czechoslovak Revolution would be prolonged and the occupation would go down in history as the rape it is.*

DOVE: *Then Dubček and Smrkovský would be dead for certain and probably the president, too. And maybe a thousand dead Czechoslovaks instead of the hundred who've died already.*

HAWK: *A thousand? Be realistic, man! Knowing the Russians, it would probably be in the tens of thousands. But it would still be better and the Czechs would win much sooner.*

AMERICAN: *My country was lucky. America won a war in seventeen eighty-one and it took almost two centuries before we really lost a war. The Czechs have been fighting the same war for three hundred and fifty years with different enemies, and sometimes you've been in on the victorious side, but you've yet to win a war.*

DOVE: *Whatever we have won, we haven't won by waging war.*

HAWK: *North Vietnam never stopped fighting, and now they've done the impossible. They never lost, so they won.*

DOVE: *But at what cost? Besides, they were up against the Americans, who always stop somewhere, not against the Russians, who stop at nothing.*

HAWK: *Gandhi's disciples practiced the Czech kind of passive resistance for years and he won!*

DOVE: *Against the British, not against the Russians.*

HAWK: *Look at the Algerians!*

DOVE: *Against the French. The French aren't the Russians.*
HAWK: *Castro started with eighty-two men on a mountaintop.*
DOVE: *Against Batista, not against the Russians.*

In this 1968 dialogue, the American is Alan Levy. The Dove is Karel Čapek. The Hawk is a Hindu named Krishna Vishwanath, a student on a Government of India scholarship to the Prague Film Faculty, who'd found the Indian vision—much as the Levys found the American Dream—in the Prague Spring that ended abruptly in August winter. And, offstage, the President who went to Moscow in August of 1968 was that Czechoslovak Hero of the Soviet Union, General Ludvík Svoboda, the hands-off "hero" whose abstention insured the success of the Communist coup twenty years earlier.

By December of 1948, hundreds were under arrest, thousands had fled the country (or been caught trying), and tens of thousands had been thrown bodily out of their offices. The year drew to a close with the Communists firmly in power and the rest of the nation locked out but sealed in.

My friend Karel Štěpán—a big, strapping lad from the Nusle district—was not very intellectual, but a good storyteller and a fine fellow with whom to drink beer or double date. Once, Štěpán and I passed by a Communist rally and stopped to listen. We suddenly found ourselves arguing with the speaker and the rest of the people there—not because we came to heckle, but just because what was being said wasn't the truth and we felt it our duty to say so. We were thrown out. On our way home, we passed a neighborhood shop that had been confiscated and converted into a party "agitprop center." In the window was one of the slogans we'd objected to at the rally. We smashed the window, tore up the slogan placard, and went home to a good night's sleep. After that, from time to time, we broke a window and talked about leaving the country.

Our parents wouldn't hear of it; mine wouldn't even discuss it with me. But, shortly before Christmas, a non-Communist secret policeman we knew (who later escaped to Scandinavia) told my father, "Just a friendly warning. I don't know what it's about, but your son had better be careful or get out of sight. They're looking into him." After nine months of Communism, one didn't have to ask who *they* were. "What for?" is all my father asked. Our friend answered, "How should I know? But I saw a card with his name and address along with some fellow named Štěpán."

When I came home, my mother was packing a bag for me. I insisted on staying through Christmas because I didn't think the security apparatus would be very active over the holidays. And I wanted to have some time with my girl, Božena.

I bought her a Swiss watch I'd had my eye on for some time. When we were decorating the Christmas tree together at her house on December 24, I hung the watch by its strap on a branch. It took Božena a couple of hours before she noticed it—and then she was so excited she almost dropped it. Her Christmas present to me was more fancily wrapped—in a box with plenty of paper and ribbon. It was a ceramic miniature of an antique car with a driver in it. While it was appropriate to my departure, I didn't tell Božena I was going until a day or two after Christmas. Even then, I simply told her, "I won't see you for a while. I have to take a trip." She must have assumed it was a sales trip within Czechoslovakia in connection with my job; by the end of 1948, nobody talked of foreign travel.

On the twenty-eighth of December, Karel Štěpán and I made a five-hour express train ride to Cheb, the last Czech city before the West German frontier. From Cheb, we took a local train to a village where Štěpán had explored the terrain on a summer visit to relatives of a friend.

It was dark when we arrived at his hosts' simple cottage. They were surprised to see us, but most hospitable. Over soup, they asked us how long we were staying. We hesitated. Our host looked at our hostess, coughed, and said, "You're welcome to stay with us a day or two—longer if you want." Blushing, Štěpán blurted out that we wanted to leave the country. Our host didn't seem surprised. "Then finish your soup," he said, "and never mind about the dinner—because the best time is now!"

The wife packed some homemade cakes (what you call

Danish pastry and we called *buchty*) for us while the husband gave us directions. The simplest instruction, though, was to follow the stars and our compass (which Štěpán had thought to bring). And, because the ground was covered with snow, the strongest warning was to move from tree to tree so that our tracks would not make us and our route too obvious.

The temperature was around 20. The stars were bright, but the moon hadn't come out yet. We didn't talk, but just followed our compass west-northwest, avoiding the two or three open fields along our way. After three hours and five miles, we saw what looked like a formation of soldiers, spaced fifteen yards apart like my notion of a firing squad. I took a deep breath, but Štěpán whispered "We're here!" The "soldiers" didn't move; they were stone pillars marking the boundary. When we were upon them, there was enough light for us to read the carved initials "ČSR" [CzechoSlovak Republic] on our side and then, by taking one step forward, "BRD" [BundesRepublik Deutschland, or German Federal Republic] on the side where we stood now.

The Iron Curtain already existed, but it was still under construction. The barbed wire and guard posts and minefields and electrified fences and zigzags and no-man's lands had not yet reached where we were.

We continued west-northwest for a mile or so and then, instead of avoiding open fields and roads, we cut across one looking for the other. We came to a crossing and were relieved, for once, to see that ugly Germanic lettering we'd been liberated from three and a half years earlier. Now we had escaped to freedom in Germany.

Štěpán and I were in the American Zone of Germany. The feeling we came west with wasn't that we were escaping to Germany—but to American-occupied Germany, which we thought would be something better than Germany if not so good as America. Our opinion of America had gone up even before our country had gone Communist. The black market had taught us to respect your field jackets, sweaters, and particularly those green fatigue caps that the young people of

Prague liked to wear as proudly as though they were the Stars and Stripes.

We followed the road west to the first German village. It was the middle of the night. In the town square, four Christmas light bulbs hung as though from a clothesline. They were turned on, but they illuminated the way to nothing that was open. At Christmastime, no rooms at the inn, no signs of life. Now and then a dog barked, but this only embellished the mood of a haunted village where nobody wanted us.

We trudged through the town, but must have been spotted. Just on the outskirts, a farmhouse light went on and the front door opened. Framed in the doorway was a lean, strong man with a German border guard's coat thrown over his nightshirt. We went to him and he spoke to us in a regional, especially guttural German dialect that sounded like a throat disease. We didn't understand his questions, but we had a few German answers prepared, which we dutifully recited whenever he paused and which seemed to satisfy him. He ushered us inside. We wondered whether we would be getting coffee or soup, but instead we got frisked and our luggage got searched. He asked us if we had any weapons and we said no. Then, relaxing a little, he made a fire and it became almost cozy in that room. He had opened our parcel of *buchty* for us while searching, so now we ate them while he went over our papers and issued us identity cards (valid for only two days) and railroad tickets (valid for only one day) to the nearest U.S. Army outpost in Wissau. Then he told us that, if we hurried, we could catch the first train to Wissau—whereupon he started chopping wood so fiercely that the splinters flew at us like sparks as he began preparing a hearty breakfast for himself.

The morning local to Wissau was still pockmarked with bullet holes from the war. The passengers on it—workers commuting to factories—looked shabby and sullen. They stared at us. Feeling out of place in the dressy city hats we'd worn from Prague, Štěpán and I tugged at the brims, trying to lower them and conceal our eyes in an effort to look more German. This was easier for Štěpán to do because his hat was too large.

At the American base in Wissau, we were greeted by a rather effeminate G. I. of Czech origin. He spoke our language and insisted on calling us by our first names. Since we were Karel Štěpán and Karel Čapek, this confused more than it clarified—but we liked it. When I remarked later that this wasn't my notion of the virile American fighting man, Štěpán shushed me with: "Americans aren't homosexuals."

How could I argue with that? It was good to know a Czech like Štěpán, who was even more patriotic about America than I ever was.

This unmanly sergeant, whom we nicknamed "Cary Gooper," had his hot little hands on us long enough to issue us railroad tickets to our next destination: the "screening camp" in Amberg. Determined to see a little of the German countryside from seats instead of on foot, we took places by the window—and slept all the way from Wissau to Amberg, where it was dark when the conductor shook us awake and threw us off.

In the screening camp, it was as if, having fallen asleep on the train, we'd been transported back to Czechoslovakia. Most of the interviewers there were Czech secret policemen—non-Communists who'd seen the handwriting on the wall in February and escaped soon thereafter. Now they were practicing their profession on the American side. Their job was to evaluate whether we were genuine political refugees or just criminal escapees. It made sense to use their talents, but it was nevertheless a jolt.

This processing took a week—three days of interrogation and then four days waiting for a decision as to whether we could stay in Germany for a while. Štěpán and I lived in a dormitory with a lot of youngsters like us, mostly from Prague. There were also rooms for families: one room to a family. The food was not bad—and there was nothing else to do except eat and sleep. Karel Štěpán befriended a Polish widow, who washed and ironed and mended our clothes and stuffed his oversized hat with some newspapers we gave her. A Lithuanian girl, in charge of dishing out the food, took a liking to me and kept giving me extra helpings, which I didn't always want.

At the end of our week in Amberg, Štěpán and I were issued displaced persons cards and sent on to a refugee center in Stuttgart—a military barracks. Here, we were fed into the machinery of processing for a new life—which we didn't want. We had come to redeem the old life and its promise that had been stolen from us by the Communist takeover. Surely, the Americans would understand what had happened to us and would use us, arm us, and help us win our own fight—for who could deny that Communism was anti-American? It seemed very simple to us.

But the subject was never raised by the Americans. Every time I broached it, I was told that I'd do the answering and they'd do the questioning.

"Where do you want to go from here?"

"Back to Czechoslovakia to fight Communism."

"The choice is: America, if you're qualified to support yourself there or else the American Zone of Germany, if there's work for you."

"I want to work in Prague for freedom for my people."

"We can't do anything in Prague for you or your people or freedom. You have yours. What do you choose? With your qualifications around cars, we might be able to get you work with Esso in Frankfurt."

"Those are my father's qualifications you're looking at. I have none—except I'm not going to rot in Germany while there's a need for me to fight in Czechoslovakia."

"Then the interview is over. Come back and see us when you're ready to think realistically."

Five of us who felt the same way—myself and Štěpán and three new friends: Vacek, Kronus, and Konopáč, all within a year of each other's age—formed a delegation and went to U.S. Counterintelligence Headquarters in Ludwigsburg, a suburb of Stuttgart. It was easy enough to find: a plain house with a shingle that said "C.I.C." hung out on the front porch.

Inside, Vacek, the son of a formerly wealthy carpet-store owner and the only one of us with a year or two of college and four or five of English, did the talking for us. He told a recep-

tionist what we wanted. After an hour, we were sent into a
large living room to talk with a redheaded man, about thirty-
five, in civilian clothes.

Vacek was eloquent. He'd been in refugee camps batting
his head against unhearing stone walls longer than any of us.
He could handle a gun. He wanted to fight. And he put all this
across in that redhaired man's tongue.

The man listened, his eyes gleaming. He didn't seem too
bright, but he seemed interested. Several times, just to make
sure, Vacek would interrupt himself to ask, "Do you follow
me?"

"Sure I do," the man would say, with a slight sneer. "Keep
talking."

When we were done, he asked, "You finished?" The answer
was yes. "All right," he said, his sneer turning into a snarl and
then a bark. "Empty your pockets!"

To our amazement, two men came out of the closets and
joined him in searching us. They took away a couple of pocket-
knives and Karel Štěpán's hat, which the Polish widow had
tightened for him in Amberg by stuffing it with newspaper.
The redheaded man ripped out this lining and uncreased the
fragments of newspaper. The paper, I noticed, was *Rudé
Právo.*

"All right," he said, ironing out the paper with his fist and
turning to Vacek. "You wanna know if I unnerstand English.
Now let's see how good you unnerstand Czech. What does this
say?" He pointed to a headline.

" 'R-revanchist wolves in G.I. khakis,' " Vacek read, quaking.
"And this one?"

" 'The Marshall Plan: Blueprint for Conquest.' "
"And what about this one?"

Confronted by a portrait of Uncle Sam with fangs, Vacek
lost his English altogether.

"All right! Get out!" the redheaded man shouted. "All except
him." He grabbed Karel Štěpán by the arm. Štěpán asked in a
quavering voice if Vacek could stay to interpret. The redheaded man told Štěpán, "You spoke perfect English before.
How come you're losing it now?"

"I don't know a word of English," Štěpán said, pointing to Vacek, who was interpreting. "He did all the talking."

"Watch your step, boy," the redhead warned. "Every word you said was recorded."

"But I didn't say a word in English," Štěpán protested. "I wouldn't know how."

"Awright, we'll do it in German," said the redhead, pointing to one of the men from the closet. "He speaks German."

"B-but I don't," Štěpán said—and he began to cry.

Now our redheaded inquisitor started speaking the worst kind of gutter Czech: "If that don't beat all! Just shove that shit, kiddo, and the rest of you clear out! You, too!" he added, showing Vacek the door.

On the porch, I marveled that "such a man could be one of us!"

"But I don't want to be one of him," Kronus said.

After two hours, Štěpán appeared, shaking his head at the stupidity of it all. "Did they hurt you?" I asked.

"No," he said, "but I want to go home. To Prague."

"So do I," the others said. Although Vacek and I made further approaches to other branches of U.S. Intelligence, their answers were less rude, but essentially the same: what we wanted wasn't possible.

A little later in life, I met men just like the redhead—but they were working on and for the other side of the Iron Curtain. Only much later did I come to appreciate the comedy of that afternoon in Ludwigsburg. The redheaded man and his cronies in the closet were playing middle-aged counterspies with a bunch of kids who wanted to play guerrillas.

I wanted to be what I was later accused and convicted of being, but I never got the chance. In the recognition of this, there is a certain admission of guilt that makes it impossible for oneself to dismiss—or wholly deny—the most absurd accusation. My conscience, at least, still finds it hard to separate thought from deed. My children have this problem, too, and I am not entirely sorry they do.

In Germany, Štěpán and I—and Vacek, Kronus, and Konopáč, too—had come to know that we would simply have to rely upon ourselves. We would go back to Czechoslovakia to work against the regime—by talking, heckling, breaking windows, even shooting. But shooting what? Shooting our mouths off seemed like the only possibility on that front—and a short-lived one at that. . . .

Until Vacek made contact with a well-known politician from Pardubice who'd fled the country right after February's coup and was now well-established in the West. He gave Vacek some addresses in Prague and Pardubice—and one in Stuttgart, where the five of us were issued a total of three handguns. Vacek took one of them as his finder's fee. Kronus and Konopáč were given one to share; Konopáč, being the son of an Army officer, took charge of it because he was presumed to know something about weapons, even though his father was a desk soldier who would cringe at the sound of a slammed drawer. Štěpán took custody of the gun allotted to him and me. As consolation prizes, Kronus was awarded a blackjack and I won a set of brass knuckles.

In return for this favor, the politician from Pardubice saddled us with a hometown runaway named Sýkora, two or three years older than any of us, though he seemed much younger and more naïve. Lean, sallow, and pit-faced, he would tell everybody he met, without waiting to be asked, that "I'm a student rebel from Pardubice. I planted a bomb that didn't go off, but they know I did it and they're after me, even here." When we asked him about his bomb exploit, he didn't seem to know much about explosives. When we asked him how and when he became a student rebel, he replied primly, "For ideological reasons"—but he knew even less about ideology. He struck me as a dangerous fool, but the politicians, who must have wanted to get rid of him, too, had insisted that we take Sýkora back with us because "he'll know what has to be done in Pardubice." If Sýkora did know, he never said so—and he talked so much that if he *had* known anything, he would have blurted it out many times. The others must have smelled danger emanating from him because I noticed that none of us would tell him where we lived in Prague.

We split up into two groups for the trip back home. Štěpán

and I were saddled with Sýkora, and we would go the way we'd come, via Cheb; Vacek, Kronus, and Konopáč had come by another route and would go back that way. On the afternoon local train from Wissau to the border town, with all those same workmen watching us with listless curiosity, Sýkora started to tear up his documents—his displaced person and I.D. cards. We had to stop him. It was, after all, against German law as well as Czechoslovak law to cross the border illegally in either direction. While the authorities in the American Zone gave sanctuary to refugees, they didn't favor shuttle traffic across the border. And breaking *into* Czechoslovakia would, in fact, carry even greater risk of penalty than breaking *out* had. So we didn't destroy our papers until we were in the forest about half a mile from the frontier.

It was February 1, 1949, and I knew life would be hard for us. Like the others, I'd given up my job without giving notice —and my disappearance had surely been noted and reported. I'd even sent my parents a postcard from Germany. I didn't know at the time whether it had reached them (it had), but surely it had been read and probably they would be watched from time to time. So I couldn't go home again, and neither could Štěpán, Vacek, Kronus, Konopáč, or, for that matter, Sýkora. We would have to live like outlaws in a police state. Nevertheless, leaving Czechoslovakia, I'd felt sorry. Going back into that beaten, bleeding land, I have to admit that I felt happy. I even think I'd feel that way now, too.

The first night in February was much colder than the night in late December when Štěpán and I had crossed this same border. By moonlight this time, we followed our compass, the stars, our memories—and the wind, which was so fierce that it was better not to go against it. We filed along, a few feet apart, and I was in the lead when, right after passing the stone border markers, I heard a clink of metal. On a swift down-hand signal from me, the three of us halted. Fifteen yards away and coming right at us were two fur-hatted Czechoslovakia border guards and a big brown dog (like the ones that now patrol the Chicago subways); it was his straining at the leash that had caught my ear.

We saw them, but they didn't see us. Falling to the right in the new snow, we slithered behind a tree. The dog lunged toward the tree, but the guards were in no mood to follow him. They wanted to get on with their patrol and to follow their prescribed route all the way to some warm soup or Cognac. They went past us, so close we almost could have touched them.

Five minutes after they were past, we slipped into the shadows of the woods and took a windier but more solitary route that brought us, at dawn, to the outskirts of Cheb. We didn't try to call upon the friends who'd directed us to the border in December. They could do nothing for us now and a visit from us would do nothing for them except perhaps make trouble. Anyway, we knew they'd be much more afraid than when we'd seen them last. From outside, in Germany, we already knew conditions had worsened in our absence. Police searches on trains had become commonplace—not just on the few international expresses, but on the domestic locals, where any passenger with too much or too little luggage, too many or too few documents, or any other suspicious possessions would have to "come along with us and answer a few questions." Which was why, when Sýkora had wanted to bring back a carton of American cigarettes from Germany, we'd argued and finally ordered him not to.

We knew that spies and provocateurs abounded. We suspected that some of the Czech ex-cops who were now interrogating refugees for the U.S. Army of Occupation in Germany were double agents. Not only did some of these policemen go back to serve their former masters, but they took with them (as tickets of readmission) names and sometimes even photos of refugees who'd fled to Germany and then changed their minds and quietly slipped unnoticed back into Czechoslovakia.

Even within the borders, thanks to provocateurs, anyone the authorities were out to "get" could be had. In early 1949, their principal targets were wartime émigrés who'd fought in the R.A.F. or other Western armed forces. Their military know-how and experience of freedom made them a threat to the regime. Some had already been arrested and executed on trumped-up charges. Other veterans would be approached by provocateurs with plans to flee the country. The veteran might decline. But he would be arrested the next day anyway— for "failing to report an illegal plot" to escape. In some cases, the penalty was as high as twenty years in prison.

Knowing that the trains were closely watched, we stayed away from public transport. Instead, we went to a truck depot in Cheb and hitched a ride to Prague. There was room for only one of us in the cab of the empty cattle truck. The driver said, "Two of you have to ride in the back. Which one of you wants to sit up front and keep me company?" Sýkora answered first, but I said quickly, "If you don't mind, we'd all rather stay together in the back of the truck." The driver did mind my un-friendliness, but we couldn't risk letting the talkative Sýkora spend even five minutes up front with the driver.

He let us out in the Square of Charles IV that afternoon. My parents lived within walking distance, just one tram stop away, and Štěpán's family not much farther on, but we didn't dare to go see them, and we wouldn't let Sýkora know where we lived. So, taking a tram right through my old neighborhood and Štěpán's without a glance, we delivered Sýkora to the railroad station in Vršovice and put him on the next train to Pardubice. When it pulled out, we began to breathe the Prague air— though we knew there was still danger from him. After a week, we had a series of designated meeting places (a different one every night) for connecting up with Vacek, Kronus, and Kono-páč. Since the politician's contacts in Pardubice would have work for us to do that would be relayed through Sýkora, we'd been forced to share this schedule with our least reliable member.

That would be a week away—and we hoped we'd never see him again. He was unreliable enough for this to be possible. Now that Sýkora was out of sight for a while, Štěpán and I could function again. We needed to find a hideaway and, since we were in Vršovice, we thought of a married couple living nearby whom Štěpán knew well and I knew, too. The Jeřabeks, in their thirties, were childless—and would always be so, for she'd been sterilized in the Ravensbrück concentration camp by Nazi medical experimenters. Neither he nor she was Jewish, but they'd met each other in the camps, where they'd been imprisoned for being passionate anti-Nazis. Married after they'd both survived the war, they were now passionate anti-Communists; and compassionate people who, when we called upon them at nightfall, offered to put us up for as long as we needed.

While waiting for Vacek, Kronus, and Konopáč, we kept busy delivering the politician's message to his friends back home. That week, we had one close shave with the secret police. They were never hard to spot in their inevitable disguise of brown leather jacket and black beret, as well as from the way they worked so busily at looking unsuspicious. But they were also getting bolder: pointing and even shooting pistols at bystanders who got in their way. And they no longer waited in the street for their victim to come out; they went inside to get him. On our second or third day back, I was delivering a message to the wife of a man who'd fled to Germany while Štěpán stood lookout on the street—Revolutionary Boulevard, it was now. I stood in the doorway while the woman made me repeat the message twice. Then she asked me in for coffee and cake, but I declined because "I have someone waiting for me." I left a minute later.

On the street, Štěpán fell into step behind me and then we both stopped short as a black Tatra car roared around the corner, clipping the sidewalk and nearly amputating our toes. It pulled up in front of the building I'd just left. Six men in brown leather jumped out and raced into the building. Štěpán and I kept walking, apart, and when we were a safe distance away, we stood and watched. The men came out of the building dragging the woman I'd just visited and flinging her into their car. She had two children in school, I knew, and I wondered what would happen to them when they came home to an empty apartment. But I didn't dare to go back there.

The time came to connect up with Vacek, Kronus, and Konopáč—and maybe Sýkora. Štěpán and I arrived right on time the first night at the rendezvous spot: the little park between my old employer, Linhart's, now nationalized as part of the

State Textbook Enterprise, and the old Woodrow Wilson Station, already renamed Main Railroad Station for the second time. Nobody came. The next night found us—but not our three friends—across the river in the Angel Market of Smíchov. And the next night in the courtyard of Strahov Monastery.

By the light of the moon over Strahov on a clear winter night, Štěpán found the brighter side: "Well, at least we're done with Sýkora." He had only known our first three meeting places. Now that he hadn't shown up, he wouldn't know what the next prearranged step was—a card to Vacek's girl friend indicating where we were staying.

We sent her a picture postal—with a black-and-white photo of flowers—and on it was a routine girl-to-girl missive that Mrs. Jeřabek penned for us with her return address at the top.

(What *we* didn't know was that Sýkora had been "apprehended" in Pardubice and had talked freely to police about Čapek and Štěpán and Vacek and Kronus and Konopáč and their meeting places. Those last three had shown up early in the park near the railroad station and had been grabbed— after a struggle in which Vacek sent one secret policeman to the hospital for treatment. They had been hauled away, tortured, and interrogated—keeping the police so busy that they almost forgot that there were two more of us and the park should have been staked out for a few hours after the capture. By then, the other two nights had passed, but the police placed all known contacts of the trio under surveillance, wiretaps, and mail intercepts.)

We came home to the Jeřabeks' two nights after sending that fateful postal and took the elevator to the fifth floor—using keys our hosts had lent us to open the house's front door and ride the coin-operated elevator free of charge. Štěpán and I each had a set of keys. When he tried to open the apartment door with his elevator key, I had the right key ready, so I said, "Out of my way, stupid!" and took over the job. So I was the first to step into the apartment.

From the vestibule, where I took off my shoes to put on the carpet slippers we call "house shoes," I could see Mrs. J. sitting in her living room. I was surprised she didn't greet me, for she was usually quite animated. Tonight, she looked pale and tense.

With my slippers on, I padded into that silent living room to say good evening and find out what was the matter with our hostess. No sooner had I passed through the doorway, though, than a brown-leather bear of a man, who'd been standing against the living-room wall to my left, came bounding out and pounced on me, shouting, "Hands up!" while pushing me to the ground. A smaller man in brown leather, who'd been covering Mrs. J. with a pistol from the far side of the sofa that she was sitting on, turned his attention from her to me by jumping up and down on me once the big bear had me down.

A third man, who'd been crouching on the balcony behind Mrs. J., raced through the room to catch Štěpán. Not having begun to remove his shoes, Štěpán simply turned around and ran. He was closing the apartment door when the big bear, still working me over, pushed my head aside and fired one shot that hit Štěpán in the left thigh.

It was when that shot exploded and blazed near my ear that I first began to believe what was happening to us.

Part 2

Little Speck of Dust

Štěpán didn't stop running when he was hit. The two-minute push-button light in the hall had just gone off and he knew the building better than his pursuers, so he managed to dash two flights down the stairwell before three secret policemen, racing up from downstairs, caught him. Knowing Štěpán had a gun, I'd been almost hoping he would shoot it out with our three tormentors in the apartment—but when I learned that fifteen to twenty men were staked out in and around the building, I was glad he hadn't. Štěpán's three captors and the two men who'd been chasing him from the apartment didn't carry him, but dragged him, up the stairs and back into Jeřabeks' flat.

I must say I was relieved to see them, if not Štěpán, because they diverted the attention of the runty little brown-leather man who'd been left with Mrs. J. and me—and who'd been spending the time jumping up and down on my neck. Štěpán was paler than I'd ever seen him. Blood was seeping through his gray trousers and down his leg, but it seemed to disappear into Mrs. Jeřabek's living-room carpet, which, I'll always remember, was red.

I stuck my chin into the carpet to support the weight of the little man, who was now just sitting on my neck. The Jeřabeks may have had a fine quality red carpet, but it made such a coarse towel that it gave me my only wound from being captured: my chin began to bleed.

We were handcuffed and searched. The little man took away my brass knuckles. The big man, who had the immature beefy red face of a butcher boy, whistled when he found Štěpán's gun. Mrs. Jeřabek had already been searched; now she was handcuffed, too. She kept moaning, "I want to be with my husband! I want my husband!" From her laments, we learned that her husband had been taken away by the police three hours earlier, but she'd been kept behind as a decoy for us.

We were taken in separate police cars to the Bartholomew Street police headquarters, which is a square block of buildings built around a courtyard. The outer ring, facing the street, is the side used by the public and by uniformed police and civilian employees; the inner ring, entered through the courtyard, houses the secret police. There, I was marched upstairs, shut into a room, blindfolded with a rag, and then beaten. The men formed a circle around me and lashed out from all directions. Still handcuffed and never knowing quite where the rain of blows was coming from, I concentrated on defending my groin; I knew where *it* was and wanted to hang onto it.

After a few blows had been struck, the blindfold fell off and my assailants didn't bother to replace it. I could see there were five of them—including the three who'd been in the apartment —and now I could defend myself a little. But this was, in a way, worse than being blindfolded. Flinching from or dodging a blow left my groin vulnerable. All five wore brown leather, but one I hadn't seen before, who wore a belted leather trenchcoat instead of a zippered jacket, was especially interested in his work and my groin. He would grab me by the hair and pull my head back hard in an effort to pry my hands away from his target and then he would smash at my balls with knees, shoes, or whatever he could get on me. He was a small, unhealthy-looking man with pale, yellowish skin. He was trying so hard to hurt me that his breathing grew heavy and labored and then red spots erupted on his face. Never, before or since, have I seen someone so passionately involved in his work. It was incredible to me that I had done anything

to make someone that angry with me—and what had I done?
I hadn't done anything yet!

Throughout my beating, the men shouted questions at me—
but they weren't listening for answers and I wasn't talking
back. Besides, they would have had trouble understanding
anything I said because several well-placed blows to my mouth
seemed to be mashing my teeth and lips into an impenetrable
mess. Thus, they found out nothing from me. But, by listening
closely to them, I could find out what they knew—which was
everything Sýkora had known about me and not much else.
(Vacek, Kronus, and Konopáč apparently hadn't broken under
"questioning" yet.) They knew about Vacek's visit to the
émigré politician in Germany, who'd sicked Sýkora on us, but
they didn't know about our visit to the C.I.C. in Ludwigsburg.

They knew I'd come from Germany to Prague via Cheb and
a cattle truck. "You still stink like spoiled swine!" "Nazi!"
"Hitler Youth!" "You come from Germany to make an uprising
here!" "We overthrew Hitler and now we've got you!" There
were German epithets, Moravian epithets, Slovak epithets, and
Czech epithets. After forty-five minutes, the beating stopped,
but the insults went on.

"Swine!" said the man in the belted trenchcoat. "Why don't
you go back to Germany and shit up the place instead of here?"

"I'll be glad to," I managed to spit out through the gap where
two teeth had been an hour earlier.

This earned me a hard slap on the face and "Why, you
swaggering young punk!"

I picked up the cue from them—and swaggered. They
seemed to understand and even respect a swaggering young
punk. It was a pose I adopted for all future "interrogations,"
whether verbal or physical. It gave me a big advantage and
even played a part in my survival. If I swaggered just a little,
I didn't crawl and wasn't humiliated. They might slap me for
my cockiness, but it worked psychologically: they stopped
thinking of me as a deadly ideological enemy. They could cope
with me in their mental box of "swaggering young punk" and
I was no more and no less than that as a threat to them.

"Why did you go to Germany?"

"I like to travel."

"So you admit you went to Germany! What for?"

"I wanted to see other countries."

"Why did you come back?"

" 'East, west, home's the best!' " I replied.

"So you admit you crossed the border illegally twice! What made you an enemy of the State?"

"Communism." For that, I lost another tooth.

As the serious questioning began, I took stock of Karel Čapek, Prison Beginner. I was minus several teeth and a huge pile of hair that the man in the trenchcoat had torn out of my scalp. It lay before me like a mat. And it never grew back.

When they called it a night at 3:00 A.M., they had elicited little or nothing more from me than they already knew from Sýkora. I merely filled in and embroidered details they already had. Then, in the middle of the night, I was delivered from secret police headquarters to my own neighborhood jail, Pankrác.

It took such a long while to get *into* Pankrác that I wondered if it would be any easier to get out. My butcher-boy captor rang the night bell. Nobody came. He rang it again and still nobody appeared. We drove to the day entrance, but it was closed up tight—with a sign there telling you to use the night entrance. Back we went to the night gate, where Butcher Boy rang some more—in vain. Disgusted, he went off to find a phone and left me in the care of his two partners from the apartment ambush. After half an hour, he came back and, a few minutes later, a grumbling turnkey opened the heavy steel gate.

"Not supposed to be any new arrivals after midnight," he complained.

I was the only one who answered him: "Then suppose I go home and come back another time, maybe."

He didn't smile. He'd heard all this before—at more civilized hours. My captors gave me a hard shove that almost tripped me. The whole situation was funny, almost like operetta, but it was too cold for laughter. Besides, my escorts-in-brown-leather took this runaround all too seriously. They'd had a long, hard day's work, might even have been shot and killed by Štěpán, and now they wanted to get home to their loving families.

I was not especially depressed by my ordeal with the secret police. I had met the enemy and they were just as bad as I'd assumed them to be. But, having survived my capture and my first night in their hands, there was some comfort in finding out that the evil I'd been fighting against was evil, after all. When Butcher Boy's bullet had gone off near my ear, I'd known I was in Big Trouble—which, if I measured it, might mean a five- or ten- or even twenty-year sentence, I thought. The duration wouldn't matter much to me, because I would be in jail *only till the end of Communism.* I emphasize this because, at the time, I was not the only one who still charted the future of Communism in units of months or a year. Even the most optimistic Communist, like my old professor Cibulka, might have given it two years—and perhaps only Klement Gottwald (who'd succeeded Beneš as president) and Josef Vissarionovich Stalin (born Dzugashvili) were thinking in terms of generations. So going to prison struck me not as a fate, but as an interlude—like the times themselves.

Inside Pankrác, I was led through ten grilled doors, which were opened, before anyone had to knock, by men peering through the grillwork. After the second door, my handcuffs were removed and the three secret policemen disappeared. As I left the custody of my captors and entered the custody of my jailers, I felt a certain euphoria. I'd heard that Pankrác, in particular, was still staffed by old-time prison guards who might shout at you or hit you, be unkind or even brutal, but they would not do you any serious or permanent damage. "Jailer" had long been an acceptable profession in Central Europe and—until the Nazis, at least—nobody had been more aware than jailers that today's prisoner might be yesterday's Cabinet minister and he might be tomorrow's corpse, but he might just as likely be tomorrow's prime minister. So their practice was to treat prisoners harshly if necessary, but decently—as job insurance in case the political winds shifted.

Under Communism, their professionalism was being tested by new demands to be barbaric and inhuman. But they were so well-trained that they knew only the right way to cope with a prisoner. They had dealt in a civilized way with thieves, murderers, perverts, and rapists—and sometimes even seen them respond to kindness. Thus, when hundreds of respectable people were brought to them, starting in 1948, they knew no other way than to be kind to them, to give a cigarette to a beaten man, even to smuggle out a letter to the family of a man who'd "disappeared." Having been decent to indecent people, how could they be expected to be indecent to decent people? The answer to that question is that many of those guards wound up as prisoners themselves.

I was ushered, not flung, into a cell on a basement level. A man who'd been sleeping on two mattresses and a pile of blankets on the floor jumped to attention and stood under the little barred window near the ceiling, at ground level. He was wearing blue exercise togs. The door closed behind me and my cellmate greeted me with a sympathetic smile and then some water and a wet rag, with which he washed my wounds.

"You're bleeding," he said.

"I was beaten, y'know," I said.

"Yes, I was, too. It hurts less after the first time."

"My name is Čapek," I said, extending my hand.

"Houžvička," he said, shaking my hand. The name means "miser," but I knew he wasn't one from the way he handed me one of the mattresses and a couple of blankets. The latter were coarser than Mrs. Jeřabek's rug, but I slept in them—and my clothes—past daybreak.

When I awoke, my cellmate was already dressing. As he donned his collar, I discovered that he was a priest. Father Houžvička, in his mid-thirties, had been the pastor of a popular church in the Karlín district of Prague. Before he asked me anything about my case or told me any details of his, he wanted to know the latest Prague happenings, the news of the world, the sports standings, and every scrap of current events that I had in my head.

He was a large, heavy man, but not fat because he kept him-

self in excellent physical condition. He combed his thick black
hair a lot and paid great care to grooming; he gave me some
good advice about this: "Here, more than ever, it's important
to keep up your appearance. When you start to decay, you start
to die." He worried, too, about his posture and spent the days
exercising. At night, he slept on his back with his stiffest clothes
piled beneath him. "Back home, I always slept with books beneath me to keep my back straight," he explained, "but here
they won't let me have books, so I use clothing instead. It's not
the same, though."

He never raised his voice, but he must have preached a good
sermon, for that's what he was in jail for: preaching sedition,
alias Catholicism.* Once or twice, I saw him put an intem-
perate guard in his place with some well-chosen words and a
fierce blaze in his eyes. He was the only priest I've ever lived
with and I was surprised at the extent of his ability to live
among and deal with all kinds of people.

Once I'd absorbed the revelation that I was rooming with a
priest, I looked around our monklike cell. There wasn't much
to look at: on one of the four brick walls, two shelves, one for
each of us; on each shelf, a bowl for drinking and a steel dish
for eating; a ceramic pitcher to be used for washing; and below us a toilet. The toilet was actually a hole in the floor, with
footprints showing you where to stand—as in a Parisian pissoir
—and it had a flushing mechanism below. Unlike a pissoir,
however, it had to be used for all other bodily functions, too,
including crapping and puking. It was also our source of water
to wash in.

---

* "The last religious census of Czechoslovakia, made in 1947, showed
that 77 percent of the Czechoslovak people consider themselves Cath-
olics. This made the Church a natural authoritarian rival and target for
the Communists, who . . . formed a 'Peace Committee of Catholic
Clergy.' It was headed by a 'peace priest' named Josef Plojhar, who was
immediately suspended by the Vatican. Nevertheless, Father Plojhar
headed the only 'Catholic Church' with which the government dealt
regularly for two decades—[during which time] Father Plojhar also
became the minister of health and, still wearing his clerical collar, a
familiar figure on East European lecture platforms: a churchman who'd
seen the light of the red star." (Alan Levy, *Rowboat to Prague.*)

"You may be used to better plumbing," Father H. remarked, "but having even this much is a tremendous advantage. If you stay clean, you stay well longer, you stay alive longer." I didn't really appreciate this until I was lodged elsewhere without all the conveniences of Pankrác.

The most important part of any prison cell is the door. Ours had a peephole for the guards to look in on us from outside. This the guards did several times an hour—at no regular intervals, but on a spot-check basis. They relied on the element of surprise and, for this reason, wore sneakers, which enabled them to move on silent soles. One of the most intimidating shocks in prison is the first time you glance up at the peephole and see it filled by an eye watching you. It happened to me that first day.

Prisoners called this omniscient peephole "the eye of God." Of course, one could always block the guards' view by putting one's head in front of the hole—and this is what one of us would do whenever the other prisoner was doing something unauthorized, suspicious, or just private that he didn't want the guard to be watching. Sometimes, the guard would go away. Sometimes, he would grow angry and unlock the door. But that took him a little time and made enough noise to warn us—so that all was in order by the time he was inside the cell. Still, the punishment for obstructing the view could be solitary confinement.

The door also contained what looked like a mail slot, except it could be opened only by the guard with a key. Meals were sometimes served that way. First, there would be a signal for all prisoners to stand by with their steel plates. Then, when the slot opened, we'd shove our empty plates through and they'd come back a few seconds later with food on them. More often, though, the guard would simply open the door and a prisoner (known as "food man" or "passage man"), pushing a wagon, would dish out our meal to us under the guard's watchful eye.

No matter which way it was served, the food was always the same. For breakfast, at 8:00 A.M. or after: a piece of bread and a bowl of coffee that tasted of acorns. (Once, when a prisoner

complained to a guard that "acorns are for pigs, not people"—
well, you can guess what the answer was to that one.) Lunch
was around noon: a bowl of greasy soup and a plate of noodles,
sometimes in a sauce. Once a week, lunch was a meat dish—
tough, stringy, and small, but nonetheless appreciated. On
Saturday, lunch was served in the late morning and it consisted of one big *buchta* ("Danish pastry" in the singular) that
had to tide us over to Sunday breakfast because the cook took
his day off from Saturday noon to Sunday noon.

Similarly, the daily supper—potatoes in an onion sauce—
was served between 4:00 and 5:00 P.M., so that the cook would
work only one shift. This meant we went without food from
4:00 or 5:00 P.M. to 8:00 or 8:30 A.M. On such a schedule, no
matter how much you eat, you'll be hungry at night—and the
guards at Pankrác never had any trouble waking us for breakfast.

At first, I didn't feel much like eating and my mouth wasn't
in much shape to receive food, but Father Houžvička said,
"Start eating right away. It's important," and I obeyed. The
Pankrác menu was the traditional Czech prison diet—just
enough to live on. But Pankrác was just about the last prison
in the land where they were still practicing basic, if minimal,
nutrition; within six months, this vestige of humanity would
be gone, too.

At Pankrác, then, the hunger at night was the worst part of
the diet. But, even in this, there was an advantage: Most of
our interrogations were at night—and it was better to be beaten
on an empty stomach.

Three or four nights a week, I was taken through the ten
doors and then by police car to the Bartholomew Street headquarters. I was locked into a room and sometimes I was interrogated, sometimes not. There were so many new arrests and
new arrivals that the secret police wouldn't always find time for
me. But they never sent anybody back to Pankrác without
something to show for his travels. Toward daybreak, the pallid
man in the brown-leather trenchcoat could come around to
visit anyone who hadn't been interrogated. He carried a cane
and, as soon as one saw the cane, one knew what to do: take

off shoes and socks and kneel in a praying position, but on the seat of a chair, not on the floor. The pallid man would then handcuff me to my chair and beat the bottom of my feet with his cane. People who didn't cooperate with their interrogators (some refused to talk with them at all) not only were given extra beatings by Pallid Man at headquarters, but their cell doors at Pankrác were decorated with red bull's-eyes—meaning that they were to be kept awake at *all* times.

Naturally, one came to appreciate interrogations more than unproductive visits over to Bartholomew Street. One was beaten during questioning, too, but at least there were human contacts, rather than just the dread of Pallid Man's rounds. My first few interrogations were by three to five men, including my captors. Later, I was entrusted to a young man who always wore high boots. He was twenty-one or twenty-two, not much older than I, who was just turning nineteen. He would slap me every now and then—and I even suspect he saw through my "swaggering young punk" pose, but he knew and I knew that he had no real power over me. Whenever I gave him a rough time, though, he would step out—and I would be worked over by either Pallid Man or Butcher Boy.

Still, I stuck to my "young punk" role—using slang, speaking in neighborhood dialect, drawling my words and then biting them off at the ends. My interrogator ate it up. He was composing my confession for me—and he had to make it jibe with those that other bright young clerks like himself were making up for Štěpán, Vacek, Kronus, Konopáč, the Jeřabeks, and others who were being "implicated" in our conspiracy. Sometimes, he would go out (obviously to a room where one of the others was being questioned) and then come scurrying back to say, "How come you didn't mention ———?" or "Why do you say October when you mean December?" If I didn't "correct" myself, I'd get slapped. If I didn't see the light then, he'd send for Butcher Boy or Pallid Man—and then I'd see stars.

The most important thing was to keep talking—even if I talked nonsense, the more nonsense the better. When I was talking, I had control—and they were listening or taking notes.

When I wasn't talking, *they* had control—and that meant pain. There was no way of not talking; even a mute would have been forced to scream. So, after they found out from someone else about our visit to the C.I.C., I said I would "tell all"— which I pretty much did, stringing it out with as much suspense as I could. I kept them rapt and happy—until the ending. They didn't like the part where we all failed to qualify for the C.I.C. What particularly gnawed at them was that several of us seemed to have conspired to trump up this same absurd story; to their mentality, truth is the greatest hoax of all. So they hit me a few times and ordered me to "tell it over, but tell it right this time."

I retold my tale with a few more flourishes. I could see them practically drooling in anticipation of a happy ending, with Karel Čapek and his friends all falling into the receptive arms of U.S. Counterintelligence. But I dished out the same stranger-than-fiction climax, where we wound up as rejects "because what kind of organization wants swaggering young punks working for it? I mean, would *you* want the likes of *me* in the secret police?"

For those two questions, I was answered with four blows— but the kind of ceremonial ones that a cop might direct at an incorrigible punk rather than the vicious ones reserved for a traitorous conspirator.

I even invented a man named Herbert in Germany: a well-dressed American with a slight Continental accent who cultivated young émigrés from the Communist states, spent many dollars on them, and induced them to go home and work against their Motherlands. Of course, I kept the others out of my contacts with Herbert—and I never admitted doing any spying for him or anybody else.

On two occasions, when I couldn't remember something, a "contradicting witness" was brought in to confront me. This was Sýkora. I didn't try to hide my contempt, my disbelief. I would look at him with quite honest contempt and great interest—asking with my eyes and my mind, though not with my mouth, "What kind of creature is this that has brought such a fate upon me and Štěpán and our friends and families?"

Sýkora was dressed as a prisoner—still posing as one of us, but clearly not one of us. For one thing, he had cigarettes. When he offered me one, I declined it. When he tried to say hello, I wouldn't speak. Then the interrogators would turn to him and he would recite his "contradictions" of my lies; his truths, I noticed, were no more truthful than my lies. Then the interrogators would take him away—and I observed that they showed him no deference, for even users must despise, as well as depend upon, the source of their poison.

After two or three confrontations between Sýkora and, at separate times, Štěpán, Vacek, Kronus, and Konopáč, we were spared the unpleasantness of these meetings with our undoer.

Karel Štěpán had arrived at Pankrác two weeks after I did —with his bullet wound still untreated. The secret police had held out medical care as an inducement for him to talk. He had been interrogated and beaten lying down, but he hadn't broken faith with any of us. After a fortnight, they'd let him go to Pankrác, where a doctor went to work on his festering wound.

At Pankrác, in the daytime, the high point was always our morning walk. There were three floors to the secret-police prisoners' wing and, starting at 9:00 A.M., inmates of each floor would be given an hour's airing in the courtyard. We were allowed to walk and talk, but only with our own cell-mates. Still, it was a chance to see Štěpán and even to murmur quick messages to him as one couple passed another. There were other channels of communication, too, within Pankrác: Morse code knockings on the walls; shouting through the over-head windows at night; smuggling spitball messages with the "food man." But the exercise hour was the best means of keep-ing in touch with each other and the outside world. Just by seeing who was arriving—more and more non-Communist politicians, parliamentarians, former ministers, and the first few Communists, symptomatic of the party purges to come— was a better newscast than any that Czechs and Slovaks "on the outside" were getting from their controlled press or radio. (TV didn't reach Czechoslovakia until 1954.) It seemed to me that the Communists were clinging to power by putting the rest of the nation into jail—and I didn't think this would work.

As prisoners arrived who'd passed through other jails, Štěpán and I were able to piece together the whereabouts of our partners-in-crime: Kronus and Konopáč were in the secret-police jail right in the Bartholomew Street headquarters. Vacek, having broken a policeman's finger while resisting arrest, was in maximum-security solitary confinement at the Ruzyně jail on the other side of Prague.

My parents, who'd assumed for a long time that I was still safely in Germany, learned that I was in jail less than a mile from them in a way that seems curious now, but was typical then. Since Pankrác was still adhering (for a few months more) to the vestiges of civilized Prague prison traditions, prisoners were allowed to send their clothes home once a week for laundering and replacement.

Soon after my arrest, the secret police had visited my folks, asked them a few questions, and searched their apartment. My parents guessed that the authorities had just discovered I'd escaped to Germany. They didn't tell the secret police much. Even to admit knowing his son was in Germany would have made my father guilty of not reporting my escape. And the secret police didn't tell my parents anything.

Then, a week or two later, an unmarked truck delivered a carton of dirty laundry to them and a driver from Pankrác prison asked them to replace it with some clean clothes of mine. My parents obliged him—but they thought it must be some new Communist way to extort clothing from relatives of escapees. They had no notion I was at Pankrác as they sliced the rope wrapped around the box. True, the clothes inside were mine. Then they found a spitball in my shirt pocket. The spitball said, "Open rope." They looked at the rope my father had just cut with his penknife—and inside it they found a long letter from their son in Pankrác.

In my letter to my parents, I devoted a paragraph to Sýkora's role in our arrests and interrogations. My father quietly

noised it around to friends he knew or thought would be heading westward.

Shortly after we stopped having confrontations with Sýkora,
word galvanized Pankrác that a man had "escaped" from police
headquarters during interrogation. This being the first getaway
we'd heard of from there, it fueled our gossip for several days.
We all took hope and wanted to learn how.

After a few days, however, word came that there was something "fishy" about the "escape." A day later, the identity of
the "escapee" became known: "a certain Sýkora." Štěpán and
I were able to certify to our jailmates that none of us could
ever go his route.

Later, I learned that Sýkora soon turned up in West Germany again—in the camps, posing as a refugee. But my father's
warnings about him had crossed the frontier by then and
Sýkora, like the rest of us, wound up in jail—but in the relative
comfort of a West German jail as a Communist spy.

No visits from parents were allowed in the secret-police
jail—but there was a possibility of a visit *after* the prisoner had
signed his confession and been moved from Pankrác's secret-
police wing to its pretrial wing. Hearing this, I stopped inventing stories and got on with satisfying my young interrogator as quickly as possible.

Five months after my arrest, he presented me with a nine-
and-a-half-page typewritten document "freely given in my
own hand." Its facts were not far from wrong, but it presented
a picture of me that I would never recognize even if it had
been in language I might conceivably use. According to this
confession, I was the notorious Karel Čapek, who'd been born
into an old-line National Socialist family and had (in one sentence spanning seventeen years of my life!) grown up to join
the Friends of the U.S.A. Club in order to work against the
will of the Czechoslovak people. The rest of my confession
dwelt largely on my escaping to Germany illegally—an offense that meant a sure five years in prison—and mentioned
the C.I.C. visit and our Prague activities very perfunctorily. I
was amused to see, though, that a sentence was devoted to my

mythical Herbert. But it was a much milder and less damag-ing-looking confession than I'd anticipated, so I signed it gladly.

Standing up to say farewell to me, my young interrogator actually shook my hand and wished me good luck. I thanked him for "putting together such a nice confession. It doesn't sound very serious, I think."

"Well," he said, "I would take the charges rather seriously if I were in your shoes."

The actual crimes I was confessing to weren't mentioned anywhere in my confession, so I thought, belatedly, to ask him what they were.

"High treason and espionage," he replied. Then, seeing me nearly faint, he started to leave—adding reassuringly on his way out, "The prosecution will ask the death penalty, of course. But, if you're lucky, you'll just get fifteen or twenty years."

I never saw him again and there were no further night in-terrogation trips. But I wasn't moved right away to the pretrial wing. It was full—and meanwhile our cells started to be crammed with new arrivals. In the middle of one night, our door opened and, as Father Houžvička and I jumped to our feet, a gaunt, sallow young man in a bank clerk's black smock was thrust in between us. The door shut and the young man didn't move. He was absolutely frozen—like a black-and-white still photo of a man in shock. To be specific, the man I thought of was Kafka—because there was a physical resemblance and Kafka had been a bank clerk in Prague, too.

Father Houžvička touched him gingerly, with a finger, and the young man came slowly to life. He began to shake. After a minute or two, he said, "They have arrested me! They have arrested me!"

This was no news to us. I asked him the standard prison question: "What have you got?" This meant "What are you accused of?" without having to ask an innocent man "What have you done?" Young K. didn't comprehend this jargon, though, so Father H. asked, "What do they say you've done?"

"They never said!" young Kafka moaned. "They just came to the bank and took me away and beat me. They have arrested me! I have never done anything in my life." I suspected this was true—and, with that, I could at least begin to comprehend his outrage.

He kept shivering, even after the father and I had given him all our blankets and I'd lent him my sweater. He was unable to get up the next day or the day after, so they took him (still wearing my sweater) to the prison hospital, with what we soon learned was "pneumonia, but he'll live."

Two months later, a guard brought back my sweater and said, "The fella you gave this to won't need it anymore."

"What'd he do? Die of pneumonia?"

"He died, but not of pneumonia." I learned later that he'd recovered, but had jumped out of a window during a night interrogation.

Young Kafka had been a most unusual cellmate. Our next was the most ordinary Czech man one could have imagined —starting with the name, Novák. He was delivered to our cell in the middle of the night, but they had neglected to beat him up while arresting him. This was a mistake, for now he didn't quite comprehend the enormity of the fate that had befallen him.

Mr. Novák was a big, strong man in his fifties with fine teeth. Behind his eyeglasses, I saw fear—but the rest of him was anger. "Where am I? What am I doing here?" he wanted to know. "I don't belong here," he went on. He ran a well-known shop, a small one, where excellent hand-knit men's underwear was made and sold by him and his family and relatives. "I'm a decent man, a family man, a good provider, and an honest man. What am I doing here?"

"I suppose," Father Houžvička said softly, "you're here because you're a shopkeeper, a private entrepreneur."

"What's wrong with that?" Mr. Novák barked back. "Since when was that a sin? To run an honest shop? Why should I be thrown in with a bunch of common criminals?"

"No criminal is common," Father H. observed in his kindly manner, but I bristled at the scorn with which Mr. Novák looked through us and spoke about us as though we weren't there. "This man is a priest," I reminded him.

Mr. Novák snorted. He was so entirely out of the picture that, if Father Houžvička had been Saint Houžvička, it wouldn't have made any impression on Mr. Novák. After a few months in prison, we must have looked entirely alien to such a man.

We tried to persuade him to take breakfast, but he said he'd wait until he was released to "break decent bread with decent folk." I don't even think he meant to be unkind when he said this. His attitude was more *Don't bother about me. I'm a tourist here myself—just passing through on an excursion carrying a heavy case of mistaken identity, so don't disturb the natives.*

We knew what was bound to happen, and we tried to warn him what was coming—and advised him to be prepared, to compose his stories, anticipate the questions, and have his answers ready somewhere in his head. "That's good underworld advice," this solid citizen said, almost benignly, "but I've done nothing wrong, so nothing bad could happen to me." It was hard to imagine any man in the twentieth century actually believing that!

When the guards came to open our cell, Mr. Novák didn't stand up—and was cuffed for that. The next time, he not only stood up, but grabbed the guard by his lapels and told him to "tell your supervisor he's got an innocent man here." The guard sent him sprawling. From the floor, Mr. Novák demanded the guard's name and number. For that, he was kicked, too.

On the third night, toward 11:00 P.M., the cellblock's gates clanked open, a face appeared at our grillwork, and a voice said, "Novák, get yourself ready for interrogation. You hear me, Novák?"

"*Mr.* Novák," our cellmate corrected. "I'll be ready in five minutes." The guard could scarcely believe his ears. Mr. Novák dressed himself, almost trying not to hurry. But he could hardly contain his excitement: "If they come for me in the middle of the night, it must have been all straightened out."

There was nothing we could tell him in those five minutes that we hadn't tried to tell him for two days. We watched him go and we knew what he didn't know awaited him. A minute later, he strode out, casting a disdainful "last glance" at the prison rabble he'd been forced to live among "temporarily"— the bogus priest; the kid who thought he was Karel Čapek. Oh, what stories he'd tell at Sunday dinner!

At 4:00 A.M., the guards came back carrying an entirely different man: a broken Mr. Novák, several years older than the Mr. Novák who'd left us that night. During my years in prison, I would see men ruined by beatings, but I've never seen a man beaten so badly in a single night. He was sobbing with pain— "*Ohhhh, ohhhh, ohhhh!*" All his fine teeth were gone. His face and body were smashed. His back was blood and open skin. The bottoms of his feet were like goulash.

We bandaged him and soaked him in cold water from the toilet. Father Houžvička was an expert at giving succor. I helped, too, but I couldn't resist saying, "We tried to tell you, *Mr.* Novák." And Mr. Novak's answer, which made me drop the subject, came back: "*Ohhh, ohhhh, ohhhh!*"

Mr. Novák and I never became friends, but a different kind of adversaries: chess opponents. We played long-drawn-out games on a homemade chessboard: a cardboard with the white squares formed by toothpaste and the chess pieces made of bread. When he told me to stop calling him "*Mr.* Novák" in my ironic way, I said all right and addressed him as "Cellmate Novák." And he, never conceding the reality of jail, addressed me as "Chessmate Čapek." It was our parody, I guess, of how people on the outside had begun to call each other "Comrade."

By the summer of 1949, as the Communists kept filling the jails and nobody who went in was coming out free, there were nine cellmates in a cell built for two. A secret policeman was put in charge of our wing, the professional prison guards were placed under his orders, and—as our ration of bad air was shared by more and more cellmates and as the midsummer heat burned its way into the Pankrác damp—it was decreed that the overhead window was to be kept closed at all times.

One of the nine of us was the former chief of police in the Sudetenland city of Liberec. Like many Czechs there, he had a German name: Umlauf. Having been active in the Catholic

People's party, he had fled to Germany when the Communists came. There, he'd worked as an interrogator for the Americans and tried to organize some kind of underground resistance that would counterattack in Czechoslovakia. Like us boys, he had come up against a stone wall in Germany. He had to move on to France, where he found no greater success. Then he, like us, had decided to come back as an outlaw and work from within.

I had once met Police Chief Umlauf in Liberec—a strapping, husky blond hero-cop of the kind used on recruitment posters. He had shown my father and me snapshots of his family; if we'd had more time, he would have shown us his family. He was arrested even before I was and, knowing this, I rather hoped I'd meet up with him again. Finally, in July, Umlauf was thrust into our nine-man cell at Pankrác.

Umlauf was now thirty-five, but completely bald. His face now had the complexion of an albino. From his skin, one could see bad bruises still healing from months of brutality down at secret police headquarters. His interrogators had also experimented on him with the "truth serum" scopolamine and, when he still didn't give the right answers, had beaten him while under the influence of the drug.

If Umlauf was a beaten man, however, it had nothing to do with his beatings. A member of his family (I never found out whether it was his wife or a child) was the one who had betrayed him to the authorities.

Physically, Umlauf was still vigorous and active—a compulsive worker who buried his sorrows in manual labor. Later, in the uranium mines, we would call people like Umlauf "crazy workers." They were working to forget—to forget the tragedies of the worker's republic that had shattered their lives.

We had to wash our cell floor once a week. For this chore, we were issued a cloth and a ration of foul-smelling powder. The first time this happened, Umlauf grabbed the cloth and set to work washing and scrubbing. As he kneeled on the floor, he fell flat on his face. Father H. and I helped him up and leaned him against the cell wall.

"Stand back and give him a little air," Father H. said. The

others did so and Umlauf began to revive. "You feeling any better?" the father asked him.

"Yes, I'll be all right," Umlauf replied—and, with those words, he fainted again.

This time, we laid him down on the blankets. Then I climbed up to the overhead window and opened it, despite the new regulation, while Father H. asked Umlauf, "What's the matter, Chief? Smell bother you?"

"No, no," he insisted. "I *want* to work." But we wouldn't let him up. Just then, the secret policeman in charge peeped in and opened the door. "What's going on here? Who opened that window?" he wanted to know.

"I did," I said, "because this man fainted. He couldn't stand this stinking smell."

He gave me a fist in the face—so hard that it not only raised a new cheek upon my old cheek, but sent me banging into the wall. "Go close the window," he commanded. I obeyed, flashing an apologetic look to Umlauf.

"It's all right," Umlauf told me. "I don't think it's the smell. I think it must be the beatings." He was right. Later, the doctors found that, from so many blows on the brain, he had lost full mastery of his center of balance.

To help make room for the new arrivals, the Pankrác authorities added a double-decker bunk to our cell furnishings. As senior inmates, Father H. and I were entitled to this comfort. But, as the youngest resident, I gave my berth to an old man, around sixty, who'd just arrived and talked about nothing but escaping. He took the lower and Father H. the upper. But then the old man started dismembering the bunk to arm us with bed pins and bedposts as weapons with which "we can overpower the guards, liberate Pankrác, and start a real revolution in Prague."

I declined to participate, though I was tempted. But I shrank from the idea of hitting anybody with a big ugly iron bar. "I'm not a violent criminal!" I protested, which made Mr. Novák laugh. I laughed, too, adding, "I'm a political criminal. I've never hurt anybody in my life and I'm not going to start now."

How could I add that, to join such a plot, I'd want more formidable leadership than this grubby, fanatical old man nobody could take seriously. Grimly, Father H. put his bed back together every night so that he could sleep in it and the authorities wouldn't find out about the insurrection that was being hatched (not to mention armed) in our cell. Maybe the authorities caught on by themselves or maybe there was an informer among the many transients passing through—because one day four guards came in and dragged the poor crazy old man off to solitary confinement.

(When I met him again, in the posttrial jail, I learned that he'd had ten years, for plotting an escape, tacked on to his five-year sentence for having made an illegal trip to Germany in 1948. I never saw him again after that—but I heard his name once more, five years later, in the uranium mines. A special formation was called by our camp commander. As a warning, he read to us the details of an escape plot that had been suppressed in a neighboring camp. A guard had been hurt and the ringleader who'd assaulted him had been executed. This was when I heard the old man's name one last time.)

One afternoon in Pankrác, a prisoner was taken out for his hour of exercise all by himself. This in itself was unusual. So was the afternoon hour; only mornings were reserved for exercise. He wore a gray raincoat, which was also unusual; somebody must have been taking especially good care of him. He was a pale, blondish young man of medium height and ascetic, scholarly mien. Watching him pace the courtyard felt like intruding upon a monk's retreat. The nine of us in our cell took turns at the overhead window watching him and even trying to communicate with him, but a guard was watching him carefully. Occasionally, though, this special prisoner would wink or nod at us.

"Who is he?" we asked around—and the grapevine came back with word that his name was Milan Choc and that he was under sentence of death. "For what?" we wondered, and the word came back a day later: "For murder. He shot a big Communist named Major Schramm. The Russians want him to hang for it." And, a little later, one inmate managed to exchange a few words with Choc. And Choc told him, "Major Schramm killed Jan Masaryk and I killed Major Schramm."

Thus was prison more informative than civilian life in Prague in those days. In 1949, we had a name for the likely killer of Jan Masaryk: Schramm. On the outside, it took almost twenty years before any public light could be shed on who killed Masaryk—and, in 1968, the most frequently named suspect was Major Augustin Schramm of Soviet Intelligence and the Czechoslovak Communist party.*

All the younger inmates of Pankrác idolized Choc. He was our hero: a decisive young man who'd done something about the situation. We sent him signals on his solitary afternoon walks, and he answered them so serenely and confidently that we were sure something would happen. Something big was in the works because Choc didn't look or act like a man about to die.

Then, one morning we heard he'd been hanged. Later that day, reports of his death were confirmed by his absence, forever, from his daily walk.

The first Communist in our cell was named Pinky. He, too, was a source of information that the outside world didn't know yet. His profession was, he said, waiter—but he also admitted to being an informer, a provocateur, a Communist agent, and, at other times, a double agent reporting to the Communists he was supposed to be betraying.

Pinky still considered himself a good Communist. Like the early Mr. Novák, he would have nothing to do with the likes of us. We despised him even more than he did us. But, being young and curious, I did try to talk with him. He blamed his arrest and jailing on Klement Gottwald's biggest rival, Com-

---

* Miloš Forman, the Czech movie director, had just moved into an apartment on a street called Major Schramm in the Dejvice district of Prague in early 1966. Asked then if he knew whom his street was named after, Forman replied, "I don't know. But he must have been some kind of Communist war hero." Two years later, Forman found out.

munist party secretary general Rudolf "Slánský and his gang. They put me here because I know too much—and they're murdering me for it."

Whoever *was* doing it to him *was* murdering him—because he had leukemia and wasn't getting the medicine he needed. to stay alive longer. Pinky insisted it was "Slánský's clique, but I'm a better Communist than all of them put together. All I want is to stay alive until I see them die here, too."

Pinky didn't make it. Slánský and Foreign Minister Vladimír Clementis (Jan Masaryk's Communist deputy and successor) hadn't even been arrested by the time Pinky began to fail and was carted off to the prison hospital to die. And yet he seemed to know the fate that Stalin would eventually dictate to Gottwald for Slánský, Clementis, and nine others (mostly, like Slánský, Jewish) who were hanged at Pankrác in 1952.*

The second Communist I met in prison was the first I ever came to respect anywhere. He was a locomotive engineer who'd been arrested, interrogated, and tortured in the work clothes he was still wearing when he landed among us— beaten, but still proud and erect. A man in his fifties, he was so robust that our heckling of him began just as soon as he spat out all but two of his teeth and said of his interrogators, "They even had the nerve to call themselves Communists! That was the worst insult! I've been a Communist all my life! My father made me one and we had to leave this country twice because we were Communists." Once had been to the U.S. just before World War I; the second time to Russia in the 1920s, when it was hard for a Communist to make a living under Masaryk.

I pointed to the rest of Pankrác jail and said, "So look what your people have made of this country in one year." And then I had to duck as he swung at me, saying, "Call those

* When Mrs. Clementis asked for her husband's remains, she was told that his ashes had been flushed down a drain in Pankrác. Actually (she learned from the Prague press in 1968), the ashes of all eleven men had been taken in a sack to be scattered over fields outside Prague. A Soviet adviser, who'd witnessed the execution, went along to make sure this was done. Along the way, the pavement was icy, so the driver and the Russian instead spread the ashes over the slippery roadway.

bastards Communists again, son, and you'll have two fewer teeth than I do."

Twenty years later, Erika Levy, four, undergoes extremely delicate surgery in Prague. During Erika's second week of recuperation in a children's hospital (during the tenth month of Soviet occupation), her taxi driver Karel Čapek comes to call on his tiniest client. When Čapek says good-bye, the doctor in charge of Erika's floor takes Karel aside and says, "Those Levys. They seem like very decent Americans."

"They are very decent Americans," Čapek replies.

"Communists?" the doctor asks.

"Certainly not!" says Čapek. "They were here last August and they weren't even Communists before then."

"But there must be something bad about them," the doctor insists. "Or else why would they still be allowed to stay here?"

And Karel gives the doctor his own prescription: "Don't ask around about them and just be glad they're here somehow. Treat them as a talisman."

In August, 1949, I was called out in the daytime—not to be interrogated, but to be searched and marched upstairs to the pretrial jail. I was put in a cell with five others. Here, the food was the same as before and the routine much the same—except that I was allowed to write one letter a week to my parents. Unfortunately, while I'd been waiting to be transferred upstairs, the rules had been tightened: pretrial visits were no longer allowed.

I did, however, have a visitor: my lawyer. My parents had hired him. He didn't stay long and he didn't impress me, even though he acted as if he was going to save my life: "You could get the death penalty, y'know, but I'm not going to let them."

"Good," I said, "thank you."

"And do y'know how I'm going to do that? I'm not going to deny your guilt—we'll admit everything."

"And that will get me what? A life sentence instead of death?"

"I hope so. We won't dispute the charges at all. We'll just

argue that you were very young and didn't know what you were doing."

"Well, I'm still very young, but I knew exactly how little I was doing and I had a pretty good idea of what I wanted to do, but I never got to do anything."

"Listen, son, if you just do what I say, I think I can get you off with fifteen or twenty years."

He sounded to me as though he knew less than my young interrogator in high boots. But the numbers seemed to be coming out the same.

A few days after his visit, a guard escorted me to a clerk's office inside the prison. There, a man in a green eyeshade, who never looked up, droned out the charges against me: high treason; espionage; and "acting against the Republic by leaving it illegally." Then he handed me what he'd just read—for signing. I signed that I'd been notified of the accusations. I was never asked how I pleaded.

In this part of Pankrác, there were many comings and goings. As men came back from their trials and were led down the corridors, there was only one question about the outcome: "Years or death?"

If the answer was "years," there were friendly smiles on both sides of the bars. Nobody asked, "How many years?," for, with everybody concentrating on surviving for the few months that Communism had left, the difference between two years and twenty years didn't matter.

If there was no answer, then the answer was "death"—and the condemned men never reentered their cells, but were led to Death Row. There, they didn't linger long: only hours or days, seldom weeks or months.

On a Friday morning, I was told to get ready for my trial three days later. A barber came and shaved me every day. A prison tailor came with my best suit (obtained from my parents) and had me try it on. If I had lost much weight, he'd make alterations so this wouldn't show. Fortunately, I hadn't—so he told me just to wear my suit around the cell for an hour or two each day: "That way, it won't look out of place on you." Instead, I wore it all the time because it felt good for once to wear a suit. And I slept in it, too, so it would look rumpled and truthful at my trial.

Late Monday morning, I was led in handcuffs through a maze of tunnels and corridors to a Court of Justice within the prison complex: a court that the public and the officials could enter from the street, but which the defendants entered from jail. Everybody left the way he or she had come.

In an anteroom, my handcuffs were removed and I was then let into an impressive courtroom with high ceilings, paneled walls, solid wooden furniture, and blue carpeting and drapes that gave it a surprisingly restful appearance. I took a place with what eventually came to twenty-one others on the prisoners' bench—and, like my codefendants, immediately started looking around for my folks.

Relatives were permitted to attend our trial. With twenty-two defendants, however, there was barely room for all our kin—and, of course, no space for press or public. My parents were seated in a back row. It was the first time I'd seen them since the last days of 1948—nearly nine months earlier. My father looked the same. My mother looked like a widow.

In a blackish-gray suit I'd never seen on her before, she was grieving for her only child. She was also wary, watchful, and defensive-looking—which was not the way I remembered her. Throughout the trial, I tried to steal a glance at my mother when she wasn't looking back at me—to catch her in an unobserved moment of composure. And, when I did, I discovered that this new look on her face was not put on as a courtroom mask. It was the way she looked and lived and thought now.

Several of the other mothers sitting back there looked the same way as mine. For the family was under attack as an outmoded institution. The Gottwald regime was smashing like a tank through such bastions as motherhood and the "old bourgeois ties" between parents and children. In the schools, children who challenged the official truths with innocent questions that began "But my father says . . ." often wrought official vengeance upon their parents' heads. Thus, sitting in that courtroom and seeing her son on trial for his life, my mother showed she knew she was in the fortress of *her* enemy as well as mine.

Whenever our eyes met, she waved. Sometimes, I'd wave back. Much of this went on between defendants and relatives, but the court transcript doesn't show that the most repeated admonition to the defendants was: "Turn around and face the court!"

The mother of my codefendant Konopáč was there, but not his soldier father—who had publicly denounced and disowned his son in order to retire from the Army with his pension, if not his honor.

I looked down the defendants' bench next. The leader of my conspiracy was a man I'd never seen or heard of before, but I wished I had. He was a man in his fifties: firm, commanding, soldierlike in the way he held himself, unhesitating in his answers, more eloquent in his arguing than all five of our defense attorneys put together, and never pulling any punches in expressing his utter disdain for Communism and the "socialist legality" that had put him in jail. He wouldn't even let his lawyer talk for him. Instead, he told the court, "I can't stop you from saying nonsense against me, but I won't allow nonsense to be said *for* me!"

Following his example, each of us at every opportunity started to tell how he had been beaten by police. But, when we did, the court stenographer immediately stopped taking notes. I knew this long before I ever saw her transcript (years later) because I rarely took my eyes off her. She was an attractive young thing in a green dress who looked all the more gorgeous because she was the only one of the five people on the judges' bench who wasn't wearing robes.

The four people in robes were:

. . . a People's attorney, who was some kind of Communist party watchdog. He spent the whole trial doodling and daydreaming. He was probably there to see that nobody grew tenderhearted toward us—and, in this particular case, there was hardly any work for him.

. . . a professional lawyer, serving as legal adviser to the court. He was a dark, dignified man with an aristocratic visage.

His sharp features expressed cynical enjoyment of this charade he was sanctioning. He seldom spoke and, when he did, out came only a sentence or two, but each with a double edge or several meanings. He looked like a hard drinker, squirreling up his ironies as tidbits to be washed down with booze that night.

. . . the prosecutor, a neatly dressed middle-aged woman named Kolarová. If she hadn't been trying to put a noose around my neck, I'd have taken her for a high-school teacher—in a rough neighborhood boys' school, because she talked that way to all the defendants. Whenever we'd open our mouths, she'd snap "Keep still!" or "Don't talk so much!" She had read our confessions, and when we'd deny the slightest detail, she'd thump the documents hard and say, "It's your word against *this!*"

"Well, which is truer? What I say here and now or what you say that paper says I say? And the paper was made after I'd been beaten by—"

"You don't ask the questions here—I do! Speak only when you're spoken to!"

"Well, *you're* speaking to me."

. . . At this point, the fourth person on the bench—the presiding judge—would silence the court with "SHUT UP!" He was a very strange-looking man. He was already in place when I arrived in court on the first day, so it took me a few hours to see what was the matter. He had a big, shaggy bearlike head and no neck. At first, I thought the judicial robes were creating this unfortunate effect until, at the end of the first session, he rose to leave. Or, rather, he stood up and was no bigger standing up than he'd been sitting down! Now everybody in that paneled courtroom could see that he was a congenital cripple with a tiny body and a birth defect that required him to swivel from side to side as he slowly made his way from bench to chamber. The courtroom was swept by a gasp, which the judge either didn't hear or had learned to ignore.

This was my first time in court—and I watched the ritual enacted there almost critically: as a kind of theater, inadequately done. Witnesses were sworn in, but not on a Bible.

Sometimes, when I felt myself maligned, I actually interrupted —and was silenced more as a heckler than a victim of this theater.

By trying to follow my prosecutor's logic, I often ended up telling her that she was wrong and trying to show her the error of her way of reasoning—not out of malice or even self-defense so much as just to improve her performance for the sake of the drama.

"You're jumping to conclusions and your conclusions are wrong!" I interjected once.

"Stop fighting it!" she snapped back—in such a way that I knew all our punishments were preordained.

I had a funny feeling of freedom in that courtroom. Mrs. Kolarová was so abusive that I couldn't think of her as an official of the law. I felt myself in a shouting match with some Communist agitator on the sidewalk of Wenceslas Square— except this was indeed in a courtroom and, besides, such street arguments hadn't happened in Prague in more than a year. Thus, for me, the illusion of Hyde Park was as strong and re-freshing as a flagon of Czech beer from the tap.

When my turn came in the witness box, Prosecutor Kolarová was gunning for me. She reviewed my written confession while I argued that it was inaccurate and coerced. Then she un-leashed her full arsenal of sarcasm on me: "So, my poor in-nocent little boy, you went all the way to Germany just to make contact with your bosses in the C.I.C. And now you want us to believe that they didn't understand you, didn't want to see you, didn't give you any work to do in Czechoslovakia, didn't give you any weapons, and didn't ask you to betray your homeland?"

"Well," I replied, "you have a few details wrong. For in-stance, they never got to be my bosses."

"They didn't, you say? Well, we *know* otherwise!"

"You do? This is my account you're basing your whole case on. I was there and you weren't. How could *you* know if I know differently?"

"I've had experience with liars like you," she snarled. "I've had experiences with C.I.C. men like you. You're not the first one to say what you're saying! I happen to know that people like you are trained in Germany to give answers like these if you're caught."

"We are? Well, if you know this, you must have had more experience with the C.I.C. than I did."

"SHUT UP!" the judge bellowed. He presided without a gavel. He didn't need one to make my teeth rattle.

It's a tribute to the female sex that Kolarová didn't make a misogynist out of me. But, not having seen a woman in some time and knowing I wouldn't be seeing any where I was going, I feasted my eyes on the luscious court stenographer. I studied and memorized every detail of her. She couldn't have been more than twenty-one—well-built, with a slim figure and a lovely oval face; soft skin, fresh complexion, all setting off a pair of big, gray-green eyes. She wore hardly any lipstick and her wavy hair was either dark blond or light brunette. But her most provocative feature was that, for all her expressive good looks, she maintained an absolutely poker face.

It became virtually sexual for me—trying to enter her consciousness with my eyes and my will, if not my heart and my body. I caught her eye several times and she never avoided my gaze. On the third or fourth day, we exchanged glances that suddenly locked. We looked deeply into each other. She gave me a little smile and two big eyefuls of compassion. After that, every look we exchanged was long and lingering.

It was not, for those times, a casual flirtation. She was a year or two older than I. And, if I, at nineteen, still happened to be a teen-ager, I was also a man on trial for his life.

The dominant personality on that bench, however, was the presiding judge—that dwarf, deforming justice as he himself had been deformed and ruling with infinite variations on the motto of "SHUT UP!" in a croak that sounded far away even when he was quite near. His body, his motions, his gestures, and his words were all warped. He was addicted to Napoleonic poses that never quite fit his words or the situation. And his name was Prášek, meaning "little speck of dust."

The testimony, which had started on Monday afternoon, lasted through Wednesday's sessions. Each night, we were taken back through tunnels to our cells. But, first, a kindly guard would put all twenty-two of us into the same detention room while he phoned for escorts to fetch us. We were supposed to be isolated from each other, but he simply said, "I know you haven't seen each other for a good long time. Please try not to make too much noise." Saying nothing about the risk *he* was taking, he went away, locking the door behind him, for a good fifteen or twenty minutes before the first escorts appeared.

How we hugged and embraced our old chums that first night! We exchanged experiences, advice, and gossip. Štěpán and I even had the chance to apologize to the Jeřabeks for the trouble we'd brought upon them. "Doesn't matter, son," said Mr. J. paternally. "Sooner or later it would have to happen. We were natural enemies of their system and we didn't stand a chance."

On Thursday, there were the lawyers' summations. Prosecutor Kolarová recited (or, rather, repeated) the ugliest of her accusations against us. She reminded those men on the bench —who didn't need much reminding—that we were "enemies who'd declared war on the working class." She implored the judges—who didn't need any imploring—not to be swayed by such considerations as Mrs. Jeřabek's physical impairment (saying this, Kolarová glanced almost compassionately at Judge Prášek) or "Čapek's and Štěpán's age. In their cases and the other boys', the very fact of their youth made them stronger and more physically dangerous to every responsible person in this courtroom."

The five defense attorneys spoke in succession after she was finished. They didn't change their prepared summations even though she'd answered every one of the arguments they delivered. They all spoke in the same monotone. Probably, they had shown their texts to her. Or else the same party had prepared both sides of the argument.

The lawyer representing Štěpán and me did what he'd said he'd do—but not nearly so dynamically as he'd sounded when he'd visited me in jail and said he'd save my life. If I hadn't been impressed then, I was appalled now. As he droned through our defense, I feared he would forget our names.

114 GOOD MEN STILL LIVE!

Worse still, I resented his apologizing for our "youthful mistakes." It was not our youth that had brought us into the criminals' dock.

The courts worked a five-day week, so Fridays were reserved for sentencing. No time was budgeted for deliberating; just for sentencing. In our case, the judges did "deliberate" for ten minutes—five of which were needed for the crippled Judge Prášek to make his ceremonial exit and reentrance—and then the bailiff called out, "Prisoners rise for sentencing!"

"In the name of the State," I, Karel Čapek, was sentenced by Judge Prášek to "fourteen years at hard labor plus one day's solitary confinement, with neither bedding nor light, during each month of your imprisonment." (This added punishment, which was never enforced, apparently was my spanking for talking back to Prosecutor Kolarová.)

Mine was in the middle range of sentences. The Jeřabeks and another married couple, theatrical people from Smíchov, got eight- and ten-year sentences (eight for the women; ten for the men. Štěpán, still limping from his wound, drew eleven years. Vacek, Konopáč, and Kronus—having put up more of a struggle at their arrests—got twenty, eighteen, and sixteen years respectively.* Another of my fellow "conspira-

---

* These are the fates of the people Čapek actually knew in his "conspiracy." Karel Štěpán went from Pankrác to a coal mine in Kladno, near Lidice. From there, he eventually escaped to West Germany and then emigrated to Canada. He was working as a lumberjack in the Canadian Northwest in 1957 when a tree fell on him and killed him. . . . Vacek and Konopáč were for a short time in Bory prison when Čapek was there (see Part 3). Later, as a prisoner in the mines of Kutná Hora, Vacek escaped and hid out inside Czechoslovakia for a year and a half. Because of tightened border controls, he was unable to find a way to the West, so he and another fugitive decided to cross into East Germany and make their way to pre-Wall Berlin. But even sneaking from one Communist country into another was perilous for desperate men without proper documents. In a gun duel on the Czechoslovak-East German frontier, they killed a Czechoslovak border guard and made their way into West Germany. There, in another gun battle—this time with the *Volkspolizei* (People's Police)—Vacek's partner was slain and Vacek captured. He was returned to Czechoslovakia and executed. . . . Konopáč's route through Bory and various slave labor camps was almost identical with Čapek's for a while, although one was always arriving just

tors," an elderly man whom I'd met for the first time at our
trial, got twenty-five years. And the soldierly man who'd "led"
our "group" was given a life sentence. When he heard this, he
laughed and laughed. "What's so funny?" we asked him, wondering whether it was relief at escaping the gallows. He
laughed again and said, "I'm already under a death sentence
I can't appeal. I have cancer."

(Nobody thought of appealing anyway. The State tribunals
resented such burdensome requests and, if granted, the ap-
peals or new trials often led to death sentences.)

Our sentencing was the most impersonal scene of the trial.
All of us on the prisoners' bench felt like players in a game
(very much like cops-and-robbers, though our adversaries
would have called it "Brave Communists vs. Class Enemies")
or participants in a charade with very specific roles to play.
But the game was for our lives. And the answer to the charade
was our destiny. Both sides knew the accusations were illusory,
but the procedure lent substance, if not credence, to them.
Then, with the sentencing, all these distorted procedures were
wrapped into one Big Lie that became the Greatest Single
Truth of our lives.

Living creatures passing sentence upon living creatures in
high-pitched times of improvisation! We didn't know yet that
this was merely the overture to decades of madness. And who
would have thought that these absurd sentences would prove

---

after the other left, so they never met in the camps again. Konopáč, always the most delicate of the boys, had been badly hurt by his military
father's disowning him. In the mines, he fell in love with a civilian clerk
—a married woman—and, in despair at the hopelessness of their
romance, he hanged himself in 1955. . . . Mr. Jeřabek served six years in
jail—and then fled the country in 1955, but not as far as everybody
thought he had. Still a sworn anti-Communist, he was next (and last)
heard from in 1956 in Hungary (!), where he was shot to death by the
Russians for his part in the revolution there. His wife, childless and
alone, lives in a furnished studio apartment in a modern Prague housing
development where the buildings look like oil drums (with acoustics to
match). Čapek says he never had the heart to visit her. . . . She and
Kronus, who lives in Prague with the tuberculosis he acquired in prison,
are the only survivors—besides Čapek.

lasting? Certainly nobody in that courtroom—not the judges, not the judged. We had survived. We would get away with our lives for the time being. And, having gotten away with their charade, now they could get away on Friday noon for the weekend. *For the time being . . . for the weekend . . .* it all seemed as ephemeral as that—*at the time!*

Part 3

A Pound-and-a-Half
of Feathers

On our way out, we waved to our relatives—and they waved back happily, rejoicing. We would all be together again soon —whenever this aberration of Communism had gasped its last. The last person I saw as we left the courtroom was the girl stenographer. Seated at the far end of the bench, she watched the prisoners impersonally, more as though counting sheep than seeing men and women. But, when I passed between her and the door, she gave me what I'd call a good-bye look: an intimate nod, a holding of the eyes, and a brave snap back of her wavy hair. And then she was gone—or, rather, I was.

Led back to our cells in Pankrác, we were peppered with the same question: "Years or death?" Even when the guards forbade our well-wishers to shout at us, they'd make a slit-throat gesture and we'd shake our heads no—adding for emphasis, with our fingers, the number of years that lay ahead.

My three postsentencing weeks in Pankrác were a happy time. The treatment was good, calm, and clean. Secure, too, for in Pankrác you knew that the guards wouldn't let sudden death or violence attack you out of the gray. I would not have that security again for more than a decade—and I'm not even sure I have it now.

There was also the relief of a known fate—with only the details to be determined. I felt this particularly when two of us, on whom sentence had already been passed, were detailed to clean up a courtyard of Pankrác that I'd never visited be-

117

fore. Its centerpiece was a plain wooden bar that looked like the kind of backyard rack upon which Czech people hang out rags and beat rugs. Beneath it was a platform, and underneath the platform was a small pile of shit, which was what we'd been sent to clean up.

"Do they let dogs in here?" I asked my partner, an older man.

"Don't you know what this is?" he asked me, pointing to a hook on the rack.

"A coatrack with just one hook?" I wondered.

The man laughed and pointed to a trapdoor in the platform beneath the rack. Then, glancing upward again, he said, "That's a hook on which you hang a man." He pointed down to the pile of shit: "Until this morning, that belonged to a student named Bacílek." I hadn't recognized the gallows because it had no arm and no rope. The latter, my partner told me, was wrapped around the man and then tied to the hook. We did our work in thoughtful silence.

When I was issued my first prison garb—gray denim with a brownish tinge (from sweat, rust, or blood?)—it meant that I would be transported from Pankrác soon. And so I savored those last lingering days in Pankrác the way a vacationer on a beach might watch the sands of time dwindle away.

The high point of those last three weeks in Pankrác was my first visit from my parents. I was taken to an L-shaped room on the main floor. The room had two entrances: one from civilian life, the other from prison life. After a prisoner had traversed the bottom of the L and turned its corner, he was in a normal room with a built-in divider—cement wall from floor-to-waist level; double-meshed barbed-wire cage from waist to ceiling. By the time I was admitted, after a search, there were ten prisoners on my side of the wall and twenty or twenty-five visitors on the other.

My mother had a smile on her face. She was making a special effort not to cry, too, but her eyes bore evidence beneath them of months of weeping; of tears that were now nightly, and perhaps daily, routine in her life. When she saw me in prison grays, the smile vanished. And when she reached out but couldn't touch me, the tears came.

"Germany, Germany," she moaned. "We thought you were in Germany. If only you had stayed in Germany." My mother was a strong woman who would have done anything in the world for me—but, in this bizarre situation, she didn't know where in the world to begin. I felt very sorry for her.

My father—that dissatisfied man who moved from job to job and never quite made a go of his life—had risen in my esteem from good dad up to pal up to friend in need. He accepted reality, even if he didn't always participate in it (when it would have invited such moral sacrifice as joining the Communist party) and sometimes miscalculated it. Now he was a pillar of strength and reassurance. "What's done is done," he said. "It won't last long. So just don't get hurt while it's happening, Son." He was listening to the BBC again (although there were severe penalties and jamming just as there had been in the past) and he would keep me posted throughout prison life by smuggling me news in toothpaste caps.

(Throughout the next decade, my father would persist in probing the weaknesses in the case against me and, when nothing worked, he would keep on trying again—just in case the winds of repression were shifting in the slightest way. He never succeeded, but my greatest peace of mind during those years came from knowing that someone on the outside was calmly, coldly, and continuously trying all possible means to help me out of prison.)

My father and mother brought another visitor with them: my "fiancée." She proved to be my girl friend Božena, who'd been presented to the authorities as the girl I'd planned to marry. Once the custodians of the Big Lie had accepted this small distortion, even *they* couldn't refuse her a visit.

Božena had grown from girl to woman since I'd seen her last. I liked pretending to be her fiancé, talking to her like a fiancé. But I feared I might be carried away by my performance and ask her to wait for me. And this I didn't want to do. It was probably the first time I acknowledged to myself that I might be out of circulation for some time. I had already been thinking of escape as a possibility. Either way, as a prisoner or as a hunted outlaw, I would not have liked to wish any part of my fate onto Božena. And yet I was nineteen—an age at which the tongue is impelled to say, "Will you marry me?" because it sounds so romantic yet possible (or, in some cases, because the tongue has nothing else to say). In this situation, my tongue wanted to say, "Wait for me, my darling?" but I knew it shouldn't.

Božena made it easy for me. We chatted about mutual friends and a fire that had consumed the old houseboat where she and Štěpán and I used to hang out. (The fire, she'd learned, had started a few minutes after secret police had raided the houseboat in search of evidence against Štěpán and me.) Then, in a gentle, bashful way, Božena said what I wanted to hear without either of us speaking the words or tying us to an un-keepable vow. I will always remember how she put it: "This is just my first visit to you, Karel, dear. One day you will visit me."

"Many, many times," I murmured. So was it said—without ever having to be unsaid if, inevitably, we should go separate ways—and so, in a sense, was it done.

This visit lasted half an hour. After twenty-five minutes, the guard in charge of the L-shaped room at Pankrác sounded a five-minute warning. The visitors started pushing cigarettes through the barbed wire and the prisoners went fishing for them. Even other prisoners' parents were pushing cigarettes at me. All this was strictly forbidden, but the guard's spoken five-minute warning had been an invitation to do it: "I know you're all decent people who won't pass weapons. So do whatever else you have to do, but please be quiet about it."

Then he'd turned the other way to stand lookout—not over us, but for other guards who might report him. And I'd been most impressed by how, when he'd said, "You're all decent people," he'd addressed himself to the prisoners as well as their relatives. Good men still lived—even inside the prison guardrooms of our jailed land.

Very early a few mornings later, in October of 1949, two truckloads of us were assembled for transport from Pankrác. In the dark before dawn, we were counted, marched to the trucks, recounted, seated on the truck floors, recounted, and sent off to an unknown destination.

Just outside the main gate, the other truck developed mechanical trouble. During the half-hour it took to repair it, our two-truck convoy was stalled on a deserted street in the "free" city of Prague. Two women were the only civilians on that street. They were mothers of prisoners, both from nearby Vyšehrad, who had been taking turns keeping a vigil and alerting each other whenever a transport seemed to be looming. The delay in our departure had given both mothers the chance to see their sons leave Pankrác for the jails beyond.

Both mothers looked very much alike. Their faces and their posture bore the same outlines of grief and devotion to their sons. One wore a red coat; the other, my mother, wore a blue coat. In the otherwise colorless early-morning street outside Pankrác, my mother waved to me and I waved back. She waved again. I waved again. She waved. I waved. This went on for half an hour and I kept hoping they would hurry up and fix the truck because I wanted this to end. It was breaking my heart and hers—a terrible experience for both of us.

This was the last time I would see my mother for more years than we could have imagined. But that morning street scene hardly ever left my mind: a pastel of those two women in blue and red waving to gray men on brown trucks in that drab street at dawn.

The sixty-five-mile ride took three hours. Each turn, each bump in the road, each glimpse of scenery through the back of the truck told us what we feared—that we were going to Bory, the worst of the prisons in the Czech Lands. All my life, Bory had been a word that mothers used to frighten their children into behaving. In the First Republic, only the most violent criminals had been confined there. During the war, the Gestapo had put Bory to prodigious use. After the war, Bory had housed the worst collaborationists and Nazi war criminals incarcerated on our soil. Then, in 1946 and 1947, a typhoid epidemic had made any time in Bory a death sentence—and purged Bory's decks for the wave of repression yet to come.

In Pankrác, at least we had been in Prague; from its court-yards and an occasional cell, one could see the city's spires and a little civilian housing, if not civilian life. In Bory, a concrete octagon on the outskirts of Pilsen, not a blade of grass grew and not a shred of outside life was visible. In Bory, one saw only Bory.

From the moment one arrived at Bory, one was shouted at. A prison number—8210—was shouted to me and, from then on, whenever an authority entered my cell, I had to jump to attention and shout out my number and then my name.

Thanks to the typhoid epidemic, Bory wasn't overcrowded when I arrived in the autumn of 1949—though the Communists would remedy that before long. I was given a cell to myself, which I welcomed because I needed "to be alone" and "to think out" all that had happened to me, as well as face up to the future as realistically as I could. Unfortunately, as soon as I began to brood, I saw some reddish-black spots on the white walls of my cell. Examining them closer, I discovered they were blood.

There was no plumbing in the cells at Bory. If lucky, one was issued a pail with a lid, but most of us drew open slop buckets.

The principal "hard labor" at Bory was feather-plucking. A four-pound bag of mangy feathers was brought to my cell by an older prisoner, who simply said, "These are your feathers, and you're supposed to pluck sixty-seven decagrams of them a day." A pound and a half of feathers!

They were to be used as pillow and comforter stuffing. Glancing at this sack of hard-stemmed, virtually hairless plumes, I stopped pining for my feather quilt at home and wondered how any soft down could conceivably be pulled off that barren center shaft. But I gave it a try.

I began to empty the bag. There was no end to these feathers, which had been tightly compressed inside the sack. Now I found myself half-covered with them—feeling as though I'd started to grow feathers and feeling . . . as if . . . I had . . . excuse me! . . . I had to . . . SNEEZE!

My first sneeze sent the feathers flying like the birds they'd once adorned. Plucking only those that remained on my person, my fingers were so blistered and bloody within half an hour that I stuffed all the feathers back into the bag and ignored them for as long as I could—which was a couple of days.

On the third day, the old prisoner collected my feathers and gave me another bag without saying a word. I let these sit around, untouched for just a few minutes—which was when two guards came in and hauled me off to a week in solitary confinement or, as it was called in Bory, "on Correction with Mr. Brabec."

Mr. Brabec was a swarthy, bushy-black-browed man whom I'd first noticed at Bory's initial "welcoming ceremony"—a ritual at every prison, where new arrivals turn in all the clothes on their backs and, stripped naked, have every opening in their bodies searched before being issued their new home's wardrobe. In the crowd of new faces screaming commands at us, Mr. Brabec had stood out because he neither shouted nor spoke. He had simply dropped in to look over the new talent that would eventually find its way to him in Correction.

Mr. Brabec had deep-set eyes that he shielded under a visored officer's hat. I caught a glimpse of them only once and saw what he had to hide: eyes even darker than their brows, eyes with no sparkle, no glitter at all. He was also, I learned later, an alcoholic.

Almost tenderly, he took away my belt and trimmed my fingernails, explaining "no sharp objects." For his aim was to destroy me, not to let me have the privilege of destroying myself. And he told me that "any day when you're in Correction, if I don't do you any harm, something's seriously wrong with me!"

Then he ushered me into a dark cell, where I could see nothing, and told me to keep walking. The cell seemed to be a square—four paces long in every direction before I'd walk into a wall. After a few minutes of this, waiting for my eyes to begin to fathom a little of Mr. Brabec's darkness, there was a blinding flash. Mr. Brabec had switched on a high-intensity floodlight. Now I could see everything, but the light was so dizzying that I felt the walls swirling closer and closer around me. Now, when I bumped into them, they all had sharp edges. Somewhere, Mr. Brabec was murmuring, "Keep moving, Eighty-two ten, keep moving. The Eye of God is watching." After a while, when the light went out, I was sure Mr. Brabec hadn't switched it off, but that I'd gone blind.

Mr. Brabec always marched. Standing still, he'd mark time. In Correction, he marched up and down the corridor—always in full uniform, including his visored officer's hat. And every one of his "guests" had to march. During the night, which was Mr. Brabec's prime time of day, we were summoned to our cell door at irregular intervals (but never more than forty minutes apart) to report and keep marching, while Mr. Brabac counted cadence. Each man's daily trip out to puke, piss, or shit (on Correction's diet of one piece of bread every second day, we could hold it in with little trouble) into Correction's only toilet hole was done by the numbers, too. "Three steps forward. Halt! [For guard to open cell doors]. Right turn! Halt! [For search.] Forward march! Left! Right! Left! Right! Left! Right! Left turn! Left! Right! Left! Right! [Before toilet hole.] Ready! DUMP! About face! Forward march! Left! Right! Left! Right! Right turn! . . ."

When I emerged from Mr. Brabec's domain after a week, a guard handed me a sack of feathers on my way to my cell. "I can't do those," I told the guard. "The feathers bother my eyes. I must be allergic to them." The guard started to beat me and I said, "I want to see the prison doctor." "Fine" said the guard, dragging me back the way I'd come. "Mr. Brabec is the prison doctor at Bory."

Mr. Brabec came marching out to meet us. The guard said, "He says the feathers hurt his eyes."

Mr. Brabec doubled over with laughter. "It hurts his eyes!" he said chokingly. The guard laughed, too, and I found myself smiling—briefly. For Mr. Brabec came up from his crouch with a truncheon and smashed me in the face. "It hurts his eyes!" he repeated, beating time to his words on my face, particularly on and around my eyes. He led me back to Correction, beating out his ominous chant all over my body, as he led me back to my dark-and-light little cell. Only then did his words change: "Now I have something else for your eyes." It was at that moment that I saw his own eyes for the first and only time —and perhaps perceived not just the soul of such a man, but the soullessness of evil.*

After another week of Mr. Brabec's dazzling hospitality, I was resigned to a career of feather-plucking and determined to make the most, if not the best, of it. The quota of a pound and a half of feathers per day was so unrealistic that, when I was allowed out for an airing in the courtyard, I would skim little stones and handfuls of sand into my pocket and, at the first opportunity back in my cell, transfer them to my sack of feathers. I cleaned my cell by stuffing each speck of dust into the feather sack. Even with this help, I never achieved more than 80 percent of my quota—and my rations were therefore cut by 50 percent. And this is not to say that I didn't work hard on the feathers, too; plucking them from their stubborn shafts, I saw to it that I cut and ruined only one finger at a time. Then I would use up another finger, and then another and another and another, until the first one had healed enough to be used and maimed again.

I was not the only one at Bory stuffing his feather sacks with sand and, inevitably, a complaint came to Bory from the State Feather Enterprise. Individual weigh-ins were decreed. Each feather-plucker would be called out of his cell to deliver his bag of plucked feathers first to a dumping room. There, under the supervision of an officer, I would have to dump the contents of my bag onto newspaper. A pound of feathers being light and a half pound of sand being heavy, the sand stayed on the paper while I, under the officer's watchful eye, loaded the feathers back into the bag and took it into the next room for weighing.

A fellow prisoner named Mirek Zástěra taught me a trick. On the morning a weigh-in was due, I would fill my mess canteen, immediately after breakfast, with spit and piss. As soon as I heard the guards coming to take me and my feathers to

---

* Mr. Brabec committed suicide in 1962.

the scales, I would dump my slime into the sack. By the time I got to the dumping room, my moisture may have soaked a little sand into staying up top with the feathers. Certainly, on the scale, my urine and saliva added a decagram or two to the total.

Mirek had shared his secret with others, too. After several weeks, the State Feather Enterprise complained that feathers from Bory were decomposing prematurely. Our mess kits were taken away from us after the morning meal on weigh-in days—and we had to proceed to the dumping and weighing rooms with nothing more than a quick spit. And now, in addition to an officer in the dumping room, there were two officers manning the scales. Fortunately for all of us, a new prisoner was assigned to do the actual unloading at the scales. He was a middle-aged Communist secret policeman with a real Ph.D. from Charles University, and he had played such a key role in the 1948 upheaval that his "superiors" feared he knew too much, which he certainly did. Through other connections within the system, he managed to stave off execution and even land himself a relatively good job at Bory. But he had no respect for the system he had helped bring into power, so he took special delight into distracting the two officers while adding a toe or even his baling hook to the pressure on the scale.

I could never thank him enough, so one day I paid him a compliment. "Thank God you're one of us," I told him, "because if we ever had a man like you *against* us, even God couldn't help us."

"All my life," he replied, having cheated the scales once more, "I've been practicing to be a butcher."

He was, in fact, a professional prisoner—one of several who taught Karel Čapek the tricks of his trade. Karel's 1969 utterance in my presence in Prague—"I guess . . . you might say . . . that what I am . . . is . . . a professional prisoner!"—rings in my ears as he tells me in Cicero of his mentors at Bory. I remind him of the 1969 conversation and he says, "I said it hesitantly then because, even as I spoke it, I was already calculating whether it could be used against me. That's one reason why we had to leave—because, by 1969, you had to make calculations like that whenever you spoke. Speech itself becomes an impediment. But I spoke the truth then. It's hard to consider myself anything else but a man who is a professional prisoner. Prison was my life's Greatest Single Truth. I can only hope it isn't its direction, too."

The best way to beat the feather-plucking quota at Bory was to latch onto another assignment. One of the best jobs, making leather purses, belonged to an old man named Bacílek, who never spoke. On our morning walks, I sidled up to him and asked how he'd done it, but he never answered with even a nod. Finally, I asked another inmate if the old man could talk at all. "He used to talk a lot," I was told, "until he learned his son was executed." Then I realized that old Bacílek was the father of the young student whose last excrement I'd mopped up and erased beneath the gallows at Pankrác. Now I was glad old Bacílek hadn't allowed himself to get to know me.

Another desirable job was called "Valdes," which was the name of a big safety-pin manufacturer with a branch factory near Bory that the Czechoslovak Socialist Republic had recently nationalized. At the final stage before Valdes merchandise went to market, prison labor was used for sorting by size and for mounting. Three or four pins—or, better still, garter snaps!—would be inserted through precut holes onto cardboards preprinted for retail sales. Mounting garter snaps was just about the most coveted job in all of Bory. A remarkable feel of intimacy came from working so close to women's underthings. Longing, too—but it kept a man in prison thinking civilian that much longer. We could think, but not touch. . . .

Unfortunately, we didn't control who was put on Valdes duty and who wasn't. I could draw Valdes instead of feathers only as a temporary fill-in when someone else was visiting Mr. Brabec.

I had more luck with the job of making sisal hemp into rope. The raw hemp came in long, knotted strands—which we had to untie and cut into strands of uniform length. Each man's daily quota was five hundred identical strands of rope. It was boring, to be sure—the only time in my life that I've looked forward every day to being at the end of my rope. But sisal-hemp duty was sociable. Because we had to cut the hemp with knives, we could not be allowed to work in the privacy of our cells. Instead, we were sent to a basement workroom with two guards to oversee twenty of us. There, we were forbidden to talk—but, of course, we did. Going to unload a bag of hemp, two of us would drape a couple of bags over ourselves and disappear for two or three minutes, deeply immersed in conversation. And, once or even twice a day, a few of us younger, stronger prisoners would actually be sent to the next wing of the Bory octagon to carry the bags in for unloading. Such travel meant the chance to meet more people—and maybe to pass an office or a garbage pail with a page of newspaper in it.

The newspaper was *Rudé Právo*—but even that was forbidden to us. In those days, it was as stupid as ever, but not dull. The farmers were being liquidated as a class—*kulaks*—and we were already seeing these "class enemies" among us: bluff, baffled men for whom prison was just more unrelenting seven-day-a-week travail, but their eyes asked why couldn't they spend it with their families? Soon, the sons they'd sent to the universities by dint of hard work would join them at hard labor —for the crime of having been "kin to landed bourgeoisie." We knew they were coming—and now, as we read of big trials looming, we learned that Communists were doing unto Communists as they had done unto us. Some of our persecutors might soon be joining our ranks. Others would not be so lucky as we were to leave Pankrác alive—for, on the outside, party members in good standing were signing petitions demanding their executions (even before some of them had been tried). Did the people who signed these petitions to save their own skins have any realization that *they* were dooming others? Bory didn't seem so degrading to me when I read such stories.

Everybody who used to be anybody seemed to be coming in —and nobody was coming out. Nobody who was inside and still in his right mind could even think about release or amnesty. It was in Bory that I stopped considering Bory or my own suffering just temporary. I had been granted very little experience of the world and business affairs, but I already recognized the wisdom of older prisoners who nodded sagely about our fate and agreed it was an "economic necessity. The Russians are going to need our uranium and the mines are going to need slaves to take it out of the ground for them." That was how I caught the first real whiff of what lay ahead.

Only much later would I comprehend that the whole terrible history of Stalinist Czechoslovakia was shaped not by actual conspiracies bigger or smaller than ours, not by Stalin's paranoia or Gottwald's fears, but by gold and uranium. It was all a matter of money and metal, not men and events. Even *we* in Bory, in those days, thought we were there as convicted anti-Communists or potential enemies of the State. In this, we overestimated Communism as an ideology; we were strictly economic casualties of the Cold War.

In Correction, I'd thought some of this through for myself. The Communists had flung down a gauntlet for us "State prisoners." It was a challenge they thought we could never meet. And we had taken it up the only way we could—in a sportsmanlike manner. It was a race, a contest—and we rose to the challenge, even though the rules were rigged against us. We rose to the challenge because we were sure we could outlast them. Or thought we could.

If we had known then what we know now about how long *they* would stay in power, we could never have lived that long. But we didn't know—and so we survived on the illusion we could endure beyond our limits.

Bory taught one that resistance led one to quick destruction. The system broke the strongest man very quickly once he made himself visible as a man. Better to bend rather than break— to "Schweik it" as much as possible without overdoing it. With the most cheerfully servile demeanor, the Good Soldier Schweik made slaves out of masters, flunkies out of bosses, chaos out of order, and a national attitude out of satiric fiction. In Bory, every man found a little of Schweik in himself. For, aside from Brabec, the faces and uniforms oppressing us were not much unlike the policemen and Army officers who were harassing Schweik.

For all its limitations, the food for thought at Bory was far superior to the food to eat. When one wasn't in Correction, one was privileged to enjoy the same Continental breakfast every morning: vile acorn-flavored coffee to wash down the sour-smelling, puttylike "Bory bread," baked on the premises and tasting like raw potatoes. Lunch was a soup that you might find quite tasty if you didn't look at the worms writhing in it. "I don't mind them," a prisoner named Janko told me. "They add to the flavor and, if the soup hasn't killed *them,* maybe it won't kill me." Supper was a starchy white dish that would turn blue before your eyes if you didn't eat it right away; it was better not to wonder why. And, worst of all, there were no second helpings.

The special-treat dinner was on Fridays: goulash. One Friday, there was so little goulash that we clamored for more. We were lucky that the kitchen didn't oblige us, for what little goulash we did get that Friday was enough to give the whole prisoner population diarrhea. And even this emphasized the challenging nature of our existence and survival at Bory. Although our slop buckets ran over with our own waste, the authorities insisted that we "carry on normally." The next bucket-emptying was fourteen hours away. For once, it was impossible to keep clean, no matter how hard we worked— and so, without any organizing, without any signals, we all decided to take a holiday from cleanliness and let ourselves get as dirty as possible. The diarrhea went on for several days and it became a contest to see which of us smelled the worst. So this, too, united us against our oppressors. It became such a bond of unity that, to this day, when Bory alumni meet, those of us who were there during the Big Diarrhea find a special kinship, if no nostalgia.

At other times, keeping clean and preserving one's appearance and health were essential. One big advantage of sisal-hemp duty was that it afforded occasional chances for me to exercise by toting the bales of raw material. Exercising grew to be an obsession with me. I quickly came to realize that confinement is indeed the essence of prison. Lack of fresh air and the absence of any chance to exercise can make just twelve months in jail into a life sentence or even a death sentence. Years after he's served his time, those unhealthy months can hasten the end for an ex-convict.

In Pankrác and at the beginning in Bory, I'd gone for long walks in my cell, which never allowed me to pace more than five steps in any direction. But, after my visit to Mr. Brabec's four-by-four cell with his dark-and-light show, I gave up pacing.

Instead, I started to do every exercise I could ever remember doing: push-ups, sit-ups, deep-knee-bends, handstands, breathing exercises, duck walks, and a few others I invented to exercise muscles that weren't getting any activity. There was no known rule against exercising in the solitude of one's cell. But one day I felt that the guard's quick periodic glance through the peephole had lingered. I stopped exercising, stood up, and stared at the eye I couldn't see but knew was there. Whereupon the guard opened up the part of the door through which meals were served so he could have a conversation with me: "We don't work you hard enough? You don't get enough exercise?" He wasn't demanding an answer, so I stood silent and dignified, waiting for him to go away so I could get on with my exercises. This infuriated him more. Eventually, he slammed the Eye of God shut and went away. But, five minutes later, I felt God's Eye upon me again, so I stood up once more. The meal compartment opened and the guard said, "I caught you! You're not allowed to exercise. Once more and you'll be doing chin-ups for Mr. Brabec on the gallows."

He had no right to deny me exercise, but I never exercised again while he was on duty (though I more than made up for it on all other shifts). I couldn't be punished for exercising, but I could be punished for disobeying an order.

Some of the other prisoners took up yoga, which must have been invented by a monk or a prisoner in a small cell. One fat man did headstands, and I would have liked to see the face on my nemesis, the guard who forbade me to exercise, if he'd ever looked through the Eye of God and seen an upside-down prisoner.

In 1973, Alan Levy tells Karel Čapek, "All the time that I was writing Rowboat to Prague *there—a block and a half from the Russian Army's city occupation headquarters—prison was a very real possibility that I had to prepare for in the back of my mind. When a Reuters correspondent, just released from several years of solitary confinement in Communist China, emerged from his ordeal surprisingly fit and gave yoga as the secret of his survival in cramped quarters, I sent to Brentano's in the States for an English-language yoga manual. I received in the mail a book containing Olivia de Havilland's secrets of staying young and beautiful through yoga. This didn't fill the bill, so I sent to Blackwell's in Oxford—and, through the posts, there came a British war hero's memoir (complete with specific instructions) of how yoga carried him spiritually and physically through the Japanese prisoner-of-war camps. This looked to be much the better of the two books for my purposes, so I stuck it into my briefcase—and, as often happens once the key to such a laudable intention is in hand, I never found time to read it. This yoga book was still with me, however, when I went for my secret-police interrogation in 1971, but very early in the game it was confiscated as 'evidence' of my 'Green Beret training.' "*

And Karel Čapek tells Alan Levy, "Even without it, Alan, you'd have made an excellent prisoner."

With such praise from a professional like Čapek, I am immensely complimented. But I ask him, "Why do you say that?"

He replies, "You proved yourself with the Prague police. But you had it in you even before then: enough detachment to see the humor of whatever bad is happening to you and to laugh a little at whoever is doing it to you—not in a way that makes outright defiance, but in such a Czech way that he alone knows you're laughing at him a little bit and he fears you a little for this."

Bory was filling up rapidly. Vacek and Konopáč arrived shortly before Christmas, 1949—and, while I saw them only once or twice because we were in different wings of the octagon, Vacek managed to smuggle me half of the Christmas cake he'd received from home. As one who'd spent two stints in Correction with Mr. Brabec, I was still on half-rations with no mail, visitor, or gift privileges. It was my first Christmas in jail and I was reliving my last Christmas decorating the tree with Božena, so I was feeling particularly low when Vacek's coffee cake was inexplicably stuck through my slot like manna from heaven, where I hope Vacek is now. I never got to thank my doomed partner-in-crime for it.

In the spring of 1950, Bory grew so crowded that I was given two cellmates. Both were big-city boys, but more primitive than sophisticated—and I found myself being exposed to new views of sex and bodily needs, which was as far as their universe went. One was Janko, from Prague, the chap who'd expressed his preference for soup with live worms. He was a sort of Dancing Dan ladies' man who said he'd rather do anything physical with a girl than talk with her.

My other cellmate, Vokoun, was from Pilsen and prone to terrible rages. They stemmed either from syphilis, which he insisted he'd had when arrested, or else from anger he felt because his complaint wasn't being treated or even examined.

Thus, the topics of conversation in our cell were largely internal medicine—but this was true even among more cerebral cellmates, since the politics outside were so incomprehensible and unthinkable.

One question—such as "Are they putting saltpeter in our food?" to keep our sex drives down—would arise in one cell, spread to others, and then, during the daily one-hour walks, be discussed democratically and farmed out voluntarily to each cell for more specialized research. After comparing notes and questioning a couple of prisoners who worked in the kitchen, just about everyone came to the conclusion that yes, there was saltpeter in our diet—most likely in our morning coffee. Only one man stayed strangely silent, and that was Janko, who ordinarily might have been expected to be the first to volunteer his personal case history. Then, one day, when the rest of us were all in agreement on the saltpeter issue, Janko proclaimed, "I want you all to watch me at tomorrow's walk."

Next morning, without telling us what he was up to, Janko made a point of drinking not only his coffee, but Vokoun's and mine. Then, at our morning exercise, with all eyes upon him, Janko paraded around the courtyard sporting a giant erection that was clearly visible, even through baggy prison denims.

Strutting and swaggering like the cock of the walk, which he was, Janko nevertheless did not attract the guard's attention. It was the other prisoners—doubling over with laughter or sputtering with rage at the irrational logic of this demonstration—who caught our jailers' eyes. They even questioned some of us to find out what conspiracy was afoot. This made us laugh all the more and rendered us totally unhelpful. Later, when the guards lost interest in what we were up to, we prisoners reopened our inquiry in the light of Janko's "new evidence," which the more academic among us wanted to dismiss as a sexual boast.

There was only one guard in our wing of Bory who was approachable by prisoners—and he happened to supervise the food and water deliveries. His name was Mašek—a "white gypsy" of a tribe that had migrated, over a few generations, through Rumania to Hungary to Slovakia, from where they had spread across our land as "lunaparkers"—carnival-ride operators. Mašek must have been an exceptional "white gypsy" who'd wandered all the way to the horror house called Bory. Regardless of tribe, though, he was an exceptional man— exceptionally stupid and, for a Bory guard, exceptionally gregarious. He just couldn't ignore people—which put him one notch above his colleagues on the human scale.

We were brought a jug of water every morning for the day's washing and drinking. It was never enough, and, in hot weather, it was much too little. Only when Mašek was on duty did we dare demand more. Mašek would appear outside the cell door and ask such a question as: "What do you need water for? You're only gonna piss it out anyway."

"But, sir," I would answer. "I can't piss *without* water."

This made perfect sense to Mašek, so he would fetch the water. And, because I was one of the few men in Bory who could keep a straight face while conversing with Mašek, I was designated to ask him whether it was true that our coffee was being doctored to dilute our sex drive. My tactic for seeking information was to pretend to knowledge.

"Sir," I began, "about the saltpeter in our coffee—"

"Out of the question, Eighty-two ten," said Mašek. "I'd get you some if I could, but the kitchen says no special privileges."

It took me a while to transmit what I was after and, to heighten the urgency, I added, "I need to know because I haven't had a hard-on in two months."

"Well, neither have I," Mašek said, "and I don't drink the coffee or anything here. Say, do you think my wife's putting that 'peter stuff into my beer?"

That's as far as my saltpeter research with Mašek went—but, several years and several labor camps later, I was still hearing impotence referred to as "Mašek's Disease."

An even more fiery argument erupted in our cell over the issue of "Do farts burn?" Vokoun, who prided himself on his unfailing ability to "fart on demand," said yes, they did, because they were gas and, besides, *he* ought to know. Janko, on the other side, said that farts were natural gas and the product of fermentation "like beer and wine, which don't burn." The debate spread through the other cells and the courtyard. It took about two weeks to arrange a properly scientific experiment, but finally a candle and some matches were smuggled into our cell. Then, with me lying on the floor as the impartial witness, Vokoun pulled down his pants, squatted like a rower without a seat, and spread his cheeks. Janko stood by with candle ablaze and, as Vokoun cut loose with a volley of farts, Janko stuck the candle up his ass. To my amazement, looking upward, I soon saw a small bluish flame licking around Vokoun's asshole as though it were some sort of hot rum dessert.

"Liquid gas!" I proclaimed. "It burns!"

The next day, one who dissented from my finding consulted the oracle Mašek about it. His answer: "Well, when I fart, my wife burns."

One day, going to fetch a bale of sisal hemp, I laid hands on a page of *Rudé Právo*. Ten minutes later, a guard came over to

me and said, "Eighty-two ten, I know you have a newspaper."
I started to deny it, but when he said, "Give it to me and I'll
punish you myself. Otherwise, it's Mr. Brabec for you," I
handed it right over and he slapped my face just once. I spent
my reading time wondering how he'd known I had the paper.
The answer seemed to point to the prisoner who'd been sent
with me on that same errand: a young Rumanian named
Dumitrescu, who'd been caught passing through Slovakia in an
attempt to escape to the West. Later, when similar incidents
happened to other prisoners, we compared notes and rosters
of all possible informers. Dumitrescu was on every list.

Seven of us who'd been his victims formed a delegation. We
approached Dumitrescu quietly one day and told him to stop
informing on us. Dumitrescu's answer was to shove the two of
us nearest him, deny everything, and say, "I'll fix you for saying
this!" We walked away from this confrontation and scattered
quickly. A few minutes later, we saw Dumitrescu pointing us
out to a guard. The guard, however, looked sheepish. Informers aren't supposed to communicate with captors in public.
The guard eventually just walked away from Dumitrescu with
an embarrassed shrug.

Nothing happened to us seven, but Dumitrescu's usefulness
as an assigned informer was at an end. Nothing more would
have happened to him at our hands if he hadn't continued informing on a voluntary basis. Even the guards despised him for
this, but every now and then they acted upon his information.

One day, he found a note in his pocket: "The next time you
tell on us, you'll have nothing to tell with." The note had been
stuck in his pocket six hours earlier, but, not being very bright,
Dumitrescu assumed it had just arrived. He swung hard at the
surprised prisoner standing nearest him. Seeing the opportunity, eight other prisoners formed a circle around the two men,
struck Dumitrescu a blow apiece, and scattered quickly. Before the guards could respond, Dumitrescu was unconscious.

By the time he was back on his feet, about ten minutes later,
we'd all been ordered to our cells. The commandant of Bory
ordered a complete search of our wing—in the course of which
a concealed ax was found (or else planted-and-found. To pun-

ish us for punishing Dumitrescu would be to admit they used informers). The next day at dawn, our entire wing of Bory was ordered into the courtyard where we usually took our daily walk. We were paired off, as usual, but we knew this was no ordinary walk. The commandant and all his deputies were on hand—as were twenty extra guards with submachine guns. And Mr. Brabec, who was seldom seen outdoors, was in charge of this "special exercise."

He started us off at a run. "Faster! Faster! Now jump! Now duck walk! Now leapfrog! Now duck walk double time!"

On and on it went. But, immediately, from the moment we realized what was happening, we all tried to make it. I, personally, rose to the challenge and almost rejoiced at putting all my exercises to good use and maybe learning a few new ones. But even old men like the silent, grieving Bacílek came to life and performed till they fainted. Guards would run over to kick them and exhort them to "get up, we know you're faking!" —but, eventually, they had to carry them over to the submachine gunners who, as soon as the prisoners regained consciousness, made them do knee bends. One flabby young man who fainted did so many deep knee bends that morning that, for two weeks, he couldn't walk up a flight of stairs properly. He had to wiggle up, holding the banister with both hands. He reminded me of nothing so much as the deformed Judge Prášek, who, in the name of "socialist legality," had put me where I was.

Toward noon, it ended. Those of us who were still on our feet stood in that courtyard panting, sweating, stinking, and puking. Our eyes were bloodshot. Our mouths were open in the hope that our breath would fly back in; we were too tired to try to catch it. But we were one—a very funny-looking animal, indeed, but a living organism. The guards had every right to laugh at the sight of us, as they did, but we knew and they knew how they respected and feared us for what we'd shown we could take. Finally, they led us, staggering two-by-two, back to the solitude of our cells—where some of us fainted.

Bory was not done with us yet—but the rest of the reprisals were relatively administrative. Rations and outdoor walking

time were halved. All of us on sisal-hemp duty were reassigned
as a result of the Dumitrescu beating. Some of us landed better
work (with Valdes garter snaps) while others, like myself,
once again found ourselves plucking feathers. Bory was my
baptism as a professional prisoner. After my nine months of
incubation at Pankrác, I had been reborn in Bory as a hard-
boiled pro under the tutelage of mentors and tormentors whom
I will number in my nightmares to my dying day—in Prague,
I pray.

We were just numbers again—but our days in Bory were
numbered, too. The Czech uranium industry was booming—
for Russia! Bory was happy to unload a whole wing of troublemakers into the mines of Jáchymov (Joachimstal), where
Marie and Pierre Curie first isolated radium. I knew just
enough about radioactivity to fear it, but I looked forward to
the camps as an otherwise relatively healthful, if more arduous,
form of hard labor that would offer more potential for escaping. After all, nothing could be worse than Bory. So we
thought!

Thus, one morning in the late summer of 1950, when our
names were called out over loudspeakers and we were issued
the shabbiest uniforms that could be found for us in all of
Bory, handcuffed by twos, and loaded, sixty to a truck, for
transport to Jáchymov, everybody with me rejoiced. For the
two-hour trip, a couple of guards, armed with submachine
guns, perched on two wooden seats above and behind us. They
tried to shush us, but it was all they could do to keep from
falling out of the truck or into our midst, so we went on talking freely. And, through a rip in the canvas near me, some of us
could peek out at the first green trees and grass I'd seen in
almost a year. The sun was as dazzling, if not so blinding, as
Mr. Brabec's floodlight. Near Pilsen, I caught a glimpse of a
tram—an everyday object in my past life, but now so big, so
funny, and so gay that it became my vision of what Times
Square would look like. When the tram's signal light blinked,
I, too, blinked—with wonder at what I used to take for
granted.

At noon, we grew unbearably thirsty and it seemed as if the truck did, too, as it labored up dry, dusty hills. Someone who knew the territory said we were near Jáchymov, in the vicinity of the three main prison camps: Svornost, Rovnost, and Bratrství, names that mean Unity, Equality, and Brotherhood (the Communist version of *Liberté, Égalité, Fraternité*). Our first stop was at Camp Svornost (Unity), where a dozen names were called out. With weary sighs and quick good-byes, these men disembarked. As we drove away, I could see out the back why those of them who knew of Svornost had felt sorry for themselves. It was built vertically—232 steep steps pitched at a 60-degree angle with a mine at the bottom, the prison camp on top. Just about every move those men would make during their stay at Svornost would be up or down. Svornost looked like a flight of stairs carved, badly, into the side of a cliff and wrapped securely in barbed wire. I rejoice to this day that I never had the misfortune to serve time there.

Three miles up the road brought us to Camp Rovnost (Equality). Two dozen more names were called out and that many quick good-byes were said. I remained aboard the truck. We bypassed Camp Bratrství (Brotherhood), which was mainly a reception and indoctrination center for slaves delivered directly from Pankrác and other pretrial jails, not for hardened criminals from Bory like ourselves. The truck threaded its way down a winding road leading off the plateau that housed Camps Unity, Equality, and Brotherhood. Then, after a mile or two down below, it stopped—and we were unloaded at the gate of Camp Eliáš.

Actually, it was already known as "Old Eliáš" because a "New Eliáš" was being built, not to replace it, but to supplement it by housing more prison labor to work the same rich mine in between the two camps. To us, however, Old Eliáš was all new. We stood, just outside its gate, on the open road: twenty-six men, twenty-four of us with nothing in our hands, the other two covering us with submachine guns. But we hardly saw them. Eyes that had rested too long on Bory's concrete gray now roamed nature's mysteries: rich, rugged, romantic country that was far too lushly endowed to imprison anyone. It was summer now, but this particular mystery of nature would be heightened on winter mornings, when these same unbelieving eyes would watch the sun get up, all pink on the snow of steep slopes, with just a sprinkling of green from the fir trees. And one wondered, as Adam and Eve probably did, how anything evil could happen in such a beautiful place.

We barely had time to stretch our legs when the camp gate opened. We were formed up by fives and marched inside—or, rather, into the "gate hold" no-man's-land separating Old Eliáš from the public highway and freedom. Now, when our eyes gazed upward, they saw elevated wooden watchtowers, thirty to forty yards apart, manned by guards with submachine guns trained on us.

Behind the next gate, we could see the camp: ten large wooden barracks (obviously without plumbing) grouped around one latrine that might be fair-sized for a family, but not for six-hundred to a thousand men. Off to one side stood the camp's skyscraper: a two-story brick administrative building. From it emerged the camp commandant: a fat, squat Sudeten German who came strutting toward us like Hermann Göring. He barked at us in accented Czech: "Now you haff come to a place where you vill learn to obey the law! Our law! Remember that!" As he screamed on and on like this, we almost enjoyed him. Our experience with Mr. Brabec in Bory had taught all of us that the jailer who barks least is often the one who bites deepest.

His last words to us, before returning to his desk, were: "Man cannot come into *my* camp dressed like so! Who told you to come dressed like this to Camp Eliáš?" As if we'd had a choice! We knew better than to try to cope with such rhetorical questions. Anyway, his words conjured up a prisoner from Supply laden with twenty-four slightly stronger work coats and trousers than we had on. He tossed them to the ground. We each grabbed whatever looked closest to our size, undressed, and tossed our old rags onto a new pile—which the Supply prisoner took away with disdain. Naturally, he was better-dressed than any of us. But I wondered why he'd spoiled his sartorial

splendor with a red bulls-eye painted on the back of his coat
and a red stripe down the side of his trousers. The answer
came when another prisoner appeared with a bucket and began to paint our new clothes red.

"I'd rather you didn't," I said, facetiously. "It will sort of
make me feel like a moving target."

"Exactly!" he said, grinning. "And it's also supposed to show
you're a political prisoner, who tried to kill our republic, and
not just one of us harmless murderers." I noticed he wasn't
wearing any red paint and decided he wasn't kidding.

"Better paint it," I decided. "But red looks like the wrong
color for *us*."

At last we were let into Camp Eliáš and assigned to barracks. The bunks were triple-decker. As a new man, one always
began at the top of the totem pole (so close to the ceiling that
there was little air and even less room to raise your head) and
worked one's way down to a middle and then a lower berth.
After just a few minutes exchanging news of jail acquaint-
ances with the inmates already there, we were summoned by
loudspeaker and assembled to hear that we'd start work in the
mines next morning. The names of our shift bosses were read
off to us, too.

These bosses were all prisoners. None of them was painted
red. Some were thieves and murderers, but more of them were
Nazis, collaborators, and even German prisoners of war—all
of whose natural adaptation to prison routine (plus their seniority in camp) had secured them the best jobs. It was that way in
all the camps. A number of political prisoners who'd spent the
war fighting the Nazis or even as guests in *their* concentration
camps began to wonder at Eliáš—with its Germanic commander and SS shift bosses—just *who* had won the war. But,
after a while, even the Jewish prisoners mastered an axiom of
prison-camp life: inside the barbed wire, you cannot judge a
man's qualities as a prisoner or as a person by the crimes he
may or may not have committed on the outside.

For example (and for this I must skip a few months ahead
in my story), the man two bunks below me was a dashing, dark-
haired chap with wide-open eyes and a romantic pucker to his

lips. He came from Ostrava and spoke the very special local slang. His name was Erik, but everybody called his "Gary Crant" because he was sort of a mirror image of the movie actor Cary Grant. He said he'd been jailed for helping a friend escape to the West. Then why didn't he have a red stripe or bull's-eye on his uniform? "Because I was one of the first ones here, even before they started painting us red." We accepted his explanation because one always took fellow prisoners on faith and because he was convincing.

One day, though, some of us began to suspect there was an informer in our midst. A prisoner who worked in the administrative office, Honza Lang, made a routine check of the files of everyone in our barracks in case they would afford a clue to who was informing. To Honza's surprise, he discovered that "Gary Crant" was serving fifteen years for the apolitical crime of murdering his ex-girl friend with a knife through her heart.

Honza confided this to me. We decided to do nothing and say nothing unless "Gary Crant" seemed to be the informer. This seemed unlikely because he'd been around camp so long without ever arousing suspicion on that count.

After a few new prisoners had been transferred out, the informing ceased. But Honza and I went on watching "Gary Crant" with special interest. We couldn't help liking him anyway—but we observed with admiration how much he wanted to be one of us. He even, very quietly but determinedly, avoided opportunities to better his lot (there were many advantages to being convicted of a capital rather than a State offense) rather than forfeit his pretense. . . .

Until Christmas Day of 1950, when we managed to obtain two bottles of cheap Cognac and eighteen of us were sitting around our section of the barracks with a sprig of evergreen in the center of the floor. As we sipped and spoke of wives and girl friends, tears came to "Gary Crant"'s eyes and our ladykiller finally said haltingly, "Fellas, I wanna tell you something. . . . In Ostrava, I had a girl. . . . I liked her. . . . I loved her. . . . . She liked me, but she didn't love me. . . . I told her she had to love me." Now his words came in a rush: "She started going with someone else, I told her to stop, she said I was the one who had to stop, we were in her parents' kitchen and there was a knife there and I picked it up and killed her with it."

Then he began to cry—and he really didn't stop sobbing from Christmas to New Year's Day. But Honza Lang and I felt better right then and there. Soon after the first of the year, "Gary Crant" began to feel better, too. Now his secret was out in the open! And now he could see that nothing had changed in our attitude toward him.

He was indeed a fine fellow—like several of the murderers I met in prison. They were all very sad people with one trait in common. Their *crime* was the Greatest Single Truth in their lives: the high point, the low point, and, even if they overcame it or even if they killed again, they would measure their existence from that key moment of truth, much the way the rest of the world measures B.C. and A.D. In that respect, their lives were just as much over as their victims'. For many of the rest of us, *prison* would become our Greatest Single Truth, but not our crimes, such as they were.

My shift boss assigned me to a partner: a more experienced prisoner with whom I'd work and from whom I'd learn my job as a miner. I was lucky to draw an elderly, grandfatherly man named Sochor. He was a building engineer who told me right off that "My job used to be assessing stresses and strains. From that experience, I learned not to have any stresses or strains in my own life—even down here."

I have never seen a more deliberate, slow-moving man than Old Sochor. There was no wasted motion. You could even see a conscious effort when he opened his mouth to speak. When he rolled a cigarette, nothing else happened for thirty or forty minutes while he concentrated on this task.

Trying to learn from the wisdom of my elders, I emulated Old Sochor for a few days—until I learned that this man who looked sixty was only thirty-seven years old! Then I decided that I didn't want to age so carefully and well that I'd be an old man at thirty-seven. The mines and the philosophy he'd brought into them had done this to Old Sochor. I decided I'd let the mines and nature take their course with Young Čapek.

Every morning, we were sent to work, five at a time, through the "corridor." This was a passage, completely enclosed by barbed wire, connecting camp with mine. Its barbed-wire ceiling was so low that a man had to crouch as he walked. Our guards marched alongside us, but erect as free men. The "corridor" was the chute through which wild animals are let into and out of the circus arena.

By camp standards, the corridor in Old Eliáš was relatively short and humane. It took only twenty-five minutes, allowing for head counts at both ends, to traverse it. But each crouching step hurt a man's dignity until, at either end, he could stand up straight again and almost welcome being guarded merely by men in the wooden sentry boxes overhead.

Every day, we were led into a shed and issued carbide miners' lamps, rubber raincoats, and helmets of steel or leather or plastic. I tried to draw a steel helmet with the initials of UNRRA on it. This was where U.N. aid to Czechoslovakia was going—into the slave labor mines. At first, I was indignant. But, on my third day under the earth, I had cause to be grateful.

Old Sochor and I were chatting down below with a Prague barber when there was a swishing sound and a thump. The barber, standing between us in a leather helmet, crumpled to the floor. He'd been felled by a falling rock. His helmet was bashed in and he had an open, gaping, bleeding head wound. I ripped off my shirt to bandage what would prove to be nothing worse than a brain concussion that would keep the barber out of the mines for a month. Old Sochor helped me hoist the unconscious man up into the mine-shaft elevator. As he did, my senior partner remarked, "Lucky it didn't land on us. But we'd have been better off with our U.N. hard hats."

"Three cheers for Trygve Lie,"* I muttered.

Nobody gave us any instructions in the mine—not even on how to work a carbide lamp. I was lucky to have Old Sochor as my mentor; during the first few days, several other men suffered bad burns experimenting with their new toy.

---

* First secretary-general of the United Nations, from 1946 to 1953.

Every morning, after we drew our equipment in the mine shed at ground level, we were shoved into open elevators, five or six of us at a time, and delivered down, down, down into the depths of the earth. The world seemed to disappear beneath my feet many times as we passed through ceilings and then floors until we finally jolted to a halt in a big room with a dome so high that you almost felt as if you were outdoors on a sunless day. Here, it was cold and dank and dark. But, to me, it smelled of freedom.

Various tunnels led from the room. Old Sochor and I were dispatched down one of them, where the illusion of freedom was substantiated a little by our being alone, with no guards commanding us, no Eye of God upon us. As I savored this solitude, Old Sochor's slowness sat well with my mood. We were in no hurry to catch up with our fellow prisoners. Eventually, though, we did—and there were still no guards, but, on my very first day, there was a surprise.

"Be sure to stay behind the Geiger counter," Old Sochor cautioned me. I heard the clicking up ahead, but I was not prepared to discover that the Geiger counter—or, rather, the person who held it—was a girl.

She looked voluptuous and shapely even in the same lumpy clothes we wore. I could see some brownish-gold (or dirty blond) hair straggling out from under her UNRRA helmet. And, even before I saw face, the sight of her made my body tremble, my heart pound, my blood rush to my head. I had the hot and cold sweats.

She was working with a man who wrote down the readings she gave him. Every now and then, she and he swapped jobs.

When Old Sochor greeted her, I could tell—from the deferential contempt with which he said, "Good morning, me lady!" —that she was not a prisoner and probably something worse. The man working with her looked like, I guessed correctly, a policeman.

Old Sochor didn't deign to introduce me, but I caught her eye. She looked me over quickly, and what do you think her first words were? She said, "You'd like to fuck me, wouldn't you?"

She spoke in Eastern Slovak—a Slavonic tongue, almost like Russian, with a texture that, for all its softness and a distinctive *sh* sound, has a special coarseness that places its user both geographically and socially among our people. It sounds like paper slippers crossing a splintery floor. Before I could say anything, Old Sochor murmured, surprisingly quickly, "Watch out!"

So I said, with more perception than I'd have given myself credit for, "Sorry, I don't think I can afford it."

She laughed—and it was a throaty laugh that gave me a hard-on—before saying, "First time, it's free. After that, it costs. A little time with uranium and you'll need all my help just to get it up."

The man with her glared in such a way that I recognized that he and I were both being teased. Part of his job was to permit no possibility of intercourse between prisoners and Shushu, as she was called because of the way she spoke. It was only permitted between Shushu and the guards or civilian workers in the mines—and, with Shushu, it was always for money.

I learned from Old Sochor that she used to be a ranking prostitute in the ancient Slovakian town of Nitra. Among the many professions to be overhauled by the Communists, the oldest was not exempted. Shushu had been offered the choice of a trial for "parasitism" or volunteering for a well-paid position in the mines.* And Shushu had, of course, gone where the money was.

Old Sochor despised Shushu—and not only for what she was. She had propositioned him, too, on his first day under the earth with her. But he had begged off, saying, "Excuse me, I'm a married man."

---

* At that time, while prisoners were still being rounded up for slave labor, civilian volunteers were paid three or four times normal wage scales to work in the mines. It was the only way to recruit manpower while maintaining the time-consuming pretense of fair trial and conviction, which was important to Stalin because he liked to delude himself with the claim that Czechoslovakia was the one East European satellite that went Communist in a legitimate, parliamentary manner.

This had struck her as hilarious, so she'd responded, when her laughter died down, with: "What do you do when your wife's got her period?"

Old Sochor had blushed and turned away. If there was one thing this thirty-seven-year-old senior citizen had kept with him in the prisons, the camps, the mines, and the corridors, it was his dignity. But the policeman working with Shushu had grabbed him and shaken him, saying, "Answer a lady when she speaks to you!"

"We do nothing," Old Sochor had answered. Shushu, a little sorry for what had happened, had turned away, too. But not her police escort, who pressed on and made Old Sochor repeat three painful times, "My wife, when she has her period, she and I don't fuck."

Now it was over, but Old Sochor still blamed Shushu—and not her police escort—for his pain. This was why he addressed her mockingly as "me lady." And this was why, whenever she made a half-hearted effort to tease him, he'd reply, "Sorry, I've got my period."

I enjoyed the banter with Shushu more than Sochor did. She teased me every day about whether my manhood was surviving the magic potion U-235—which, believe me, was a real worry. I would have liked nothing better than to test my virility with her. But, knowing it was impossible, I settled for a kind of half-witted flirtatious chitchat about *who* should pay *whom* for *what*.

I liked having Shushu around even if I could never have her. Miners' lamps are like restaurant candles: they make a woman look much more alluring than she ever was or will be. Once or twice in our platonic friendship, I had the bad luck to glimpse Shushu above the ground: in broad daylight, the Queen of the Underworld was a slightly squat, dumpy, hairy, and moustached whore from Nitra. But, an hour later, in our deep and dim shaft beneath the earth, Shushu was once again the Everywoman my underground manhood craved.

If it was an unexpected pleasure to be following Shushu's ample behind through the Jáchymov underworld on State time, this was the job to which Old Sochor and I had been assigned. Shushu and her police escort, with their Geiger counter and clipboard, were called "collectors." As soon as the Geiger counter began to click faster and faster until it hummed, Shushu would cry out, "It sings!" Then, as the uranium-rich vein was pinpointed, Old Sochor and I would go to work. With shovels, pickaxes, and other implements, we'd clear away the walls and prop up ceilings to facilitate access to the precious uranium. Then the carpenters, also prisoners, would move in behind us to build whatever was needed for a proper extraction operation. They would be followed by the miners, mostly civilian workers.

If the Geiger counter didn't sing, then Old Sochor and I would have to clear the passageway for further probing by Shushu and other collectors. For this, we were often issued detonators and explosives—again without any training or instruction in their use.

Whichever job we were doing, Sochor and I sometimes happened upon uranium ore ourselves. The first time we did, Old Sochor moved away from it faster than I'd ever seen him move. But I picked up a stone and studied it with fascination. Prisoners and miners called it *smolinec*, which is derived from the word for bad luck (*smůla*). Pitch-black in color, it was easy to spot because it would be unnaturally smooth on one side while the other sides looked like boiling, bubbling tar that had been frozen like action sculptures. This must have been the action that took place long, long before man penetrated this earth.

Like lead, the stone of power was surprisingly heavy. At first, I thought this came from the weight of worry, fear, and grief I brought to it. But, later, loading it gingerly but hastily into the double-handled one-by-one-by-one-foot boxes that stood on the wagons waiting to roll toward Russia, I learned that a full box weighed a good two hundred pounds and required at least two strong men to lift it. I told myself that first time, "I'm going to have a good look at it just once—and that's all." But I held onto it longer than I thought I would. I was almost paralyzed by the respect I felt for that small, elusive black stone and its hidden powers. Almost like a magician, I felt the incantation in my head: "Stone of blackness; stone of death;

stone that traps me here; don't be the stone that dooms me here."

There was ample reason to fear this. Long before Mme Curie, when Jáchymov was a silver-mining center,* there had been a special miners' affliction called "Jáchymov's Disease." Local people, not all of them miners, would suffer a kind of T.B. that was not T.B., with liver, blood, and bone marrow complications. And so we prisoners, undernourished and inadequately protected, avoided uranium like the plague it was. Thirsty and dirty as we were, we even economized on the limited washing and drinking water we were granted. Shushu insisted she had once checked out the drinking water with her Geiger counter and "it was so radioactive that your balls would be empty in a month."

Sometimes, clearing out an area that hadn't registered on Shushu's Geiger counter, Sochor and I would come upon the stone. If nobody was checking or spying on us, we would quickly set off an explosion that would bury the uranium under enough debris to make it unreachable by man or Geiger counter. This was sabotage punishable by execution, but we were never caught because we took the chance only when we were sure we were alone and unobserved. That was when the calculated risk of death on the gallows gave us better odds than death from uranium.

At other times, we simply stopped and refused to work once we'd come upon live uranium. This was a breach of discipline, but we were banking on the greed of civilian workers, who were paid bonuses based upon the amount they turned in. They were happy, even eager, to relieve us of our burden. They kept reminding us, "There's nothing in it for you."

Except slow death, I agreed silently. For them, it meant money and fast death. In the mines, I saw strong, well-fed young civilian workers collapse within two months—and sur-

---

* Solid silver made Jáchymov the cradle of the dollar. In the sixteenth century, the town's founder, Count Šlik, built his own currency system around a coin, minted there, called the "thaler," from which the U.S. dollar later derived its name.

vive, if they did, as broken physical wrecks. Sometimes I would see an eager young miner grab a sandwich from his lunch box with hands coated by uranium dust and I would give him two or three months. My prognoses proved, if anything, optimistic. I could never have anticipated that I myself would spend five of my prison years under the ground—and it is only because of the day-to-day precautions I took that I'm here to tell the tale.

Only one prisoner among us didn't shirk the uranium. He was a petty thief, shoplifter, and kleptomaniac whose offenses including stealing women's underwear from clotheslines. Apparently, he was a uranium fetishist, too, for he would pocket a stone (another capital offense!), smuggle it back to camp through the very careful searches at both ends of the "corridor," and put it under his pillow at night to bring him good luck and magic. The authorities never caught him, but his fellow prisoners did. Like vengeful Tooth Fairies, we used to keep a nightly vigil and whoever found the black pebble under the fetishist's pillow would throw the magic stone away while the rest of us were throwing the uranium thief out into the cold, too, for the night.

Though we were overworked, underfed, and underslept, those first few months at Old Eliáš were among the joyous times of my life. The relief of relative freedom after Bory gave us new energy that not only carried us through long hours in the mines and those trips through the corridor, but also into the barracks, where we stayed up late at night talking and scheming and contriving hotfoots and Chinese water tortures (from dripping canteens) for our friends and neighbors.

The soundest sleeper among the prisoners was my friend the clerk Honza Lang. He was a skinny, spindly, hatchet-faced Šumava mountaineer who could contort his wiry body so well that I once saw him sleep atop a narrow pipe. He could sleep standing up. He could sleep sitting on the toilet. He could sleep riding a mine elevator. He could sleep with just his nose buried in his mess kit. So, one day, when he was sleeping on his back in his underwear, we reached through his fly and tied a rope around his penis. Honza didn't stir.

Then we hooked the rope through the bedpost, up to the ceiling, and along a rafter. When it was all rigged, we took turns standing at the other end of the room and pumping the rope. As we worked his penis back and forth, Honza got an erection. Then he began to writhe in ecstasy and, after a couple of minutes, he came—and went right on sleeping. Tightening the noose, we started Honza up again, and it was only when he couldn't come two minutes later that Honza woke up from his wet dreams. He looked at his penis, saw the rope, gave a frightened start, then saw and heard us horselaughing. He blushed—and then began to laugh, too. "I'm telling you," Honza said later, "when I first woke up, I really thought the uranium had made my plumbing *kaput.*"

Letters home were permitted—and, as soon as my father knew my whereabouts, he made contact with a civilian from Carlsbad who was working in our mine. The man agreed to deliver messages and money to me, but he was a crook who was in the mines just to make money, any money, at any risk— of which cheating the family of a State criminal was one of the safest. He took the messages and fifteen thousand crowns of my father's money without ever making contact with me before my family caught on to him.

We used to curse the Russians, for whom we knew we were working. After a while, we even began to see Russians. Overseers, officers, experts, and engineers—all of them we could smell as soon as they entered the mine, even if they were hundreds of yards and many minutes away. They all wore the same perfume and too much of it—particularly in a mine shaft with insufficient ventilation. They were all the same in this and many other ways. There was one of them, however, who smelled the same, but was very different.

He was a young Russian mining engineer of apparently so little stature or fear that, unlike all the others, he wasn't assigned a Czechoslovak bodyguard for his trips into our underworld. He worked alone and he was accessible and even eager for conversation. We all knew enough Russian to manage to talk with him.

"You've come to see your slaves?" we asked him soon after

he joined us—and he laughed, but it was a pleasant laugh. After several such encounters, he asked us, "Why do you say 'slaves' when you mean *Slavs?*" After a little more conversation, we discovered that *he didn't even know we were prisoners!*

Czech civilians with the slightest possibility of coming into contact with us were given orientation lectures on how to avoid us and report us as well as on what dangerous creatures we were. Apparently, the Czech authorities in Jáchymov wouldn't dare tell *anything* to a Russian. They must have assumed he was already better indoctrinated than they were.

When we broke the news to our Russian friend, he didn't believe us. The next day, he came back down very sheepishly and said, "You were right. They told me you *are* prisoners. They say you are all Germans and murderers." We were easily able to convince him that this wasn't so. And he admitted after a few minutes, "They warned me to report any contacts and to associate only with the civilian workers. But they are not such good people as you criminals."

"And our jailers are the biggest criminals of all!" I said quite openly. Old Sochor shushed me, but the Russian never reported me for my outburst—so we trusted him all the more. He didn't seek us out, but he kept coming back to us—with questions such as "How many prisoners are there?" "Are there really that few civilian workers?" Those were short-answer questions, but when he asked *why* this had happened, the only reasonably short answer was Sochor's: "Gold. Money. Uranium. Power."

He came to look upon us as the only decent men and our underworld as the only source of truth he could believe in this Slavonic, but alien and mysterious, land. Finding out from us that he was the master and we were his slaves had put him in our bond. Now he told us he was naïve enough to be pleading our cases with the powers above at earth level.

Their response was to offer him a guard because "they say you'll make trouble for me." And just as steadfastly, he refused —"So now I seem to be making trouble for them—and myself."

The Czech mine and police authorities spoke deferentially to even the lowliest Russian. But, when they got nowhere with him, they must have protected themselves by deferentially mentioning his open-mindedness to his Soviet superiors. One day, he didn't appear. Instead, two Czech secret policemen came to find out which ones of us had talked with him. We didn't tell, but we learned during our questioning that he'd been "sent home."

If this was the truth, then we envied our young Russian engineer *his* punishment. In 1951, nobody was sending us home. As more and more of our fellow citizens entered custody, my most urgent objective was to escape. Old Eliáš being just about the oldest of the twenty mining-concentration camps in Bohemia, there were bound to be passages from past explorations and excavations dating back to silver-mining days and beyond. Our explosions every now and then revealed to Old Sochor and me old passages that looked too frail and precarious for the "collectors" with their Geiger counters to venture into. Sochor and I were supposed to explore them a little way to see if they could be salvaged by carpentry. Then, usually on our say-so, our bosses would decide whether to go forward or wall the passage off with concrete or simply bar it with two railroad ties.

Sochor and I were just one of three shifts on the same job. We made an agreement with the other four men: on each shift, one man would work extra hard and stand lookout, too, at the entrance of any promising old passage while his partner probed deep within to see if it led toward any trace of freedom. On the other two shifts, the partners took turns. But, on ours, Old Sochor stayed put and I crawled within. "If I'm ever to escape," he sighed wearily, "I'll have to go first class—with a map, a railroad ticket, and a car waiting to drive me to the station." But he covered for me while I followed out passages that had some air in them—to see whether the air came through any outlet we could use. Whenever air or time gave out, I'd turn back.

There were many dangers. The air could give out altogether as I breathed up what little there was. Or the ceiling could cave in behind me or on me. Tons of stone could come down on my back or wall me off from air and life. (As I crawled, my rump sometimes bumped the low ceilings and I felt them tremble from the contact.)

In this airless labyrinth, not the least of the perils were getting lost or returning late or being discovered. Tardiness would be treated as an escape attempt. And I always took a deep breath before crawling the last few yards. Would Old Sochor be waiting there to welcome me with a grunt? Or a guard with a machine gun?

I was never found out. But I never found a way out. Still, those furtive crawls meant adventure, even romance. Even getting nowhere was a taste of freedom and accomplishment. It was a thrill to penetrate where no police were and no police had ever been. Sometimes, I found relics of other men: an ancient wooden ladder that was already fiber when it decomposed from my touch or else the tattered fabric of a silver miner's shirt. There were stalactites and stalagmites and gushing waterfalls from which I couldn't resist drinking.

There must have been some way out! I'm sure I would have found it in another ten or twenty years if I hadn't been transferred from the old Camp Eliáš to the new Camp Eliáš in the spring of 1951. Inmates of New Eliáš worked the same mine, but my change of address also involved reassignment to new work, new shifts, and new partners in the mine. And New Eliáš offered more fertile soil for escape right beneath my own barracks.

New Eliáš lay in a valley hemmed in by mountains. This terrain forced the guard towers to be in or right over the corridor through which we were herded to and from work. If one could tunnel under the narrow width of the corridor and a a few yards beyond, there lay farmland—and freedom, even if it were the freedom of the hunted.

I had the good fortune to be assigned to the barracks nearest the corridor. Another man obtained a skeleton key to an unoccupied room in our building (New Eliáš was so new that it would take the penal system a good three months more to fill it up) and he and I removed a square of the prefabricated floor. Then, at night, after work, by flashlight, we dug—replacing the square of floor neatly at the end of each labor.

After a week, we had a hole two yards deep. We started to dig a tunnel that needed to be no more than fifty yards long.

Unfortunately, as soon as we started to dig horizontally, we ran into a ventilation problem even worse than in the mines. It took us another week to dig two yards—and the effort was sapping our health. So we had to take four other men into the plot. We picked four who'd noticed our nocturnal absences, but had asked no questions; this rough standard, we hoped, was the measure of a qualified secret-keeper. Now we had five men to share the digging while the sixth man, with a canvas sack, disposed of all the dirt we displaced.

Still, the nightly absence of six men generated a wider ripple of interest and hope among our fellow prisoners—to the point where, in broad daylight at New Eliáš or in the gloom of the mine shaft, I would be greeted with a cheery "How's it going, Karel?"

"Lousy," I'd reply. "I think the uranium's getting to me."

"I mean *it!* Don't be afraid. I won't tell anybody."

All I could say was: "Won't tell anybody what?"

I would get at least a wink and, in one case, "I know *all* about *it*. If you won't let me help, the least you can do is let me use it when it's ready."

I'd feign ignorance, but the winks and inquiries grew so broad and blatant that my partners and I decided to lay off for a fortnight. After more than a month of hard work, our tunnel was not quite forty yards long. It was already under the corridor and we were no more than a month away from an escape attempt, but we needed to recoup our strength and silence the gossip.

A day or two before we were to resume work, the authorities found out about our tunnel. We were lucky they didn't catch us in it or we might have been shot on the spot. But it's a tribute to the solidarity among prisoners that, although half the camp must have known about our tunnel, it took nearly two months before anyone informed on us. They must have just found out about it the day they acted because it was too far advanced for them to have gone about setting traps for us.

When we came back from the mines that sunny afternoon,

there was the usual roll call. Then sixteen of us were ordered out of ranks. As the others dispersed to the barracks, the sixteen of us were marched to the other side of the administrative building—where four police cars and ten secret policemen with handcuffs were awaiting us.

They also blindfolded us so we wouldn't see where they were taking us. But we knew where we were going. Secret police headquarters for the concentration-camp belt was the former Convent of Our Lady, which lent itself to easy conversion into cells, garages, torture chambers, and an interrogation center. Anyway, our blindfolds slipped off along the way, when our escorts couldn't wait until our destination to start beating us.

In what little time our captors afforded us to think, it occurred to me that, since ten innocents had been rounded up along with us six diggers, the informers hadn't known which were the culprits and which were the winkers. From this, I could stake out a position to take during questioning.

During the twenty-five-minute trip to Our Lady, the weather changed swiftly and drastically, as it often does in the mountains. A warm, bright afternoon became a damp, cold, cheerless one that gave way to an even clammier night. To make matters worse, I was still wearing a new pair of tight, dry rubber miner's boots that I'd been lucky to lay hands on and was still breaking in. It was exactly the wrong footwear, however, in which to be broken.

At Our Lady I found the limits to my endurance. My blindfold became a gag. My eyes were covered by a pair of goggles that obliterated all sight. And I was handcuffed to a grillwork in a drafty tunnel between garages. There I waited to be interrogated, but the secret police were in no hurry. Hours and hours and hours went by. I heard men moaning near me, but I never saw them and I saw no sense in struggling to communicate with them. An occasional car came into or went out of the garages. Sometimes the men passing through brushed me aside like a rag hanging in their path. I knew they were secret policemen, but I welcomed any touch of humanity, even *their* humanity. More hours and hours and hours went by. A guard came in to tighten my gag, my blindfold, and my manacles. There was no going to the toilet. But with no food in my stomach since breakfast back at New Eliáš, it was easy to hold everything in.

The night passed. The next day passed. The next night passed. There was no food and still no chance to go to the toilet. I no longer cared. I no longer knew I was hungry. I no longer knew whether I was dead or alive.

My feet—still encased in damp rubber miner's boots—swelled until they were numb. On the second morning, a voice said, "Take him down!" My hands, still cuffed, were unchained from the grillwork. On feet that seemed asleep forever, I was marched outdoors to take a leak. The guard had to propel me roughly by hand and, when he told me to pee, I couldn't. Then I was brought back and rechained, with my feet coming awake so painfully that, had I been offered amputation, I think I would have said yes.

Fortunately, my feet fell asleep again. But the pain traveled to my mind—and I began to hallucinate. I "saw" my friend Honza Lang, the spindly clerk from Old Eliáš, trying to pass a pair of leather civilian shoes through the grillwork to me. The holes in the grill were too small, but I kept reaching for the shoes anyway. Then my mind fought back with the realization that Honza was still in Old Eliáš and would in no way be implicated in our escape plot; therefore, I must be dreaming. I opened my eyes beneath my blinders—and this was the most terrible moment of all: *when I opened my eyes, I still saw Honza Lang!*

All my efforts to keep mind and body together were coming apart in the catacombs of Our Lady. As reality became unbearable, I abandoned myself to the unreality of Honza Lang and, with my eyes wide open, I urged him forward. "Honza," I said, "you have to bring them closer to me." He didn't answer. The only sound I heard was my own voice, just a chewing gurgle through the gag in my mouth, but perfectly audible to me.

Honza pushed the shoes right up to the grillwork. I could take them by the laces, but when I did, the laces were no longer attached to the shoes. They were now tied to Honza's penis and working it back and forth. But Honza wasn't lying on his bunk in Old Eliáš; he was on the grass of Vyšehrad Park with my girl friend Božena standing over him looking down as he ejaculated upward. What was Božena doing there? She wasn't with Honza; she was strolling with my parents—and now Honza was gone. Toward them came a lady who looked familiar. It was one of the neighbors who'd seen me proudly carrying a rifle down Libušina Street when the Prague Uprising started on May 5, 1945. She was saying, "Aren't you Mrs. Čapek's little boy, Karel?," except she was making no sound. I could feel myself doing all the talking through my gag . . .

So it went into the third afternoon, when I felt myself on a merry-go-round that whirled from church to church. Christ on all His crosses was trying to say something to me that I couldn't make out no matter how hard I worked my lips—until a voice, not the voice of God, but the voice of man, a secret policeman, said, "Take him down!"

While they brought me back to *their* world, I strained to hear Christ's words as He receded. In retrospect, I think that, had I succeeded, they would have been my last words as a sane or perhaps even a living man; that's how close I think I was to madness or extinction. My tongue, in fact, was still babbling while two guards shoved me around for most of an hour until my hands and feet came alive and I could walk, with assistance, up two flights of spiral stairs to the interrogation room. On the way up, we passed a barred window. There, I tried to stop and watch a beautiful mountain hailstorm that had just erupted. I was prodded past the view, but it was there that I started to rejoin the world.

There were four secret police interrogators, but only three questions: "Your name used to be Čapek, Karel?"

"My number is eighty-two ten, sir, but my name *is* Karel Čapek."

"Did you know about *it*?"

"About what, sir?"

"Don't you try to hide anything from us, Čapek! You knew about the tunnel, didn't you?"

From the way he phrased the question, I could fathom that none of my fellows, not even the innocent winkers, had betrayed me. So I said, "Well, yes, sir, I knew there *was* one, but I didn't know where."

They didn't even bother with the usual harangue about why didn't I report it. After a minute or two of silence, one of them said, "Take him downstairs."

My remaining three weeks at Our Lady were routine barbarity—with three cellmates (disciplinary cases from other camps) in space that must have cramped a novice in this nunnery. From midnight to dawn, the four of us could take turns sleeping,—one slept while the other three had to stand. From dawn to midnight, all four of us had to stand at attention without leaning against (or bumping into) the walls that were all around us. There were beatings and days without food, but this was all, as I've said, perfectly routine barbarity. It would bore Mr. Brabec and sound repetitious to you, so let's go on.

The important thing was that they never interrogated me there again. At other times, before and after the spring of 1951, all sixteen of us might have received more torture, new trials, and longer sentences. There might well have been death sentences for those of us who were identified (as we eventually, under questioning, would have been) as actual tunnel diggers. But, during our stay at Our Lady, we all benefited from a bureaucratic reorganization in Prague. Instead of being just an appendage of the Ministry of Justice and the Courts of Law, the slave-labor-camp system was being expanded and institutionalized into a division of the Ministry of Interior and the police. Such was the uranium boom that three freight trains a day headed out from Jáchymov laden with those heavy black stones of terror, and all our rich and pillaged land had to show for it was more than a hundred new concentration camps pitting her face and her soul, with no end to the agony in sight.

The guards' blue uniforms of Justice were giving way to the khakis of Interior—and, during this transition, nobody had time to get down to the bottom of our tunnel. At dawn on our twenty-third day at Our Lady, the sixteen plotters from New Eliáš were dispersed to sixteen different camps.

Along with some troublemakers from other camps, I was delivered to Camp Brotherhood, the reception center for newer prisoners. Rather than let us corrupt the newcomers, we were all assigned "a month of disciplinary Correction pending reassignment to the mines." Camp Brotherhood's brand of Correction meant seventeen men in a small room with a toilet but no bed. We could sit and sleep all we wanted on the wooden floor, though we spent a good part of each day massaging one another whenever a man awoke with a joint or a limb immobilized. Once, standing up, I had to laugh when I saw sixteen men writhing like a slide of live bacteria on the floor. After three weeks at Our Lady, though, Correction at Camp Brotherhood was a picnic.

It became more of a picnic when we poked a hole into the next room, which proved to be a storage bin for mountains of potatoes and carrots that had already been peeled. After 4:00 P.M., when the last of the day's cooking was underway elsewhere in camp, we would take turns crawling through and gorging ourselves on raw carrots and raw potatoes (which tasted no worse than the badly cooked ones prisoners were served). It was a marvelous cure for the malnutrition we'd endured at Our Lady. Sometimes I feared I wouldn't fit through the hole on the way back.

At the end of each feast, we replaced the paneling to conceal the hole. But, in our third week, the kitchen help discovered why their rations were being so depleted so rapidly. Our hole was sealed off while we were being handcuffed by twos. Then we were made to eat "one last meal" of carrots and potatoes that were certainly unclean and possibly sprayed chemically, too. All I know is that the next day we all had diarrhea.

Perhaps because, for once, the punishment fit the crime, we took it laughing. And what a comic sight it was! One man would wake up and rush to the john, dragging his sleeping, handcuffed partner along with him. (I often wondered if even Honza Lang could sleep through this. Nobody in our group did.) Then, as soon as one or both of these Siamese twins had emptied his bowels for the moment, another pair of men would be staggering toward the toilet bowl. Our faces were a sight to behold. One of us said we were "like happy drunks laughing at both ends."

The diarrhea lasted three days. Soon thereafter, all seventeen of us were dispersed in a busload of fifty prisoners being redistributed to other camps. It was a civilian passenger bus with a deceptive destination sign that read "Recreational Autobus." And, from the outside, we may have looked as if we were on a happy lark of an outing—if the beholder didn't catch a glimpse of four guards (on jump seats at both ends of the bus) with guns trained on the riders.

Still, it was indeed a beautiful ride. In Brotherhood and in Our Lady and even back in the mines, where we'd worked from dawn to dusk, there had been almost no chance to see a sky illuminated only by nature. On that day, we could see it— particularly after the bus, with a dozen of us still aboard, left the Jáchymov area and headed south for Slavkov. In the same mountain range, but an hour distant, Slavkov was the second of three main areas of uranium mining. (The third was Příbram.) Now, in the "free man's land" between Jáchymov and Slavkov, we could see the sky without electric lights. We could perceive the pure pastels of trees, flowers, mountains, houses, and even the eyes of people who looked up at us blankly as we passed them by. Nature looks best when she doesn't wear barbed wire and floodlights.

In Slavkov, I entered Camp Prokop and became a number again—not an isolated "disciplinary case." But, from the way Camp Prokop's guards attacked us with shouts and blows, I could tell upon arrival that the whole camp was a "disciplinary case."

There had been three mass escapes in a fortnight and I had the misfortune to arrive a week after the last of them. Prisoner-miners, doing what I'd been doing at Old Eliáš, had found an opening and—eight or ten at a time—blasted their way with dynamite to freedom. Other prisoners had concealed their exit opening and organized the next escape. Three groups had made it before the jailers found the opening and sealed it off.

Two of the twenty-six escapees had been shot and killed. Their corpses had been on display in the camp assembly area until the day before we arrived. Five others, already recaptured and beaten, were still chained to poles in heat and cold and rain, day and night, as a warning to us. A dozen others were still receiving "treatment" at Our Lady after having been caught. And seven were still at large.

In each escape group, there had been somebody I'd known from Bory or Pankrác or the mines. Surely I would have been included—if only I'd come to Camp Prokop a week or two sooner. Instead, I arrived just in time to partake of the reprisals.

I was still wearing the new miner's boots that had caused me so much pain at Our Lady. But now that I was becoming a miner again, they would serve me well. Or rather, they would have—if the camp commandant hadn't spotted them and made me trade them in for a "pair" of unmatching part-rubber, part-canvas work shoes.

This was just the beginning. Each day's commuting to and from work took us through a particularly horrid corridor. It connected Camp Prokop with Mine Number 8—a shaft so new it had not yet been christened. Mine Number 8 was only a half mile away, but the trip took an hour to an hour and a half each way, thanks to the bilious yellow-green clay soil underfoot. You could not slog through this slime by yourself, so they formed us up in fives and off we'd go, four of us hugging the man in front of us and all of us depending upon the man up front. We called ourselves "The Homosexual Express" or "The March of the Radioactive Fairies." No trip was completed without at least one of us five losing a boot in the slime. Much worse, though, were the falls. All five of us had to keep the same pace or one would stumble. If one stumbled, all five would fall. If all five fell, we would be trampled by the next five-man train. This machine would not, could not, stop.

One could almost feel sorry for the guards. The terrain they marched—paralleling the corridor—was not much better than ours, though good enough for them to stumble along one by one. But any sympathy for them was negated by their insecurity, which made them tend to point (and sometimes fire) their guns when we or they stumbled. Nothing is more dangerous than an armed man who feels off balance. There was no need to shoot, as the only escape from the corridor was to work or to the camp, where there was more mud and harassment: incessant roll calls that sometimes lasted two and a half or three hours. I still ache when I remember how, during colder weather at Prokop, I spent marathon roll calls knee-deep in mud to emerge with my trouser legs caked with brown ice and my feet oozing with slime. Naturally, every little scratch or open wound was a shortcut to death from gangrene or blood poisoning.

Cold, however, was the worst enemy. At the three to ten daily roll calls, stamping your feet was the only way to avert frostbite. Prisoners at Prokop also developed a special crouch to keep our bodies least exposed to cold—and I pass it on for whatever it may one day be worth to you: lift up your ill-fitting collarless coat, but not too high, please, or you'll expose your waist. Then lower your shoulders, neck, and head as far down as possible, until just your nose protrudes. Now breathe.

The longer we stood, the fewer the necks that were visible. When the roll call was at last over, grown men grew. And, when we embarked upon our "homosexual march" through the corridor, our first steps were the most agonizing as we had to crack the glaze of ice on our coats and trousers.

Back in camp, even with twenty or more men huddled in one big room, the water in our one pail would be frozen and every warm little fart was precious to those within range; our diet was not such as to inspire giant farts. For warmth while sleeping, some miners stole the paper linings of empty cement bags and inserted them between their blankets, but then they dared not turn over much for fear the noise would waken the rest of us, who were sleeping lightly and shivering heavily. One blessed, if particularly cold, week in hell, a stray pussycat took a liking to me—so intensely that she slept with me for seven nights. On each of those nights, I would pick out a different small part of my body for her to keep warm.

My affair with that pussycat was the envy of other prisoners —and then she disappeared! Either she was unfaithful to me or, more likely, one of my jealous rivals ate her. This was definitely the fate of the Camp Prokop commandant's dog, who wound up in our stomachs as 1951's Christmas dinner. Even the dog lovers among us, who called it "un-Christian" and "semicannibalistic" at first, joined the feast—"for purely patriotic reasons," they said.

At work, there were quotas—but, for a while, I was lucky. I was assigned the job of hose repairman, which meant being on call when there was trouble, but otherwise not working very hard and not having any quota to fill. This left me free to roam within the mine—seeking out other prisoners and looking around, always looking around (ostensibly for a hose that needed maintenance, but also for another opening to freedom). My job also gave me a chance to nap—and, while Sunday was no day of rest in the mines, I always grew particularly lazy on the Lord's Day. (The only difference between Sunday and any other day was that, on Sundays, the shifts changed hours. The morning shift became the afternoon shift; the afternoon shift the night shift; the night shift the morning shift. Thus, Sunday meant that you might have to work double-time or you might get a little extra time off—and at least it kept the civilian rhythm of being, for better or worse, a day that was different from all other days.)

It was on a Sunday that a civilian shift boss came upon me sleeping atop some scaffolding deep inside the mine. He reported me to the camp commandant and, after a week in Correction, I found myself doing quota work: back-breaking labor in the mines to meet a minimum that was impossible to fulfill. When you failed, as almost all of us did, you went on half rations (soup, dumplings, noodles, and bread were the menu every single day at Prokop) with no mail privileges, no visitors, and eligibility for extra work details at night, such as smoothing out white sand to enable the guards to discern next day whether anybody had tried to escape into darkness.

I never managed to achieve more than 60 percent of my quota—and hardly anybody I knew accomplished that much. Those who did fulfill their quotas either had opportunities to cheat —the way we had at Bory with weighing our pound and a half of feathers—or else they had connections. I had neither.

Late 1951 was when the Russians stepped up their demand for uranium. Eventually, this would require still more manpower and mean still more slaves and "conspiracies" to be unmasked. But the immediate effect was felt by the slave miners they already had. Double shifts were "unofficially" decreed for us.

Here is how an "unofficial" double shift worked. Toward the end of an exhausting eight hours underground, we would gather down below at the mine elevators. The guards would load us, starting from the bottom level. Up at the top, the two hundred of us on a shift would be given "a few minutes to clean yourself up for the corridor." Ridiculous as that sounded —the corridor was an hour-long mud bath in itself!—we would stamp great clumps of mud and dust storms of dirt off ourselves before lining up at a small trickle of water for further cleaning and a little washing of the rubber on our boots.

Then we were commanded to reassemble for a roll call and to "form up in fives for the corridor." Having hurried up, we now had to wait. As soon as winter weather set in around October, one could hear the distinctive sound of two hundred freezing men stamping their feet with their rubber coats swishing as they stamped.

Now there was one last little "unofficial" formality. Having made us fully ready for the trip back to camp, the guards had to obtain a list from the "mine management." (Czech civilians handed the paper to the guards, but we all thought of the civilians as messengers and the Russians as management.) The list showed who would actually make the trip back to camp.

It was never more than a dozen names long—a handful or two of informers and miracle workers who'd somehow fulfilled their quotas. For the remaining 190 or more of us, it was back into the mine for eight more hours.

This "unofficial" pretense of a last-minute switch—with all the false hope it inspired—went on for seven days a week and lasted at least six months at Prokop. My name was never once on that little list, but every day I played the charade as intently as ever—hoping, always hoping, that something better might happen.

When it didn't, we would climb down a ladder into the mines. The shift that had followed us (and would be playing the same "unofficial" charade in eight hours) was using the elevator. The carbide in our lamps had run out and neither they nor we would be replenished. (Camp Prokop was, however, scrupulous about feeding us two meals—the one we were due plus the one we'd missed—both in one serving when we returned after sixteen hours in the mines plus two or three in the corridor.) Exhausted and depressed, we would make our wobbly way 180 or two hundred yards down a dangerous ladder by dim light and join the fresher faces on the next shift.

The same ritual was enacted with the shift that preceded mine. Looking at those men coming down the ladder, I had to smile at the sight of them descending into hell looking like shadows of their former selves. Just being in the mine for an hour would make a man filthy. Eight hours' work there was never eradicated by "a few minutes cleaning yourselves up for the corridor." Yet the sight was bittersweetly comical. I had to smile, but I couldn't laugh—for I knew, without any looking glass on hand, that these wretchedly funny men were mirror images of myself.

And I thought to myself: Whatever this is, it will have a terrible end. This is the wrong world.

Part 4

The Jaundice Brigade

Sixteen hours of work plus two or three in the corridor plus half an hour for meals left a maximum of four hours' sleep on a good day. And yet, most of us devoted at least a little of those four hours of "free time" at Camp Prokop to the amenities of decent living. A man might spend an hour brushing, cleaning, and picking nits out of himself like a finicky kitten. Of course, looking after yourself was more than a luxury in the conditions that prevailed at Prokop. It meant life just as certainly as letting yourself go meant sure disease or frostbite.

Cleanliness has long been a particular mania among us Czechs. Both before and since Communism, I've known people who've scrimped and saved and scavenged and even stolen from the State to build a house or a country home for themselves and their families. If, as often happens, the children have married or gone off by the time the house is ready, their elders—having the house to themselves at long last!—will keep it shipshape by living in the garage and coming into their otherwise unoccupied house only to clean it or entertain in it.

It is not surprising, then, that there were those among us in prison who carried cleanliness too far. I would see them shining their boots and polishing up their rubber coats in the hallways far into the night. This was dangerous not only because they lost too much sleep to work safely in the mine and because a shiny face or costume amidst the drab ranks of prisoners invariably made guards want to wipe off or wipe out that shine.

What worried me about our Mr. Cleans was that their miner's boots and coats were radioactive, which was why those particular items had to stay out in our barracks hallways.

My own fastidiousness was minimal, but enough. The luxury that mattered most to me was a porcelain bowl I acquired in Prokop. Even though it had slightly smaller capacity than the mess kits we ate out of, I liked dining off porcelain. It became my security blanket. Several times, guards tried to confiscate it because it was "not regulation" and these were almost the only occasions when I argued or even begged for something in the camps. Once, it was taken away—and that same night a prisoner who worked in Supply stole it back for me, without my even hinting, "because I knew Čapek couldn't go on living without it." I managed to hang onto it for four of my prison years before trading it for a book in English.

With nothing but bad air—and not enough of it at that—circulating through Mine Number 8 and with us working double shifts, everyone had at least a bad headache when he came out of the earth. Sickness, death, and accident rates went up—and the Russians must have complained, for after half a year of double hard labor, we finally went back to single shifts in early 1952.

New prisoners were starting to pour through the Pankrác-Bory-Brotherhood pipeline. And so were new civilian workers, responding to quintuple wages and other inducements to enter the uranium mines. But out of all this bad air came a whiff of human, family contact for me.

It started when a wrinkle-faced middle-aged civilian—each wrinkle etched by the underground chalk dust that can become a permanent face powder—came down among my group of prisoners to check our equipment. But he seemed to be searching for something else, for he looked more at our faces than at our drills and, every now and then, he'd ask a prisoner for "your name, son?" We all grew wary and I didn't like the first chill that passed through me when my drill was the first he singled out: "You shouldn't be using this. Why didn't you report the defect?"

"What defect?" I said.

"I'll show you," he said, taking me into the darkness of a deserted mine tunnel. There, to my amazement, he broke a crown himself while saying, at the top of his voice, "That crown is broken. I don't know how you could have worked this long with such a thing." That was for outside consumption, for then he whispered to me, "You're Čapek, right?" When I didn't deny it, he went on: "Soon as I saw you, I knew you. You're your father's son."

"We're all guilty of that sin," I admitted, still smelling a trap.

He chuckled and said, "I mean there's a family resemblance. Your dad sent me to you." Then, raising his voice again, he said, "I can patch it up now so you can finish your shift with it, but you must bring it in to me when you come back on top. That's an order!" Falling into the spirit of the occasion, I shouted, *"Yes, sir!"* and then listened eagerly as he told me which shack to head for.

Five hours later, I found the place—and walked in on a waiting pot of hot tea and some rolls and butter. The smell of butter was so rich and unfamiliar to me after three years in prison that I was a bit nauseated, but I took it anyway. My father's friend watched me with satisfaction. When I had consumed all the rolls and butter in sight, he brought out two cigarettes from a pack brand-named Partisans. Truly, I had ascended to at least the left wing of heaven!

My benefactor's name was Josef Nickel. He'd worked in the mines all his life, but elsewhere. When Mine Number 8 had opened, experienced talent was needed for the new shaft and Joe Nickel had signed on, at a premium, as a locksmith and repairman. And he'd remembered my dad, who'd been haunting the bus stations on weekends accosting passengers to and from the Slavkov-Jáchymov area in case they could make any contact with his son. It was a risky business, for the police watched the terminals, too, but all it had cost my father was a few scares and fifteen thousand crowns bilked by his previous contact. My name wasn't hard to remember and, when Joe Nickel found it on a roster in Mine Number 8, he looked around the bus station on his next weekend in Prague and spotted my father, as he thought he would. Yes, I was the same

Karel Čapek—and, in Josef Nickel, my father had found the missing link. Eureka!

My father, he told me, was "pretty well—and he'll be a lot better when he hears about today." My mother had gone to work in a student cafeteria—cooking for many sons when she couldn't cook for her own, but this was a good sign of activity as well as economic support for my father. I gave Joe Nickel some messages to take back home for me and then he chased me away to catch up with my shift's roll call.

I went back to see Nickel once or twice a week about "my problems with my drill." Each time, the hospitality was the same: rolls and butter and steaming tea. Sometimes, Joe Nickel drank some Cognac from a bottle while he watched me eat and sip. He himself was a drinker—not one with a drinking problem, perhaps, but enough of a drinker for me to mention it. He was certainly a cautious drinker, for he was also a cautious person. This was why he never offered me a drink of his Cognac, not even in my tea, for fear that *my* breath might betray *his* rule-breaking. He never let me take any civilian food back to camp with me. "Eat the evidence here or not at all," he told me in his shack. Joe Nickel happened to be a cautious drinker, a cautious person, and a lifelong Communist, but, above all, he was humane. And I rejoiced that, even in the hell that the Czechoslovak Socialist Republic had become above and below its plundered earth, good men still lived.

I was parted from Josef Nickel in the late autumn of 1952, when it was already snowing. One hundred twenty of us were moved from the Slavkov area back into the Jáchymov concentration-camp complex. This time, I landed in Camp Equality (Rovnost). All other things being equal, but some more equal than others, Camp Equality had an even worse reputation than Camp Prokop. Bad as Prokop had been, its commandant had not been the world's worst. That distinction belonged to Camp Equality, whose notorious commandant was known far and wide in the Czechoslovak penal system as "Tom Thumb."

His real name was Dvořák, certainly as fine a Czech name as one can be born with (though even commoner than Čapek), but—like many Communist penologists who wanted to cover their tracks from the very beginning—he had taken a pseudonym for professional purposes. His was Paleček, which means "Little Thumb." All the Dvořáks, from composer Antonín to moving-man Zdeněk, should rejoice in one resounding hymn that Tom Thumb forsook their name!

Prison commandant Tom Thumb looked like a thumb. He was a squat little pink-and-blond mountaineer with a scar on his temple. He had sparkling, very even teeth, which always showed because he wore a fixed smile on his face. No matter what he was saying, even if pronouncing your doom, he never stopped smiling. And, like Mr. Brabec at Bory, he never raised his voice.

Tom Thumb had melancholic green eyes that roamed his slave empire without his even moving his head. But those eyes never seemed to find what they were looking for.

No prisoner ever entered the portals of Camp Equality without meeting Tom Thumb in person. The smallest transport was excuse enough for the commandant to strut his stuff before a captive audience of men under his thumb. And, because he was a small man, Tom Thumb needed to single the two biggest and healthiest-looking prisoners out of any batch of new arrivals and tell them, "You won't look so fat after a month of Equality, if you live that long." Then he'd turn to the rest of the group and say, "Do you know that Camp Equality is the last stop for every one of you? Nobody goes anywhere else from here." Such grim promises were nothing new, but it was the matter-of-fact way he spoke them that made Tom Thumb so terrifying.

There were no punishment barracks or Correction in Camp Equality. Tom Thumb was punishment enough. He needed no facilities to make men squirm. A man who displeased him would have to stand outside—in any kind of weather—for days on end, "at the pleasure of the commandant," until he dropped. Then Tom Thumb would have his victim propped up again and again—until the commandant was satisfied or, as happened more than once, the man died.

Tom Thumb could decree living deaths, too. In lieu of Correction, he had "garden spots"—untilled and untillable prison soil only a few yards square. A prisoner who displeased Tom Thumb was "awarded" such a plot, plus a wooden stick to till it with, and instructed, "Get rid of all the big stones on it." When this task was completed, Tom Thumb would say, "Now get rid of all the little stones." This done, the next command was: "Now bring back all the big stones." And then: "Now put back all the little stones." Next, he would start all over again: "So now suppose you get rid of all the big stones."

Trivial and childish though this was, it could break a man after a long, airless day in the mines.

Tom Thumb knew far worse tortures. Men he considered shirkers were placed under surveillance while working *in the mines!* A bored guard stood alongside (getting in the way) while they worked. Robbed of the last vestige of privacy, the last illusion of freedom, the last tiny escape into one's self, quite a few men cracked under this schoolboy hazing. Even if they didn't, they became the butt of the guards' wrath at this absurd assignment.

Friendships formed in adversity are often the ones that last into better times and through other times, too. In Camp Equality, for once, I found myself among prisoners who were my age or younger—particularly in the mines, where I worked with other youthful prisoners as "wagon men": loading, unloading, and redistributing the underground freight cars that took uranium or just obstructive debris out of the ground. My three best friends there were all in prison for the same offense —Boy Scouting, which had been abolished as "individualism":

. . . Leopold, a year older than I, had been a philosophy graduate studying law until he'd disclosed his past as a Boy Scout. Now he had a future of ten years in prison. We called him "Polda," which could be short for Leopold, but was also slang for "police"—a derogatory word like "copper."

. . . "Snapshot" Snímek, a Scoutmaster from Ostrava, had won his nickname because prison life had made him so skinny that he looked like a two-dimensional photo of his former self.

. . . Edo "Eddie" Pelcl, a young Slovak Boy Scout who'd

wanted to study for the priesthood, was the son of an Austrian father and a Bohemian mother who'd been living illegally in Bratislava, the Slovak capital, because of the postwar famine in Austria. That sentence of biography alone had been enough to earn Eddie a life sentence in prison by the time he was eighteen. All of us in Camp Equality seemed to feel worse about this than Eddie himself. Elders like myself—I was twenty-two—shook our heads with pity at this bushy-haired blond lad spending his formative years in mines, prisons, and concentration camps. He was just barely old enough to shave, but old enough to slave.

This youth-still-becoming-a-man was too busy to care. For he was also an embryonic intellectual and no prison, no commandant, not even Tom Thumb, could suppress or confine Eddie's mental growth. He spoke perfect German and was determined to learn English. What he was doing when I first met him in Camp Equality was reading the two Communist publications in English that one could sometimes lay hands on in prison (though even these were unauthorized to us): The *Daily Worker* and the Cominform's* *For Peace and People's Democracy*. Eddie would try to puzzle them out through the similarities between the German he knew and the English he guessed. But he was having terrible trouble with the recurrent phrase "unbridled aggression." Did I think it meant rape or just unmarried intimacies?

I wasn't much specific help at that point, but I was able to tell him, "You're going about it all wrong, Eddie. Even if you're learning something that way, that's no kind of English to be learning. Who speaks Communist English? Look what they've done to the Czech language with crooked words like 'right-

---

* Communist Information Bureau, an organization formed by the Communist parties of nine countries—Russia, Czechoslovakia, Bulgaria, France, Italy, Hungary, Poland, Rumania, and Yugoslavia—in 1947 "to facilitate the exchange of experience." In 1948, the Yugoslav Communist party was expelled from the Cominform because of Marsal Tito's schism with Stalin. In 1956, as a gesture of reconciliation with Tito, the Cominform was dissolved.

wing deviationist' and 'neofascist revanchist'! And I'll bet you that, outside the jails and the courts and the radio, nobody in Czechoslovakia speaks that way."

"But how else can we learn English?" Eddie asked, responding to me instinctively as a fellow intellectual and therefore turning to me for help.

There was an old man in another barracks whose only crime was that, after ten years as a refugee from fascism in the steelworks of Gary, Indiana, he had returned to his native Slovakia to live on his U.S. pension. He was dying on his feet in the mines, but through the three years he'd already spent in the camps, he had carefully hidden and protected a ragged copy of O. Henry's collected works. With some persuasion—plus an offer to shoulder some of the punishment duties that Tom Thumb was meting out to him as a "shirker"—he agreed to lend Eddie, Polda, Snapshot, and me four loose pages at a time.

Concealing them in our rubber boots and raincoats, we'd study them, discuss them, memorize them, exchange them, analyze them—and then one of us would take them back to the old man with our unsolved riddles: "What does O. Henry mean when he says 'You're the goods'? And is there some other reason why that particular story is called 'From Each According to His Ability'?" "When O. Henry speaks, in his 'Ethics of Pig,' of being as busy as a one-armed paper hanger, is there perhaps some allusion to Hitler?" "Is it Alexander Pope or O. Henry who said that fools rush in where angels fear to tread?"

Our questions were far out of the old man's league, though he tried to cope with them. (His answer to the last question, for instance, was: "Must be O. Henry because it's right here before me* while I never seen no Pope sayin' it.") When his knowledge was exhausted, he would give our emissary four new pages for us to ponder.

We took turns as emissary not only because we thus shared the risk of being caught traveling from barracks to barracks

---

* "A kind of mixture of fools and angels—they rush in and fear to tread at the same time."—O. Henry, "The Moment of Victory."

after curfew, but also in the hope that, as happened every now and then, the old man would be spry enough to let the emissary read those pages aloud to him while he corrected accents and pronunciations. ("Tchi-car-go! Tchi-car-go!" he'd say, working on my incurably Czech rendition of the letters C-H-I-C-A-G-O, which came out like "Heat-sahgo.") Later, in the privacy of the mines, his four disciples spoke only English to each other. And what an English it was! Perhaps the spectacle of four Czech slaves babbling about Bagdad-on-the-Subway and Cabbages and Kings deep in the bowels of the uranium mines might strike a witness as grotesque or comical, but believe me that it was the only hope of a better life we knew!

The ironies and "O. Henry twists" didn't seem at all contrived to a Czech. O. Henry's rueful, bittersweet world was a real one to us—just as Franz Kafka wasn't a fiction writer to us, but a skilled draftsman who did an excellent job of blueprinting labyrinths that already existed in his native Prague, which had been Balkanized long before Communism. Many a day was spent underground at Camp Equality correlating Kafka's "Investigations of a Dog" with O. Henry's "Memoirs of a Yellow Dog." And, if O. Henry was no stranger to us, I don't think we would have been strangers to him, either. He spent a mere three years in jail (for the nonpolitical crime of embezzlement), but clearly he must have met some early-day Tom Thumb to be able to write (in his "Transformation of Martin Burney") such curse as:

> May his liver turn to water, and the bones of him crack in the cold of his heart. May dog fennel grow upon his ancestors' graves, and the grandsons of his children be born without eyes. May whiskey turn to clabber in his mouth, and every time he sneezes may he blister the soles of his feet. And the smoke of his pipe—may it make his eyes water, and the drops fall on the grass that his cows eat and poison the butter that he spreads on his bread.

It was out of love of your language that, several labor camps later, in Příbram, I finally parted with my precious porcelain bowl—in exchange for a copy of Jack London in English. I had the same book, *The Sea-Wolf*, in Czech. Thanks to the socialist tracts that Jack London alone deemed as his most important works, he was one of the few American authors sanctioned for translation into our tongue in those days. To have the same book available before me in Czech *and* English was indeed a dream come true! But it was still the America of O. Henry that I dreamed of—and it is not such a bad or unreal vision for a refugee to carry in his knapsack.

At Camp Equality, toward Christmas of 1952, Santa Claus brought me a mixed bag of luck. The good news was my transfer to the same barracks as the retired Gary steelworker whose bible was O. Henry. The bad news was that he and I were the only political prisoners in there. Our thirty-eight mates were all forgotten old-timers from the postwar, pre-Communist interim: collaborators, informers, and a handful of German soldiers and SS men. The barracks leader, in fact, was a husky, redheaded SS man from the Sudetenland. He still spoke no Czech and gave out all his orders in German.

Except for him, they were all twisted, gnarled, broken, half-crazy men. Even Tom Thumb had given up on most of them as misfits. They'd been in jail too long. The world outside—the world that their fellow prisoners brought in with them—was too much to be comprehended by such men. They didn't try. They just obeyed and kept to themselves. With them, it was every man for himself. They didn't even talk to each other, and they hoarded whatever they had. Only later did I learn that what I was witnessing in this barracks was not so remote as I thought it was. Outside the jails—in the maximum-security concentration camp that was the Czechoslovak Socialist Republic in the 1950s—the same pattern of human behavior was asserting itself.

The old man from Greater Chicago and I had to be very careful in our dealings. The man in between our two bunks was a Czech who'd been convicted of informing to the Nazis. After a few years, it had become impossible to believe that this silent man—who spoke only in monosyllables, if at all, when spoken to—could have transmitted *any* information. But my

O. Henry tutor warned me to be wary of him, so I was. Besides, he did seem to be keeping an eye on me.

Toward dawn one December morning, I found out why. I was awakened by a feeling that something was crawling down my belly. Without opening my eyes, I realized it was a human hand heading toward my crotch. Making a fist and a quick calculation of where the face belonging to such a hand would logically be, I lashed out hard and felt a nose squash under my fist. The hand withdrew and the invasion of my privacy had been repelled, so I opened my eyes and saw that my neighbor, the informer, had a bloody nose.

He had it all that day, but he didn't say a word about it. And it's indicative of how introverted that barracks was that nobody there asked him what was the matter. But, toward evening, I said to him, "Listen, I don't want you sleeping next to me."

He said nothing, but simply changed beds with my English tutor. Thus did my first and only overt homosexual experience in prison better my lot—and I find *that* an irony worthy of O. Henry. I know, too, that what I resented even more than the invasion of my privacy by a groping hand was the attempt *by another prisoner* to impose another way of life *upon another prisoner!*

So few choices are left to a man in prison that certainly, under such circumstances of deprivation, his sex life and sexual nature deserve to be self-determined unless they do harm to others. Remarkably few of us tampered with our selves in prison. Whenever we could, we let nature take her course with us—which is to say that there were many wet dreams; some masturbation, but not so much as one might expect; and hardly any homosexuality that wasn't already there or hinted at *before prison.*

I have heard that the inevitability of homosexuality in prisons is fashionable cocktail chatter among radical chic circles in America. Well, maybe Czechoslovak jails just aren't run right, but allow me to contribute one case history to all the research on this subject. In prison, I knew a handsome, blond young man named Zdeněk, whose good looks and bulging biceps

made him a natural prey for the homosexuals. But he stayed
clean and, after prison, married and matured into one of the
better family men I know. He was, I learned later, an identical
twin. His brother, who prospered on the outside and in Communist party functions—despite the shame of having a twin in
prison—owned a fine apartment and rose, in the profiteering
hierarchy of "crown millionaires" who comprised the Prague
"jet set" of the early 1960s, to become our town's leading fag-
got. He could even wangle one of socialized medicine's first
sex-change operations. He is now a woman, but, alas, frigid.

Christmas was coming—and even Tom Thumb had a little
of the spirit in him. We would be given the holiday off. We
would partake of the holiday fish—carp. (Just heads and entrails discarded from other Christmas feasts, to be sure. But
even the tail end of Christmas is better than nothing.) To keep
our barracks warm all Christmas Day, we were allowed to
carry back any wood we found in the corridor during the week
before.

Around that time, too, scrip money was introduced to en-
courage us to spend our slave wages—the few crowns a week
that the state was obliged to pay even its prisoners, after making whopping deductions for room and board at Tom Thumb's
spa. A one-room commissary was opened in our camp, where we
could buy tea, sugar, cigarettes, even marmalade—and, as in
the civilian market, not much else. On Christmas Eve, 1952,
just like my civilian counterparts in Prague, I found myself
with a wad of funny money in a store whose shelves were bare.
"Well, what *do* you have?" I asked the prisoner who ran the
commissary.

"Only this," he said, showing me a five-gallon glass jar of
plum compote in heavy syrup.

"All that would be too rich for my stomach," I said, starting
to wish him a Merry Christmas and leave. But then I said,
"Would it be too rich for my pocketbook?" The clerk named a
price in scrip, and it was just a crown less than what I had to
my name.

The clerk looked at me and I looked at him. The prospect of
going back empty-handed to that sullen barracks, where no-

body would even share a laugh with the other, was so depressing that I finally said, "Look, are you here tomorrow?" When the clerk said, "Yes, where else is there to go?" I agreed to pay now and pick up later—on Christmas Day, just before the noonday feast of carp heads and entrails.

The next morning's Christmas "festivities" in our barracks were just as solitary and gloomy as I'd anticipated. Toward noon, I came sauntering in with my big glass jar of plums. The others looked up, watched where I put it, and went back to themselves. The barracks were warm. The carp was delivered, as promised, and savored and eaten in silence. Then I brought my jar of plums to the table in the center of the room and, with all eyes upon me again, I announced, "These are for all of us!"

Only one man reacted—the old steelworker from Indiana, who rose slowly and tottered toward the plums. Warily, the others watched me and him and the plums.

The old man tried them, licked his lips, and said, "Good!"

The redheaded SS man ventured next, pounding his stomach either with enthusiasm or else to show that it could survive anything. But he liked what he tasted—and when he said *"Sehr gut!"* the other three dozen men in that room took it as an order and slowly lined up for their share. My former neighbor, the informer, looked at me hesitantly, but when I gave him a grandiose, be-my-guest bow, he helped himself.

When the plums were gone, something magical happened. A few of the men looked around timidly, whispered to the SS man, and then, almost furtively, tiptoed to their hiding places and brought out cakes and dumplings and other treasures they'd hoarded and hidden. They distributed them, sometimes crumb by crumb, among the forty of us. Sharing the wealth had at last come to a Communist concentration camp!

And then another miracle happened! These twisted, turned-inward men found their tongues and discovered they could talk —to each other, to me! They talked about the nicer parts of their lives: their children, their homes, their memories. The red-haired SS man suddenly found he could speak the Czech that had been in the air around him for most of his life. In the

tongue that he'd despised and ignored and perhaps even persecuted, he now spoke—brokenly, but understandably—about
his folks and their farm and his birthplace, all now in what
had become East Germany. He worried aloud whether his
homeland would take him back or would he be deported to
West Germany? "That should only happen to me!" I said—and
there was a funny sound in the room, like spitting hailstones.
It was laughter from throats that hadn't laughed in years. And
the laughter, though harsh and grating, was gentle, too. "But
you see," the SS man explained, with a serious smile on his
face, "I have nobody there in the West."

The homosexual informer showed pictures of his wife and
daughter. "One divorced me. The other denounced me," he
said—speaking his two longest sentences of the year and then
eclipsing them with: "But I have nothing against women." And
I stopped thinking of him as a pervert or an informer—just as a
sad, lonely man.

The next day and the next day and for as long as I was
among them, these people went on talking to each other. Every
now and then, they would thank me for "that funny plum
Christmas"—which was fine with me, though I prefer to think
back to it as that real O. Henry Christmas in Camp Equality.

That winter, the snow was so thick that we had to crawl on
it through the corridor; it could not be walked through. For
me, at least, this was good exercise—even though one had to
be careful not to snag oneself on the barbed wire just above.
But Camp Equality, as 1952 became 1953, was a winter wonderland—and I don't think I have set eyes on anything more
fine and delicate than the lacy webs formed by snow on
barbed wire.

Camp Equality was rich not only with beauty, but with
uranium, and, that winter, we were loading wagons in an
especially rich lode. All of us, without feeling the radioactivity
getting to us, began to move slowly, economically, as Old Sochor had in Eliáš. One was aware of every single move one
made—even when lifting a finger. After a while, one had to

plan the finger-lift before doing it. We were all on the verge of exhaustion.

By April, my urine was a reddish-brown—but that was not yet an excuse for going on sick call. Camp Equality had an infirmary, but it was there mostly to provide first aid for mine injuries. In May, during the week-long national celebration between May Day and the anniversary of "1945's Soviet Liberation," I felt bad enough to drag myself over to the infirmary. Over the door was an ornate hand-carved plaque of an approved slogan: THE END OF ALL WORK IS THE MAN. But somebody had crossed out the fourth, fifth, and sixth words. I myself felt like dying, so I knew I had come to the right place.

The doctor's helper—a prisoner—took one look at me and said, "Jaundice!" The doctor—a prisoner, too—made a few tests and confirmed his assistant's diagnosis. Jaundice was common among civilian workers, but I was Camp Equality's first 1953 case among prisoners, who took better care of themselves despite their difficulties. "I'm afraid," said the doctor, "you may be the first case of virus jaundice. We can't keep you here infecting the camp, so you'll have to go to a hospital in Carlsbad."

It was easy to feign sorrow by hanging my head, for it was mighty low already and I couldn't lift it. The prospect of a cure in the world-renowned spa of Carlsbad (Karlovy Vary in Czech, meaning the Royal Hot Baths of Charles IV), barely a dozen miles away from Tom Thumb's resort, had to agree with me. And so let it be recorded that to Carlsbad—where your President Franklin D. Roosevelt came as a paralytic and where Goethe and Mozart came by carriage and where the shah of Iran and the maharani of Hyderabad came by mini-jet —Karel Čapek came in a prison ambulance equipped with built-in manacles for his hands and feet. It was lying on my back, coming down the mountain to this gem of a city that has been described as "a diamond set in an emerald," that I passed through the worst phase of my jaundice: vomiting without being able to turn over or even cover my mouth. I thought I might die like an infant choking in my own puke.

Thus began the best month of my life—not just prison life, but *this* life, too, for one is really a continuation of the other. I was carried into the infectious-disease wing, cleaned up, examined, diagnosed (jaundice plus dysentery), bathed in my first nonradioactive water since I'd left Bory almost three years earlier, medicated, sedated, and delivered to a plain chalky-cream-colored hospital room that looked like the royal suite to me, even though a Camp Equality guard who'd been detached from the camp to keep an eye on me promptly chained and padlocked both my legs to the bed.

For two days, I slept—and then, since I had only a mild case, I awoke feeling much better, almost energetic, and quite hungry. But the doctors ordered me to "lie still and do nothing" —which, to me, meant looking around and plotting an escape. I was still too weak, though, to make a break for it. While thinking it over, I feasted my eyes and my mind on what people who weren't prisoners or jailers looked like. (Civilian workers in the mines were a little of both and looked like a bit of each.) And the nurses! Though there had been an occasional Shushu or a female clerk in the mines, the nurses were the first women I'd seen above the earth and without barbed-wire surroundings.

Young and old, the nurses handled me with special care and tenderness. One of them even admitted that they all considered my manacles a disease that, in lieu of amputation, I should be made to forget I had. They had feared me at first. A caged animal had been let out on a leash and entrusted to their custody. But then they had seen me as a man—and a sick man at that— and their eyes and hands treated me like a human being.

I wanted to meet my fellow patients, male and female, to see what the "infectiously diseased" of a sick society were like. This was not hard, for, after one or two perfunctory security checks a day, my guard would devote himself to exploring the fleshpots of the nursing stations and downtown Carlsbad. As soon as I was able to sit up and eat, other patients would stand in the doorway and—if I looked responsive, which I always was—strike up a conversation. The timidity and deference with which they stood in the doorway carried me through a few of the bad years ahead. For theirs was not the timidity of people flirting with danger from a wild beast they'd been warned against. No, their obvious respect for a State criminal verged upon treasonable disrespect for the State. *They knew what was happening!* Some of them had been compelled to sign petitions demanding the execution of a great woman, Dr. Milada Horaková, the leader of our National Socialist party, who had survived German imprisonment and concentration camps only to die on Czechoslovak gallows*—and *to me* they came either to repent or explain. *They knew!* Seeing their neighbors accused of terrible crimes (sometimes even after trumped-up denunciations by *them*) and taken away indefinitely or forever, they took over their apartments and tried to forget the means to that end, but *they knew* their neighbors, so *they knew* the accusations weren't so.

Now, as they stood in the doorway, justifying or exonerating their own conduct and trying to transmit the shock of terror *they* had lived through, I rejoiced in their awareness. Even if the State still was bent on destroying us prisoners in the name of the People, I now knew that the people weren't (though they would if they had to). In this, the State hadn't succeeded —and my month in Carlsbad heartened me with the hope that, when and if I ever got out, there might be some decency left to come home to.

In that hospital, I felt like the conscience or confessor of the whole Czechoslovak nation. It sometimes seemed as if those "free men" from the outside wanted news of the "real world" —the camps—from me, the prisoner. They *all* wanted to talk to me—from the medical chief of the whole clinic down to the lowliest whore in Carlsbad, who happened to be there, too, for venereal disease treatment.

There was a shortage of glucose and never enough food to go around, but there was always enough for me—and nobody begrudged it. The medical chief prescribed double rations for

---

* The 1950 trial and execution of Dr. Horaková for high treason was as traumatic to Czechs and Slovaks as a similar fate's befalling Eleanor Roosevelt might have been to Americans around that time.

me. But, even as I devoured my seconds, the other patients
were trying to bring me their firsts. If I hinted that I could use
reading matter, I was given (not lent) family Bibles, expensive
editions, and even banned books. (Though I had difficulty
acquiring anything in English there, I knew it was not for lack
of trying—by them and by the relatives to whom they gave
shopping orders during visiting hours.) Even the whore—a
bony young bag of a woman—wanted to donate her services
("Maybe if I give you the clap, you can prolong your stay
here"), but I said I'd rather wait for a more felicitous occasion.
I declined for a number of reasons—starting with the knowledge that a prisoner who managed to contract V.D. would
stand out like a sore thumb to Commandant Tom Thumb. And
so would the guard who'd let this happen.

I contemplated escaping, but I was almost too happy in that
hospital to ever think of leaving. I felt like part of the human
race again. Besides, I was coming to the realization that I didn't
want to escape. The risks of death or recapture were too high,
and, as an only son, my "crimes" had brought down too much
grief upon my parents' heads already; to render them childless
would be the worst crime of all. In the camps, when one
couldn't take another step or another minute of guff, a prison
saying went: "Give me a month's vacation and I could go on
this way forever." Well, I'd been granted the first half of this
truism; now I was willing to take the rest on faith.

In my room, there was an oxygen tent—and I inhaled from
that bomb until I felt dizzy. The good air made me feel so fit,
so euphoric that I started exercising. Fortunately for my status
as a patient, I still had yellow skin, yellowish eyes, and a pain
under my lower right ribs. I might have stayed much longer
than a month if, in the surgical wing of the same hospital, the
impossible hadn't happened: a prisoner, rushed there for an
emergency appendectomy, had escaped from surgery without
any clothes. (He was never found!) This led to a crackdown
on the remaining prisoner-patients. Any who could move were
moved. In the middle of one night, without any chance to say
good-bye, I was loaded into a State carriage (another "Recrea-

tional Autobus" this time) that delivered me from the royal city of Carlsbad to morning roll call at Camp Equality.

Jaundice was raging through the place. My fellow prisoners welcomed me back and congratulated me on being the first to infect the camp. My virus had cost the State a fortune in uranium. And I was to be congratulated, too, as the early bird who'd caught the bug—and the only excursion to Carlsbad. The outbreak of virus jaundice that followed my sick call had justified making a whole barracks into a one-hundred-patient isolation ward and bringing in doctors to try to keep the disease on the premises.

In addition to this, the Camp Equality I rejoined was a different Camp Equality from the one I'd left. Tom Thumb was still the smiling commandant, but now his smile was showing more teeth and less bite. The tilling and untilling of "garden plots" had been abolished. Only Seventh-Day Adventists were being tortured by having to stand outdoors overnight. A batch of them had washed in on the latest wave of religious persecutions and they were refusing to work Saturdays. Tom Thumb broke them, of course, but not with the immediate beatings, new trials, and even executions that would have been his response, a month earlier, to such outright defiance.

Had Tom Thumb got religion? No. What was happening in our camp was happening, more or less, in all the camps. For 1953 was when Josef Stalin died on March 5 and, at his funeral, Klement Gottwald caught a cold and died three weeks later of pneumonia aggravated by an earlier case of syphilis. Whether God's will or our curses or neither or both had finished off both tyrants so Biblically, we didn't know, but it struck us as fitting and proper. All we said was: "Well, they both got what they deserved." But the civilian miners talked more freely about how swiftly the puppet had followed the ventriloquist to the grave. And our jailers must have felt a strong wind of terror headed their way from the Kremlin. Their patron saint, Soviet ex-interior minister Lavrenti Beria, had waited less than a month to start baring Stalin's sins, but this was scarcely enough to stave off Beria's own arrest in June and execution in

December. Among the guilty men of power in Czechoslovakia (some of whom, with Soviet secret police training, liked to call themselves "Beria's Gorillas"), the year of 1953 was a time of watchful waiting and belated washing and wringing of indelibly stained hands.

My three buddies—Eddie, Snapshot, and Polda—had all contracted jaundice and were just emerging from "isolation." I was thrust in with them on surface labors, which had just been decreed for recuperating jaundice victims because of fear of further contamination inside the mine.

We were the envy of other prisoners, for we had found a way out of mining. They begged us to infect them with our saliva. Eddie Pelcl, being the most recent case, obliged them sometimes by chewing food and then spitting it out for them to digest in exchange for fresh chunks of food for him to consume. When this didn't work for one prisoner, he took a strip of bacon (well-chewed by Pelcl), attached it to a thread, and tied the other end of the thread around one of his teeth. Then he swallowed the bacon, but left it hanging partway down into his digestive system for a couple of days.

If you try this sometime, which I hope you won't: Even if you get to use a brand-new piece of good bacon, you will, at the very least, turn yellow. It disturbs and confuses the production of bile by the liver and you develop all the mechanical symptoms of jaundice. This particular prisoner thereupon removed the thread and the unrecognizable piece of bacon, presented his Homemade Hepatitis Do-It-Yourself Kit to a grateful fellow prisoner, and staggered off to sick call. He was diagnosed as a flagrant case of jaundice and packed off with all the other jaundice cases in "isolation," where he actually developed a real case of jaundice.

Those of us who survived the disease (a couple of older men died of cirrhosis) played it for all it was worth. This was why Eddie, Snapshot, Polda, and I and some forty others started calling ourselves the "Jaundice Brigade." We'd been placed on a special rice diet, which not even the doctors had really expected Tom Thumb to honor. Nevertheless, whenever the food was below *our* rather tolerant expectations, we would clamor for our rice diet. Sometimes we won it and sometimes we went hungry, but we were never punished for demanding rice. And, more often than not, in the prevailing political uncertainty, Tom Thumb's kitchen obliged us.

We weren't so new or so breakable as the Seventh-Day Adventists. And Tom Thumb wasn't authorized to bury any of the "Jaundice Brigade" in the mines. Thus, when he realized he had the nucleus of an organized protest in his camp, he took the easiest solution at hand: he simply had all forty-four of us shipped out. This was done in such haste that the authorities neglected to disperse us. The Jaundice Brigade went on the road intact—to Camp Brotherhood, where I'd spent an interesting month gorging on and shitting out carrots and potatoes in Correction two and a half years earlier.

Camp Brotherhood couldn't reassign us to the mines, so we were put to work "building socialism" by pouring concrete and doing other construction work on a housing project that was slowly rising in nearby Vykmanov. It was a good deal—with civilian bosses and Sundays off. If we weren't being harassed by the guards, we spent our day of rest in camp learning English and other tongues (Polda taught himself Greek, pretending to any guard who caught him that it was Russian; Eddie was tutoring Snapshot in German and, when a guard happened upon them, Snapshot explained guilelessly that it was *East* German) and arguing whether we should be "building socialism." If I reiterate that phrase, it is because billboards on huge fences, which shielded prison labor from the view of sidewalk superintendents, proclaimed that this was what was going on inside: "building socialism."

Some Jaundice Brigaders insisted we should be sabotaging the works. Others of us asked how it would undermine the dictatorship if the ceiling or wall fell in on some tenant's infant. We were lucky enough to have landed a good job, by prison standards, and civilian bosses who were making skilled building workers out of us. These old-line Communist trade unionists had started out feeling scared or vindictive or even sorry for us when we were put in their employ. Now they respected us and even heeded us when we occasionally found and instituted a better way of work. We wanted to keep the respect we'd won, for it now seemed likeliest—as the aberration called Communism became a way of life—that our salvation must ultimately come from Communists who saw us, either from inside or outside the camps, for the people we were. Besides, the prisons in the 1950s were the last bastions in which traditional Czechoslovak craftsmanship and ingenuity could assert themselves while the system outside was glorifying mediocrity and junk. So we took pride in our work—and worked accordingly.

No matter when your term began, you measured prison years from Christmas to Christmas. My first Christmas, 1949 in Bory, Vacek had smuggled me a piece of Christmas cake. On my second Christmas, 1950 in Eliáš, "Gary Crant" had confessed he was a murderer, not a political criminal. For Christmas, 1951, we had dined on the commandant's dog after working a sixteen-hour double shift in Mine Number 8. Christmas, 1952, had been that funny plum compote O. Henry Christmas in Camp Equality. And Christmas, 1953, in Camp Equality was not only a Christmas of carp ends, but also a sprig of evergreen, which we decorated with five chocolate balls and called a Christmas tree.

On Christmas Day, we awoke to find only four balls on the tree.

A Jaundice Brigader with insomnia confided in me that he'd seen the thief. It was an old professor of Marxism-Leninism who'd wound up in jail as a perverter of the young. We both agreed that the kindest Christmas deed we could do was to hold our tongues about who stole and ate the Christmas decoration.

At Christmas of 1954, twenty-five of us skilled construction workers and Jaundice Brigaders were transferred out of Camp Brotherhood and the whole Jáchymov area—to Camp Vojna, near the ancient town of Příbram, where lead and silver mining dated all the way back to the thirteenth century and uranium mining only as far back as the middle of the twentieth century. But we were not yet needed under the earth.

The first new workers' housing to go up in Příbram since the country went Communist—a project for forty thousand tenants—was just starting to rise in an open field on the outskirts of town. Prison labor built 80 percent of it. Every morning, at daybreak, we were bussed from Camp Vojna through Old Příbram to the site, where the sentry boxes had been disguised as construction shacks and where a huge fence without peepholes had been erected to make us invisible while it advertised the virtues of "building socialism." Nevertheless, the people of Příbram knew we were there and who we were. And it wasn't only because we were building workers' housing that, every day, some pedestrian on the street flashed our bus a V-for-victory finger signal. We couldn't wave back, for we were—as always on bus trips—handcuffed to each other and our seats.

We finished the houses one by one. As we did, other prisoners moved the fence in further. The first tenants moved in.

A few women were at home during the day—very few in a society where women work. Some of those who stayed home were single; others had husbands and children. No sooner did their husbands go off to work than the married women—*every* one of them, I'm almost sorry to say—would start sending us signals, and I don't mean Vs-for-victory.

Their radar, in particular, zeroed in on our strapping young virgin, Eddie Pelcl. He was a handsome fellow who must have reminded them of what their husbands seemed like when first they met. The women's eyes would survey us, rest on Eddie, and never rest again until he had responded.

We managed to smuggle letters through the fence. Eddie, being a philosopher, found his métier in writing passionate love letters to women he could look at, but not touch. Eddie made "dates" with them. By prearrangement, a dozen times a day, three or four women would disrobe for him in their windows: a couple of times a day just for him, the rest of the day for whole groups of us.

Eddie sold admissions for cigarettes, although he was liberal

with free passes for fellow Jaundice Brigaders. After audition-
ing the talent himself a few times, he would decide whether
she was a four-butt, eight-butt, or full-pack attraction. Nobody
ever disputed his ratings, but what we all marveled at was the
total tyranny with which Eddie dominated his performers. If
the apartment of one of them was temporarily obscured from
view or if her husband stayed home, Eddie would arrange for
another of his ladies to lend her apartment and window to her.
Some of us called this circus "Eddie Pelcl and his Prisoners of
Love."

We also marveled at Eddie's disdain for his performers. Even
as he egged each one on like a prompter with a prima donna,
he would murmur that "she must be a real pig to get an apartment that quick from the Communists." He stayed a virgin
throughout his time in Příbram. Even when one of his "talents"
wangled a temporary job on our side of the fence as a cleaning
lady—making apartments ready for occupancy just before the
fence would be moved inward—Eddie hid out from her behind a high girder. She had to settle, in a boiler room, for the
rest of us—and an unkept promise that, if our notices were
raves (which they were!), then Eddie would come later.

With this housewife, whose name we never knew but whose
age was around forty, we took turns and stood guard to insure
privacy. We didn't want it to be a gangbang, but something
clean and private and almost loving, which we might hope
for on the outside. She was silent, if obliging, and I wondered
whether she was thinking of Eddie or me or of anyone or anything as she wrapped her hairy legs around me to thrust
me still deeper inside my first woman in years. Eddie had rated
her a full-pack attraction, not because of her looks or her legs
or even her generous breasts, but because she had hair on her
legs, hair on her arms, hair all over her body.

Both before and after prison, I preferred women with
smoother surfaces. But somehow the thick hair on her legs,
visible even across a fence and through a window, was what
inspired the most lust in me. And in the other men, too, which
Eddie knew as he made up his ratings. We analyzed this on
Sundays. Polda concluded that the hair had been attractive

now because we could want her *now* and yet know that something better—namely, women with hairless legs—waited for us outside somewhere.

Polda's analysis was the most detached of any of us. He had abstained from the housewife because "I have a fiancée." And nobody had taunted him for this—not even the men who'd stood in line because they genuinely missed their loving wives back home. And they, like I, hoped for the best for Polda's fidelity and Eddie's virginity. "I've wanted a piece of the women I've seen," Eddie told me once, "but I haven't seen one of them yet that I'd want all of. Maybe it's my Boy Scout past."

Though we probably didn't have the virtue of a Boy Scout troop, the Jaundice Brigade had many of its virtues. When my father found a civilian worker on our building project in Příbram, we had him deliver messages not only for the Čapeks, but for relatives of any others of us from Prague. On birthdays and religious holidays (but never on Communist holidays!), the Jaundice Brigaders serenaded each other and even gave little Sunday-night choral concerts in Camp Vojna.

My father sent me Shakespeare and Shaw and A. J. Cronin and Lewis Carroll in their native tongue, which gave our self-taught English new impetus at Vojna. I found English, especially *Alice in Wonderland,* the most straightforward, outspoken language to which I'd yet been exposed. By now, Eddie and Polda and I were teaching it as well as learning it.

There were other prisoners at Vojna who knew more English than we did, but had difficulty sharing it. We took and sought help from them, which they gave willingly. But we felt the call to evangelize other Jaundice Brigaders with our wonderful discovery of the English language.

"I could never learn English," said a butcher named Jaroslav Heteš. "I'm no good with languages."

"Go on!" I said. "You know plenty of English words without knowing any English. Look, what did the doctor ask you when you went on sick call?"

"For my *symptomy,*" he said, using the plural of the Czech word "*symptom.*"

"And what was your *symptom?*" I asked.

"I think," said Heteš, scratching his bottom, "I have *heme-roidy.*"

"Good!" I said. "And if you're faking a *hemorrhoid,* where do you get sent?"

"*Korekce,*" he said.

"You go to *Correction* unless you have —?"

"*Protekce!*" Heteš exclaimed.

"And the guard you've bribed with *protection* money becomes your —?"

"*Protektor!*"

"And maybe your *protector* can get you all kinds of extra —?"

"*Privilegia!*"

"There you go, Heteš!" I said. "You're talking English."

I've often wondered why more language teachers don't start by teaching the words that are alike or similar in both languages. For, once a student has a bit of vocabulary, he is much more receptive to grammar than he would be otherwise.

Midnight in the barracks of Vojna would find clusters of three or four of us huddled by flashlight under the racks where our dirty, smelly, work clothes were hung—with a carefully constructed web of our rubber work boots piled high as a blackout curtain. Midnight would find us this way, but we had to station a lookout to make sure the guards wouldn't.

One night—by pussyfooting under the barracks window with sneakers instead of clumping in with boots—one of the older guards sneaked up on our lookout before he could sound much of an alarm. We rushed to our beds, but the guard cried "*Halt!*" and pointed his submachine gun at me while I was still quite a ways from my bunk. I froze in my tracks. Still, I was standing near the stove—and, he started to search the three of us who'd still been in motion when he'd called a halt, I dropped one of my two precious English-vocabulary notebooks into the fire. (The other was concealed beneath a floorboard.)

The guard saw me do this and was furious: "What was that?"

"What was what?" I answered.

"What was that you just burned?"

"I didn't burn anything."

"I saw you burn something. Everybody here saw you burn something."

Everybody in the room denied that. The guard searched all our beds, particularly mine, before storming out with these words to me: "I'm not done with you yet, Eighty-two ten!"

Next day, he wasn't with us on the trip back from Příbram, which was where he usually joined the night shift of guards. He was waiting for us in the barracks. He and two other guards had dug up our floor and found the second vocabulary near my bed. So now my entire English word stock was gone— and I didn't know what punishment I rated for this "anti-Soviet" linguistic affront.

The guard, however, was slightly sheepish. He was not a bad fellow, just conscientious. "I thought it would be something else," he told me. "I thought you were burning a spy code last night. But it was just another one of these, wasn't it?"

"You bet it was," I said quickly.

"Good. Look, you understand I have to turn it in now that three of us found it. But I'll tell the commandant we couldn't find out which one of the men it belonged to. And I'm sorry about this."

"It's all right," I comforted him. "But if you can ever find anything in English for me that might replace what I've lost, I'll be happy to hide it from you successfully."

He made no promises. But, a week later, he took me aside, scarcely concealing his own joy at finding what he called "a French periodical for you." I tried to conceal my own disappointment—until I saw that, while his gift had a French name, its words were in English. The magazine was *Mademoiselle*!

I asked him where he got it. He said, "I confiscated it from the old Legionnaire in the next barracks. I had to take it away from him when I caught him with it, but I haven't turned it in."

I went to see the old Legionnaire—who'd served with the Communist Legions in the Spanish Civil War—and lent him back his fashion magazine until he was finished with it. Out of gratitude, he gave me a hard-covered Spanish-language grammar book. Before long, the Jaundice Brigade had embarked upon a second foreign language. We spoke Spanish on the construction site, English in the barracks, and Czech to all outsiders. My father furnished an original of Cervantes (*persona non grata* in Czech because Don Quixote was more dangerous than a dozen Boy Scouts—an aristocrat, an individualist, and a seeker) and the works of Pío Baroja (*Memoirs of a Man of Action* and a charming fishing pastoral whose name I can no longer remember). A number of our pupils found Spanish even easier and more enchanting than English. Grammatically, Spanish reflexives ("I wash myself," "I dress myself," "It pleases me that") are very similar to Czech. And, as with English, we started with the similarities in vocabulary: *cámara* in Spanish is similar to *komora* in Czech, meaning "room" or "chamber"; *merienda,* meaning a Spanish family's light late afternoon meal, means much the same as the small celebration called *merenda* in Czech.

We, the American Family Levy, were exiles in Vienna during the longest year of my wife's life—from thirty-nine to forty. But Karel Čapek didn't forget; nor did he let Valerie Levy forget. On her fortieth birthday, June 8, 1972, she received an overnight transatlantic cablegram greeting from Cicero, Illinois: MUCHA SUERTE Y FELICIDAD A LA MUCHACHA DE CUARENTA PRIMAVERAS.

(Although he was never a member of the Jaundice Brigade, we received much help with our languages, our rights as prisoners, and our lives in general from another inmate of Vojna, Dr. Evžen Löbl. A Slovakian Jew, lifelong Communist, Marxist economist, and survivor of the Slánský trial, Löbl was best known to us—even before we met him—as a trusted adviser to Jan Masaryk and one of the creators of UNRRA as well as its chief expert in Czechoslovakia. A pudgy, jowly man who laughed a lot, Löbl was unfazed when we twitted him about wearing his UNRRA hats in the slave mines. He would puff on his pipe and laughingly admit that while we wound up in his hats he wound up in our shoes.*)

---

* Released conditionally in 1961 and rehabilitated in 1963, Löbl became director of the Slovak State Bank in Bratislava. In the Prague Spring of 1968, he publicly advocated the creation of 200,000 to 300,000 private enterprises—and, later that year, after the Soviet invasion, he left Czechoslovakia to teach in the United States.

During my stay in Vojna, I qualified for my first visit from my parents in seven years. The basic requirement for a visit was six clean months. This meant six months of meeting every assigned quota (the only way to do this was to hold a quota-free job); six months without any disciplinary punishment or Correction; and a minimum of six months in that particular camp (three clean months in an earlier camp could not be carried over to the next camp).

These matters were, in a way, so much out of my control that I seldom thought about visits. But my subconscious clock must have been ticking, for the day I suddenly decided to ask whether I was eligible to be visited proved to be the very day I became eligible.

I was given a form to fill out—and, once it was filed, I began living for that visit. In three weeks, my parents were sent a form "inviting" them to pay a visit on the following Sunday morning. It didn't say *whom* they would visit, but it did tell them *where*. Since Vojna was too grubby for public viewing, there was a special showcase area for visitors at another compound in the Příbram area, Camp Bytíz.

On Sunday morning at Vojna, those of us who could expect visitors were issued freshly laundered uniforms and civilian shoes that had been worn and returned the preceding Sunday by prisoners who'd had visitors then. Now, with all our friends seeing us off and wishing us well, we were bussed to Bytíz. There, the Potemkin Village for visitors consisted of relatively modest barbed wire and a building with two entrances and three rooms: a front waiting room for visitors, a rear waiting room for prisoners, and, in the middle, a meeting room divided in half by mesh.

Even this much of Bytíz had been rendered invisible at the time of my parents' visit, which happened to be in May. At that time of year, to celebrate Russia's race to the Elbe that "liberated" Central Europe, there was a cross-Continent bicycle marathon called a "Peace Race." Its route passed by Camp Bytíz—or, rather, it bypassed Bytíz, which was obliterated from view. In anticipation of the few seconds when the Peace Racers would zip by, inmates of Bytíz had worked for weeks

felling trees in the adjoining woods and transporting the tallest
timber back to Bytíz. There, propped up by wires, a whole
new forest had risen along the road. It lent a magical theatrical
dimension to my reunion with my parents—as though Birnam
Wood had come to Dunsinane for the occasion.

I heard the civilian room's guard calling "Čapeks!" a minute
or two before prisoner 8210 was summoned at my end, so my
parents were already in the meeting room when I entered. Our
conversation was monitored by a guard standing on my side of
the mesh—which was lucky for him. If the guard had been
standing on the other side, I think my father would have hit
him for the way he interfered.

My folks looked older, but no worse than I'd expected. My
mother was crying. My father was fighting tears. And I could
hardly talk. But if I would weep, it would be for the lack of
conversation.

For a minute or two, nothing was said. Then my mother
spoke: "Karel, how come you didn't want to see us?"

The accusation stunned me into a few more seconds of
speechlessness. Then I exclaimed, "I did! I do! I sent for you as
soon as you were eligible."

Here, the guard corrected me: "As soon as your son was
eligible, ma'm. You haven't done a thing wrong. Don't let him
put the blame on you."

He was a fatherly-looking, friendly-voiced old busybody.
My mother accepted him unthinkingly as an ally. My father,
who understood better, clenched his fists.

"If only you'd behaved yourself, Karel," my mother went on,
"we wouldn't have had to wait this long."

"You should listen to your mother, son," the guard said.
Then, basking in the rage emanating from father and son, he
added, "Of course, if you'd listened to your mother in the first
place, the three of you wouldn't be here today."

My father took his right fist with his left hand and just
gripped it hard—much the way I was holding my tongue. We
were quivering from our inner struggles, but not my mother,
whose recriminations flowed like tears: "Whenever we asked,

they said you weren't a good boy. You weren't letting them educate you."

"*Reeducate*," the guard corrected.

"Indoctrinate," I said.

After that, the guard lost interest—which was just as well, for I don't know how I could have taken much more of him on top of the news that my parents broke to me:

My girl friend, Božena, had been spending her summer vacations in the country, where she lived with a farm family that had a dashing and brainy son her age. She admired the young fellow, but had confided in my mother that she found him "too full of himself." Still, she was lonely and, at close quarters, it is remarkable that the inevitable took four summers to happen. In September of 1954, Božena came home full of him, too, and, that Christmas, they were married three months before their baby girl was born.

"This is just my first visit to you, Karel, dear. One day you will visit me." . . . *"Many, many times."*

Those words from the L-shaped room in Pankrác echoed in my head, which was suddenly full to bursting with memories of Božena. But I didn't feel grief until I asked my mother, "Where did it happen?" and she named a village on the Vltava barely ten miles from Příbram. That was when I felt caged. That was when, for the first time since Carlsbad, I thought about escaping. If only I'd had a brother or sister, I might have slugged that obnoxious guard and made a dash for it (and been gunned down before my parents' eyes). Being an only child can be a terrible responsibility.

When our fifteen minutes had dragged to an end, my father and I exchanged good-byes. My mother stared after me in silence—as if she wanted to photograph me with her mind—until we went our separate ways through the fake forest surrounding that Potemkin Village on the outskirts of limbo.

In February of 1957, I came back to Bytíz again—not for a visit this time, but for what proved to be yet another year in the mines.

"I'm a skilled bricklayer!" I protested.

The Manpower officer at Bytíz laughed and said, "So you can lay bricks down in the mines."

"No, I can't. I've had jaundice."

"So have I—a hundred years ago. But you have a choice: the mines or Correction."

I "chose" the mines, for Correction at Bytíz had been farmed out by the guards to a wolf pack of hardened, violent criminal prisoners. They'd been given the run of Correction so long as nothing spilled out into the rest of the camp. Correction also housed the criminally insane, which now numbered quite a few political prisoners. Injustice that goes on and on without end can drive an innocent man crazy. So could a few days in Bytíz's Correction.

In Barracks H at Bytíz, I took an upper bunk and discovered that I was being contemplated from below by the saintliest being I would meet in prison. "I'm Čapek," I said, extending my hand downward.

"I'm Aim," he said, reaching up to clasp hands gently. In Czech, his name was pronounced I'M.

From Jaroslav Aim's suntan, I could tell he was working on a construction site and not in the mines. He was lean, dark blond, and ascetic-looking. He wore granny glasses, which were not very common in Communist Czechoslovakia in those days. He had a lithe, muscular body with short, strong arms and legs. He moved around very lightly on the balls of his feet. And he was always on the move. He knew everyone in Camp Bytíz. Everyone in the camp knew him. Yet he didn't stand out enough for the guards to make trouble for him. In fact, the guards brought their personal problems to him for counsel.

So did everybody else. Though he looked like a young American college boy of today, Aim was the Elder Wise Man of Camp Bytíz. Prisoners of all ages came to him with their troubles. Whatever the problem, Aim's solution involved action, not advice. If a man's shoes hurt, Aim exchanged with him. If Aim's shoes hurt the man more, then Aim would exchange back— and the man would be grateful. If the man's shoes hurt Aim, he'd exchange them with the next complainer. For a man who couldn't lift a bucket of mortar with both hands, Aim would cheerfully carry two—one in each hand—and his generosity would inspire the man to carry one at a time thereafter. It was positively mystic.

Despite his boyish appearance, Aim was thirty. He'd been in prison longer than any of us. I'd even read about his inexplicable case in the Prague press when I was still a free youth. Soon after Communism seized power, a bomb had been planted in the auto of a Canadian Embassy official. Aim had confessed to it. And, unlike so many of our "confessions," it had seemed to be true. At least, in camp almost a decade later, he freely admitted he'd done it. But why? Was it meant to be a provocation? By whom? Against whom? To all of which Aim would only reaffirm his guilt. "Yes, I did it," he told us often, "and I'm not sorry. I had my reasons."

He'd been sentenced to death. But his mother had a Communist relative high in the Ministry of Justice. She'd petitioned him privately and he had said, "If your son will repent and promise to change, I can have his sentence commuted." But Aim had declined. He had, in fact, berated his mother for trying to save her son's life. His mother had persisted anyway— and Aim's sentence had been commuted to twenty-five years at hard labor.

He didn't smoke or drink. His mother's saving his life had been the second strike against her. The first had been in his teens, when she'd married an innkeeper. Even Aim had to concede that his stepfather was "a good man to be looked up to," but young Aim would not be supported by earnings from the sale of alcohol. He had run away from home. On his own, he'd worked his way up to a low-level managerial post in a provincial lumber mill. Living with a series of young country girls, he'd never married any of them, but each relationship had been as tidy and monogamous as a marriage is supposed to be. Then he had put his affairs in order, taken the train to Prague, and planted a bomb. Aim was such an unlikely suspect that he'd never have been caught if he hadn't let himself be caught.

Because I'd never met anyone quite like Aim, I tried to un-

derstand him. And because I couldn't understand him, he
became an obsession with me. I had never known anyone who
wore his spirit so close to the surface. And yet he was not a
preacher. He was the camp guru with holy qualities. And, because I could recognize but could not fathom these holy qualities, I kept trying to find his flaw.

Not that Aim had a superior intellect—or was even an intellectual. He would be the first to admit this. He stayed aloof
from my religion, linguistics. When invited, he would reply,
"I'm not bright enough for languages." He would say it self-
deprecatingly, but in such a modest way that I felt he *knew*
English and Spanish—and all languages known to man—far
better than I did.

Aim seldom made positive statements with words, just with
deeds. Yet he could condemn his mother and stepfather without accusing them—as when I asked him, "Do you know what
you'd like to be when you get out of prison?"

"Oh, yes," Aim replied. "Something I wouldn't be ashamed
of."

He was the only child of "a man who saw the whole world,
but never saw what was happening in his own home." Yet I
could never find out whether his father was a sailor or salesman, dead or divorced.

Walking together with Aim, I would argue ever so slyly and
even take positions that weren't mine—anything to get him to
take a position! I never succeeded. What's more, I always suspected he knew what I was thinking. Sometimes I hated myself for being so interested in Aim. It was the only time I ever
worried about whether I was homosexual. Or was Aim a passive homosexual? I really must say he was terribly attractive
to me. I wanted to be in his company as often as I could. Like
an interrogator, I needed to know everything I could about
him—to break him, perhaps? Seeing what I was doing, I didn't
like myself any better for it.

Aim was the only diversion of my year in the mines of
Bytíz. In 1956, Nikita Khrushchev had told the Twentieth All-
Union Party Congress the truth about Stalin and "sins of the

past"—sins that we were still living in the concentration camps. But, in that same year, an uprising in Poland and a revolution in Hungary were ruthlessly suppressed—the latter by the Red Army. The repercussions of Khrushchev's speech, which was quickly smuggled into the camps, were felt almost everywhere in the Communist orbit. But not in Czechoslovakia, whose puppet dictator—now Antonín Novotný—still took orders from Stalin's ghost. As a token gesture of "liberalization," the authorities at Bytíz allowed us to listen to a speech or two by President Novotný. Even over faulty loudspeakers, he came across as shrill, whining, and stupid. As a form of self-flagellation, some of us listened to every word. It was good for laughs of a special sort. How can you classify the humor of hearing in Bytíz the president of your country denouncing "malevolent anti-socialist malefactors" for "contriving the insidious fiction that there are concentration camps in our Republic? I challenge them—I invite them!—to travel the width and breadth of our socialistic Republic and I defy them to find one man behind barbed wire for political reasons." Of course, any journalist who'd take him up on his offer wouldn't be granted a visa: you were invited, but you couldn't come.

Starting in 1956, we heard the first few rumors of an "amnesty." They proved false. If 1956 had any real effect in our midst, it came in early 1957, when there was an influx of "casualties of the October events in Hungary," as we called the revolution there. These "casualties" were Czechs and Slovaks who had just been sentenced to two or three years for "supporting the Hungarian counterrevolution." Typical of these "counterrevolutionaries" was an old man who'd been shopping when someone had rushed into the store with the shocking news that, in Budapest, Premier Imre Nagy had broken with the Warsaw Pact and declared Hungary neutral. Instinctively, the man had exclaimed "Good!"*

---

* He fared better than Premier Nagy, who took refuge in Budapest's Yugoslav Embassy when the Red Army counterattacked and crushed the revolt. Leaving the Embassy under a safe-conduct pledge, Nagy was seized by Soviet police, tried in secret, and executed.

I found at Bytíz that I had lost all zest, all vigor, and all aesthetic feeling for the inside of a mine. And I feared that the mine at Bytíz would return my lack of passion with a painful kiss of death. Years of safety neglect in that damp mine were taking their toll. Every day, a few more loose rocks tumbled around me. But we bricklayers were not allowed to shore up these death traps. No, we were to pour concrete for new excavations in a crumbling structure that wasn't supporting its present load. Each day, emerging from the mines, I rejoiced that I'd made it—and worried because the law of averages was mounting up against me.

By the end of 1957, I'd had enough. For all my efforts to keep my body intact and strong, I now decided to cripple myself out of mining. I was willing to sacrifice the ring finger of my left hand; I was a single man and I would dedicate it to Božena. But self-destruction is no easy job. Some of us have to work at everything.

In a deserted cavity of the mine, I tried to impale the finger on the sharp edge of a metal wagon and then crucify it with a hammer. I found I didn't have the guts to go through with it. As soon as I pricked my finger, I recoiled like a child from the first touch of fire.

The next day, I made myself a little splint to isolate that finger. Then I sliced off a board to use as a tray. It would protect the knee that would serve as my worktable when I'd kneel and demolish my finger with a hammer. Then, when everything was ready for minor surgery, I hit my perfect target hard, swiftly, and often—hoping to do the damage before pain and instinct could register.

By the time I winced from the fifth blow, the pain was excruciating; the board and the splint were smashed into splinters; my knee ached from the hammer's impact—and my ring finger was bloody, scraped, and throbbing, but unbent and unbroken!

I was so angry at my stupid finger that I hammered again and again until finally I felt something snap and I stopped feeling any pain at all. I hurried down the tunnel to report my "accident" to the civilian boss, for he was the only man who could authorize me to see the doctor. By the time I caught sight of the boss twenty minutes later, my idiot finger had begun to heal! Strength and pain were seeping back into it. The blood was caking and scabbing. *I was doomed to survival!* But, pretending to hold my finger in pain, I kept pushing it out of whack even as I approached the boss with it.

Fortunately, it looked like a bloody mess to him. An hour later, I was sitting in the camp infirmary. The doctor, an unsympathetic prisoner who wanted to be left alone, acted betrayed when he saw he had a patient—and annoyed when he perceived the minor scope of my complaint. "It will mend," he said, "and you can go on working while it does. You should never have been sent here."

He bandaged me absentmindedly. In his head, I was already back in the mine. But I knew I wasn't going, so I had no choice but to throw myself upon his mercy. "It's up to you, Doctor," I told him. "I've spent five years of my life down there and I can't take any more of it. So what you're deciding is whether I'm going to be out of mining after five years and a bad case of jaundice or whether I'm going to end my days in Correction. It's *your* choice."

The doctor was skeptical, but at least he didn't say no. What he did say, thinking aloud, was: "I've sent much worse cases back to the mines. Much worse mentally and much worse physically. And if I do what *you* want, I'll either end up in the mines or Correction myself."

"So you have choices," I said selfishly. "I have none."

"It's not up to me," this gray old man said in a monotone, "but I'll see what I can do."

He kept his word. The very next morning, I was summoned to the Manpower Office. There, the official in charge—a guard wearing civilian clothes—told me, "Doctor says you can go back to the mine."

Seeing that he had a long note from the infirmary in his hand, I guessed he was bluffing. Besides, I wouldn't have been called in just to be told this. So I said, "The doctor knows better. I know better. I can't go back to the mine."

The Manpower officer threatened me with Correction. He

tried to bribe me with permanent day shifts. He even hinted at amnesties for men with good records in the mines. But I wouldn't relent and couldn't relent. I was in too deep now. If I gave in, I'd be admitting to malingering. So I tried to think what my friend Aim would do—and said philosophically each time, "Do whatever you want with me, but I won't go back to the mines."

Finally, he threw up his hands and told me, "And you won't come back into my sight either! Pack your things and report for transport."

On the spur of the moment, there weren't many places such a low-ranking jailer could send a man outside of his own camp. About the only camp he could ship me out to was Vojna— where I landed right back among the bulk of the Jaundice Brigade.

(Jaroslav Aim later caught up with me at Vojna, too, but he was never part of the Jaundice Brigade. No, Aim was a brigade unto himself!)

Young Eddie Pelcl was still at Vojna, still a virgin, still on construction duty, and still selling the favors of his harem of housewives to the voyeurs in our midst. But even this relatively good life had taken its toll on this Boy Scout growing to man-hood in prison. Every now and then, Eddie's pulse would race and his face would redden in a kind of apoplexy that lasted as long as four or five minutes. We worried all the more about him, particularly when his affliction struck while he was on a high girder, but he never fell. Nor did he take this condition seriously: "My heart just skips a beat every now and then from too much girl-watching."

I went right back to work on the Příbram housing project— building Communism from the ground up, which I now knew as a far better deal than bleeding Czechoslovakia from the ground under Bytíz. While I'd been away, Camp Vojna had acquired a new commandant, who was considered an improve-ment, and the construction project a new civilian boss, who was not. He was a heavy drinker who left everything to the prisoners as long as they made no trouble for him. I didn't consider him as bad a fellow as others did, and I lasted in his employ from early 1958 until mid-1959, when he showed up unexpectedly and heard me "defending" him thusly in an argument with another prisoner: "Sure, he's a third-rate man when he's drunk. But he's a fourth-rate man when he's sober."

The boss sent a report to the camp commandant. Without specifying our offense, he demanded a life sentence for the man who'd attacked his reputation and the death sentence for me for defending it. The other man was a former guard from Leopoldov, the prison in Slovakia, who'd been cashiered and jailed for smuggling letters out for prisoners. He and I were summoned to the office of the new camp commandant—a sturdy blond young worker type no more than a year or two older than I (twenty-nine going on thirty), if that. He had the letter and he wanted to know: "What's this about?"

We told him and he burst out laughing. But then he turned to us and said, "What am I gonna do with you two? I can't execute you the way he wants me to. But I can't send you back to the housing project, either. He has secret police connections and he'd only make hell for me as well as you. What am I gonna do with you?"

I was so seldom consulted about my fate that I suggested cheekily, "How about giving us a better job?"

He laughed again and said, "Maybe I oughtta give you both jobs in Correction until I make up my mind." But he looked us over and what he saw was a pair of experienced prisoners who hadn't given him any more trouble than a couple of good laughs. He must have reflected on larger problems of his, for he suddenly asked, "Do you think you could operate a boiler?"

We both were sure we could.

"Good!" he said. "Because I've got a boiler room that's run in three shifts by a collaborationist, a homosexual, and an alcoholic. The Nazi's no trouble, but the other two are gonna blow this place up one of these days. So I gotta get them outta there before the cold weather comes—and that's a good place to keep you two out of sight of that guy in Příbram."

The collaborationist broke us in on what proved to be the last of my many prison jobs. Thus, I spent the winter of 1959–1960 in a warm boiler room. To a prisoner, this was almost, but not quite, the equivalent of a trip to the Riviera. It was the first winter I wasn't cold. I had plenty of time to read. There were occasional, but not many, visitors: prisoners and even guards who'd drop in to chat and keep warm.

I had another visit from my parents in late 1959—again at Bytíz, now defoliated of its fake forest. My mother was more composed this time and she had a plan: "You must apply for a conditional release." This was the kind of parole that Communist prisoners and a few non-Communists (who sometimes had to "reconfess" their initial "guilt" or even turn informer to qualify) were receiving.

How could I tell my mother that her idea bored me? That my boiler room represented, for the time being, solitude and sanctuary and warmth and staying myself? That making deals with the system that had dealt with me so unjustly was reprehensible to me? She wouldn't understand. I had sprung from my mother's womb, but now we belonged to two different worlds. Would sharing civilian life ever bring us close together again? My world was already that of the professional prisoner. Just the folk wisdom of my world—"They can fuck us, but we won't get pregnant" or "A short-timer can coast the rest of the way sitting on razor blades"—would repel and elude even a mother whose eyes had seen her country and her family raped by more than a decade of Communism. So all I said was: "Mom, you won't like what's left of me if I get out that way."

My father soothed the blow with: "Besides, they say there'll be an amnesty next May."

And, for once—but it took only once!—he was right. Though there were three amnesty rumors a day in 1960, I wouldn't let myself believe any of them. Nor had I ever counted the days until my fourteen-year sentence would officially be up in 1963. There were too many ways to deflate hope and inflate time. But I did believe that "freedom" would come sooner rather than later, for the State hadn't succeeded in exterminating us— and now there were too many prison-camp alumni back in the society, even on "conditional release," for the society to ignore our existence. Turning thirty that April in Vojna, I must have been hoping against hope. As the likeliest amnesty time

came—first May Day, then the May 5 anniversary of the
Prague Uprising, and then the fifteenth annual "Soviet Liberation Day" on May 9—and went, I began to despair and even
wondered how one went about applying for a "conditional
release."

We weren't even given the day off on Monday, May 9, 1960.
But, when I came back from my boiler room that evening, I
found that one whole barracks had been fenced off and its
regular inhabitants evacuated. One of them was lying in my
bunk. "Where am I supposed to sleep?" I asked him.

"In my old barracks, you lucky bastard," he told me. "There
was a roll call and your name was read out. You're supposed to
move in there tonight."

"What for?" I asked, my hopes rising.

"They won't say. But a lot of the guys who weren't called
are calling it Amnesty Barracks. The guys who are going there
call it Barracks X."

As soon as I passed through the fence and checked into
Barracks X, I knew it was indeed Amnesty Barracks! We
weren't allowed out of the building for the night. Nobody
wanted to leave it. Inside, we were issued our personal belong-
ings from the time of our arrests and whatever old civilian
clothes of ours that could be found. The wardrobe I'd worn to
my trial had long ago disappeared during my odyssey through
the camps, but I was allowed to buy the clothes (including a
horse blanket of a brown jacket) that had once adorned a
a man who'd gone directly from Camp Vojna to the grave.
Once this expense was deducted, I was paid the rest of my
prison earnings and savings and allowed to convert my scrip
into crowns. All of this amounted to less than two months'
living on the outside. Then I was handed the contents of a box
with my name and number on it. Inside it were my old wrist-
watch (rusted to death); my driver's license (long expired);
and my membership card in the Friends of the U.S.A. Club
(long extinct). I hardly glanced at these souvenirs, for all the
transients of Barracks X were busy winking at each other.

That night, the sympathetic young commandant of Vojna
delivered a lecture in Barracks X. He warned us that what

we'd seen and where we'd worked were military secrets. Mentioning them in civilian life would insure our immediate return to the prisons, the camps, and the mines.

"Tomorrow, it can all start over for you," he said. "But, if you come back here, I can promise you it will end here, too."

He spoke so candidly and with such sincerity that I'm afraid I believed him. (I think he must have believed it, too.) And I wondered how I could ever return to a society whose worst injustices were national secrets. Well, I would take my chances! My month on the rim of civilian life in the Carlsbad hospital was enough to propel me forward with hope.

None of the three hundred men in Barracks X that night tried to sleep. We sat up talking, playing cards, and waiting for daybreak almost like condemned men—condemned to the world that had put us in Vojna.

At dawn, a convoy of six Recreational Autobuses came growling in empty and lumbered out twenty minutes later with prisoners bound for Prague. It was the first bus ride I'd taken without handcuffs in a dozen years. The four-hour trip allowed only one rest stop—in a Bohemian field, where we were solemnly warned that "the guards have orders to shoot to kill" any urinater who made a dash for freedom. And the guards really did cover us with their submachine guns as I pissed at gunpoint for the last time.

We entered Prague by the road that had been rerouted away from Lidice and Lány (where the Masaryks were buried), but still went by Ruzyně prison and White Mountain (Bílá Hora), where Bohemia's defeat in the seventeenth century's Thirty Years' War passed a three-hundred-year sentence of Hapsburg domination upon our Czech Lands. One expected Ruzyně and Bílá Hora to look drab, but not the Prague Castle and St. Vitus Cathedral and St. Nicholas Church on a sunny Tuesday noontime in May. And yet, for all my bright memories —which should have helped—these landmarks of my native city looked gray. It hadn't occurred to me how the Communists had neglected our treasures, though it should have. It didn't even occur to me that Tuesday. I thought the trouble lay with me and my prison vision.

The bus panted along the left bank of the Vltava and made

its first stop in Smíchov, near the Angel Market, which was open for business, but barren of fruit. I could have disembarked there and made my way across a bridge or by public conveyance to home. But the next stop would be the Square of Charles IV, just four or five blocks from home. So why not stay a prisoner for ten minutes more?

Emotionally, I wanted to get off that bus right there in Smíchov—to hurry away from the armed men still guarding us; to escape the prison air that was all one breathed in that Recreational Autobus. But my prison training told me, "Never hurry, Eighty-two ten, and never be among the first in or out." And, to my astonishment, a dormant civilian instinct awoke and asserted itself in agreement: "You've got to stop living in fear, Čapek, right now!" So I stayed aboard.

A dozen of my fellow passengers disembarked at Smíchov and dispersed. As I watched them walk away unfettered and unfollowed, the bus heaved a huge groan and started up again. I began to believe what was happening to me.

On our way to the Square of Charles IV, I said good-bye to Eddie Pelcl, who would remain aboard the bus for two more stops and take the train to Bratislava. (And, since he leaves my story here, I want to tell what little more I know about Eddie's fate. I saw him in Bratislava two or three years later. He had lost his famous virginity within his first twenty-four hours back in Slovakia—to the kid sister of one of the boys who used to be in his Scout troop. He had played the field and was more attractive than ever to women, but now he was settling down to a long-lasting affair with a lovely girl who still had a husband. "I like good women," Eddie told me then, "and there are probably many I could have. But I still want more out of freedom than the life of a super stud—which I'm not, anyway.")

Bidding Eddie farewell, I was the last man off the bus at the Square of Charles IV. I stepped down onto something so hard that it hurt me! For a minute, I thought I had broken both my feet. What had taken me by surprise was—pavement: my first since leaving Bory a decade earlier! In the camps and even on the construction site in Příbram, I had never set foot on that magical modern convenience called a sidewalk.

The cars startled me. Hardly any of them looked like any I'd known. A trolley clanged its bell. While the sound was the same as ever, it went through me this time and I jumped—fortunately, away from it. I gazed wistfully after the bus that had deposited me in this terrifying city where I'd lived all of my first life.

When the bus was out of sight, I started studying people's faces—hoping, I quickly realized, to see some I'd known in prison. Even a guard's face might have been welcome at that moment. Nobody looked at me, even though I was the only person standing still in that busy square. A few pedestrians detoured around me—but without glancing at me, until one young man stared back at me with a what-are-you-looking-for? look that was probably more helpful than belligerent. Not knowing what to say, I shuffled away.

Once I started moving, my feet ate up that hard pavement with steps that turned into strides—past Faust House and down the hill that dips toward Vyšehrad and Libušina Street. It was early afternoon and nobody was home. I hurried over to the student canteen where I knew my mother worked. My route took me along the riverbank. I breathed the air of my boyhood—of days with Štěpán and Božena and my idyll with my first woman—but it tasted so rich that I felt menaced. I'd have been more at ease breathing the stale metallic prison air of the bus that had brought me to Prague. But at least this air in Vyšehrad was not totally unfamiliar and it made echoes in my blood.

I found the kitchen where my mother worked. I stepped from the sunlit purgatory of my native city's streets into a steamy white cloudland that stung tears from my eyes, but comforted me with an institutional air that made me feel a little closer to prison and the boiler room I'd been running just yesterday. When I regained my vision, a bossy, hefty woman in white was looking me over with her hands on her hips. She was either about to cook me or tell me I didn't belong in her kitchen when something about me made her take a second glance. Then she started calling, in an unexpectedly high, sweet voice, "Mrs. Čapek! Mrs. Čapek! You have a son here!"

From behind a soup tureen stepped my mother—a warm,

grandmotherly woman (without grandchildren), flushed from work, heat, and surprise that had not yet jelled into joy, and momentarily perplexed by what might happen if her soup went unstirred. She still had a ladle in her hand and, as she threw her arms around me, I caught some sizzling metal and a trickle of hot bouillon on the back of my neck. I hugged her and we both cried together and all work stopped as all eyes in that kitchen made their own salty soup water—until the boss lady with the incredibly sweet voice stopped sobbing long enough to tell my mother, "Rose, please get out of here and be a mother to your son."

My mother said, "Thank you" and I realized that these were the first words she'd spoken. And I had yet to speak my first word as a free man. Would it embarrass you if I told you that the first word that came out was "Mother!"?

My father had to take a bus and then a tram home from the automotive plant where he worked. After a few hours of being mothered (of listening and eating), I walked down to the Number 21 tram stand on the Marx-Engels Embankment, to sit by the water and watch for my father. Five trams came and went before Tony Čapek stepped down from the sixth. I took a minute to look at him before he'd see me: a stocky, hunching man in his fifties with more lines in his tired face than there ought to be, but with a glint of eagerness, anticipation, even hope for a surprise or two yet to come. Oh, I could see this good man haunting bus stations and searching other faces for a link to his lost child! He didn't yet know I was out of prison, so I ended our separation by walking up behind him and putting my hand on his shoulder—not like a policeman, but like a son.

Two men kissed and hugged and wept on a tram stand in Vyšehrad and walked home with arms around each other's shoulders, father and son, for the first time in a dozen years.

Part 5

A Free Agent

On my first weekend at home, I was awakened in the middle of the night by one chilling howl that came from several directions. It sounded like a pack of hounds baying at the moon or after a hunted fugitive—and this was enough to make a man of thirty, just four days out of prison, go whimpering to the bed of his sleeping parents.

"Oh, that!" said my father, when he figured out what was bothering me. "That's just the taverns closing." For this was the hour when Czech men cut loose with all the pent-up anger and frustration and expression that they'd repressed on the job, in the streets, and in the crowded housing, where neighbors could listen and inform. This sound was the foam at their mouths that they hadn't been able to drown in the good beer. And this was a society in which men had to stand out and scream on Saturday nights and women worked and an awful lot of people had ulcers or gall bladder or migraine or marital trouble. This was a society where other people could sleep through those pitiful howls as though they were a little night music. This was the society I'd come home to.

In those first few weeks as a free man, I ate too much and drank what I could, but I didn't feel the need to howl. With my parents, I made the rounds of relatives and old family friends. I was treated like a returning war hero, not a disgrace to the proud name of Čapek.

I myself looked up some boyhood friends. But I had difficulty communicating with most of these people who'd been on the outside. Frankly, I found them dull. Even when they didn't let me get a word in edgewise (and those who'd gone into cultural fields were the most overbearing!), I found they had nothing to say to me. We spoke the same Czech words, but we talked in different meanings and laughed at different jokes and pursued different interests. We had no shared experience, no shared truth.

So many of them seemed obsessed with their economic and material worries, ambitions, and achievements that I began to think of them as intellectually crippled. Sometimes I had the feeling that they'd voluntarily lost or wasted those years that I'd been deprived of. I particularly felt this when I met a schoolmate who, while I'd been in prison, had married twice and divorced twice—and all he could talk about was his Saturday-night date and how much it cost to support his families. He was thirty and I was thirty. I was unmarried and unemployed and just starting out in adult life with a criminal record, but I suspected I had a better chance in this world than he did. I also began to suspect that, on the inside for eleven years, I hadn't missed much on the outside—just a few more bad times.

My friend Polda had been freed during my time in Bytíz. The fiancée, for whose sake he'd abstained from loving up the housewife on the project in Příbram, had been waiting for him. Polda was married now. His Jana was worth his vow of chastity and Polda was worthy of her. Linguistically, from Jaundice Brigade English and Spanish and the Greek he'd pretended (to the guards) was Russian, he had moved on to Latin, Sanskrit, and Hebrew—and a dozen foreign embassies in Prague were trying to steal him away from each other as translator, chauffeur, and policy adviser.

I found myself interested in talking about prison. And I could only really talk about it with people who'd been in. We could talk all night about who was in, who was out, and who was dying; who might be coming out in the next amnesty and whether there would be one. On any weekend evening and most other nights, too, I could drift down to the Mánes coffeehouse along the Vltava (or any of a dozen other places around town) and find men with prematurely white or lost hair and badly yellowed teeth (if any were left) smoking a lot and drinking a little as they talked—sometimes about jobs they knew of, but mostly about prison.

There was almost always somebody I'd known, but even if there wasn't, I was welcome. Every now and then, an outsider would appear—sometimes, a secret policeman to check our identity cards and advise us not to congregate. We would disperse, but come back the next night. The management of the café liked us.

More often, the stranger in our midst was a construction boss looking to recruit skilled building workers. In a workers' republic, the work habits of a nation had been deformed, destroyed, and forgotten—but we prisoners, who'd been walled off from civilian vices, were now workmen in great unofficial demand. The State had just begun to restore the decaying landmarks it had inherited or confiscated. I remember a man, who'd just been hired as a bricklayer, letting his new boss buy him a Cognac and saying to him, "Won't it be nice for you to have a former history professor helping you restore that palace?"

I wouldn't have minded a good construction job, but it was out of the question for me. A week after I'd registered with the Prague police (as I was required to do), I received a notice to report for induction into the Czechoslovak Army. I had no wish to defend socialism with a gun. What was more, I knew the Army had "special regiments" with a special slave-labor regimen for "security risks" like myself and student rebels (who suddenly found themselves conscripted over the holidays). The Army would be yet another two-year sentence. Having done eleven, I was unwilling to try for thirteen.

I thought about fleeing the country. But first I went to see my doctor.

He took a thorough inventory of my health and was able to certify, quite honestly, that I had a delicate liver (and should drink very lightly, if at all) and a heart murmur and a slight blockage of my right heart chamber—all related, he was sure, to my bout with jaundice. I was also the first balding male in my family—thanks to my hair's being pulled out by the roots during my first night of interrogation in 1949—but this complaint wasn't grounds for military exemption. The others were.

My dentist pulled nine teeth and then certified that, even after the two years of dental work that needed to be done, my mouth wouldn't meet minimum Army standards. (In most camps, there had been no dentists at all. In Eliáš, one prisoner had been a dentist—but he had not been allowed to practice there, except by night in the barracks. I had felt my teeth disintegrating and the process was not completely arrested in civilian life. I am now down to the last five of my own.)

These two certificates kept me out of the Army, but they also disqualified me from any physically strenuous employment. Even if I landed a strong man's job, if the Army found out, I could be reclassified and inducted.

Thus, my sphere of employment was limited largely to jobs ordinarily done by women or disabled men. Twice a week, I'd report to my District Manpower Office and be handed two to four cards with a job opening on each. Several times, I qualified and was hired on the spot—until I mentioned (for my employers would find out sooner or later) that I had a prison past. Once, at a book-publishing cooperative that needed a warehouse clerk, the personnel officer said, "No matter. You start tomorrow."

When I showed up next morning, however, the warehouse foreman had a message that I should report back to the downtown office. There, the personnel man was looking sheepish. "I'm very sorry," he said, "but we can't employ you. We have a security officer who's hired for us by the party, and he says we can't have any C.I.C. agents penetrating our stockroom."

He gave me the address of a personnel officer at another publishing enterprise who might be just as sympathetic and even more flexible "because he's also the acting security officer over there." I rushed over by tram—and the conductor who punched my ticket was my first Pankrác cellmate, Father Houžvička. "They won't let me go back into the clergy," he said, after we'd compared notes and I'd admired his uniform, "but, yes, I'm still in costume."

The second publishing official seemed almost as impressed by my prison past as by my bookselling apprenticeship at Linhart's. "Of course," he said dryly, "that diploma you have from a bourgeois publishing school is worse than *no* qualifications at all. But I'll take a chance on you. How would you like to work with fifty women?"

I said that would be just fine, though it turned out it really wasn't. But, next day, I rejoined the book trade—as a stock boy carrying and loading bins of diaries and appointment calendars (some imprinted with a Communist slogan for each day) through a bindery where fifty of the coarsest and ugliest cows in creation glued the bindings together in the hope that they might not come apart for a year. These women were all middle-aged, somehow all married, mostly Communist party members, and, even if they didn't reek with the perfume of glue, I would have found them offensive. In all my life, I had not heard so much explicit talk about men, not to mention men-and-women, as I did in my first week on that job. As I moved back and forth on my errands, at least one of them would comment loudly that I didn't wiggle my ass when I walked and another would shout back knowingly that I saved it for after hours.

Prison seemed to lend me a certain sex appeal—as though making love to me would be, by definition, illicit love. Some of my co-workers even seemed to have some knowledge of the jails.

"That Čapek moves around here like he's the cock-of-the-walk!" one of them would proclaim.

"You mean *cat*-of-the-walk!" another would screech. "The cat walks of Bory!"

That particular time, I snarled, "Go back to your cathouse, Granny." But, usually, I just ignored them, though they contended I always acknowledged them with a blush—which is to my credit.

Fortunately, my employer had underestimated the job. There were fifty-one females—and the fifty-first was Marta, the only woman there who didn't stink of glue. She was twenty-one and wore her brown hair in a pert bun. She was not unduly bright and not at all demanding—exactly the kind of pretty young thing with whom a man just out of prison should have his first affair. Morals had been such in postliberation Prague that one could now, one generation later, safely presume, without bothering to ask, that a girl over fifteen was not a virgin.

Marta had worked many months amidst all that smutty talk, so she knew what was expected of her the first time that legendary uncaged stud Čapek asked her out. When I brought her home, her two brothers went next door to sleep with their parents. I suspect six or eight ears were listening through that thin wall while I unleashed my manhood for the first time since Příbram—and came up impotent!

I tried several times again with Marta, but the result was the same. She tried harder and harder—and even blamed herself. No matter how often I assured her (and tried to reassure myself) that a man in prison gets out of training, out of practice, and out of touch, Marta wanted to try, try again—even at work, in case that could excite me more. Just what those fifty lecherous biddies would have needed! They'd have drowned in history's first Marxist-Leninist mass orgasm. Oh, they were enough to make any man impotent or even homosexual! And I will forever love Marta a little because, during our time of torment in her bed, she never confided her frustration to anyone in the bindery. I know she kept my secret. If she hadn't, I would never have heard the end of it.

One Saturday afternoon, without consciously remembering how I'd arrived there, I found myself standing alone on a staircase. It was in the building where my old girl friend Božena and her mother used to live. Božena's mother had died, but Božena had kept the apartment in her own name and I knew, from a passing mention by my mother, that Božena now lived there with her little daughter most of the time. They had a place in the country in her husband's name—and he spent most of his time there, but visited Prague on weekends. Even under Communism-*cum*-housing-shortage, a couple could live quite well and quite legally in two homes.

"One day you will visit me, Karel, dear."

She and I used to stand on this staircase for a long hour or sometimes two, saying good-night before she went in to her mother, who always waited up. We'd talked and kissed and necked and petted—and once I'd even had an embarrassment inside my jeans—but that was as far as we'd gone. Now I found myself standing there again, just remembering.

After an hour, the familiar door on the next landing opened and it was Božena who stuck her head out. At thirty, the pretty girl I'd wooed was now even more attractive—"a nice piece of woman" is how we'd have described her, longingly but respectfully, in prison—and her dark blond hair had turned a rich reddish-brown. She didn't show the least trace of surprise at seeing me. She just said, "Oh, it's you, Karel. Come on in." When I was through the door, she added, "I'd heard from poor Karel Štěpán's mother that you were out and I was going to drop around to ask how you were." (My parents were getting ready to celebrate their tenth anniversary on the waiting list for a phone.)

Božena introduced me to her five-year-old daughter—very much like her and clearly her closest companion. I stayed for coffee and cake. We talked about prison and people we both knew. I called her the following Monday and we met several times that week. She never talked about her marriage or her husband. By the time I met him two weekends later, Božena and I, at long last, were intimate—and I was no longer impotent.

Consummation of an old desire had overwhelmed a new barricade. From the first, I proved sufficient unto the woman I used to love. Now I marveled at how a relationship that was so gently romantic when it was interrupted eleven years earlier could be so violently passionate—though it all made sense.

"This is only the first time, Karel, dear. One day you will visit me."

I liked Božena's husband. A researcher in an agricultural institute, he was also a skilled technician and farmhand who could thrive in any world—and a daredevil weekend motorcycle racer. Upon meeting him I could only wonder that Božena had resisted him for three or four summers. And, though he could sweep almost any girl off her feet, he was not a skirt-chaser or a drinker or a man with any vices—just a faithful husband, good provider, and a much better catch than Karel Čapek, ex-convict.

From a man's point of view, he was a nice guy to know. But I could see that he was also a very private person who led his own life. He loved his wife and daughter. He listened to every trivial or important thing they said. But he never asked them anything and he never consulted them about anything he was going to do or they were going to do together. He simply told them his decisions and that was it.

Now that I knew him, I still coveted his wife, but I could no longer bring myself to go see her. Even if I hadn't liked him, he was now a real man we were betraying and not an unknown quantity. A few days later, with much fanfare and bad-natured railery, I was called to the phone at the bindery. It was Božena calling to ask why I wasn't seeing her. I told her, quite honestly, that "I can't talk here" and promised to come around that night. When I hung up, I noticed someone standing quietly in the third row of my otherwise raucous gallery. It was Marta—who hadn't given up on making a man out of me and who hadn't been given any after-work opportunity to meet the new me.

"Karel, dear. One day you will visit me." "Many, many times."

That night, I went around to Božena's to tell her that I didn't want to make up for lost time, at age thirty, by having an affair with a married woman—not even the one I might have married in an earlier life. She said she understood—and then I spent the night with her. And, once again, we were going out every night to a restaurant or theater and I was sleeping over at her flat and going to work from there. My parents hardly saw me, but didn't complain. They knew where I was and I think they even approved.

Naturally, Božena's husband found out about us. He rang me up at work one day to tell me he knew everything and he didn't want there to be anything else for him to know about. Before I could say anything in reply, he hung up. That was his way, I knew.

Again, I stayed away from Božena. Again, she called me up at the bindery. Again, I went back to say good-bye and stayed —and stayed.

One Monday, her husband—in full cyclist's regalia and with three other men dressed like him (in their brown-leather jackets, they looked much like a secret police raid on wheels) —buzzed up to the bindery and parked in the loading area. The husband and his three friends stormed through the bindery, where I wasn't hard to find. He pointed me out to them: "That's him! Make sure you remember his face while he has it." Then he turned to me and said, "You'd better be careful crossing the street." I started to promise I would, but he warned me —in the presence of everybody present—that if I ever went near his wife again my services wouldn't be worth having.

He gave the most virile rendition of cuckoldry I ever hope to see. But, before he and his storm troopers (who were actually, I imagine, just nice young country cyclists) could make their exit, a taxi drew up. Božena had intercepted her husband— and, after ascertaining that I was unharmed, she pitched a raging quarrel with him. She bawled him out for never listening to her, hardly living with her, and demanding chastity of an undesired female. He gave it right back, telling her that in his house, the man was still the boss, that she drove him away, that he didn't think I was the first, and that she'd damn well better keep her fucking chastity or he'd take away their daughter. While Marta watched in flushed silence and my Greek chorus of fifty witches took sides (some of them even took bets), Božena announced that she should have waited for me even after he got her pregnant. And he dished it right back by saying that I just wanted to fuck her, not marry her.

With that observation—which, I recognized, had more truth than untruth in it—all eyes turned to me. Almost unconsciously, but very decisively, I reached out for little Marta, put one arm around the sweet young thing, and said, "I don't know what all this commotion is about. *She's* my steady girl friend."

Božena burst into tears. Her husband's friends tried to comfort her and the five of them spilled back out to the loading zone. I was relieved to see Božena ride off with her arm around her husband's waist on his motorcycle. Back among the biddies, someone brought out some warm beer—which went so well with the smell of glue that I almost puked on the spot—and we all celebrated Marta's and my "secret romance."

That night, she and I consummated it. And, even as I made love to Marta hot and heavy, I couldn't help thinking—in a cool corner of my otherwise inflamed mind—that, in so short a time as a free agent, I'd managed to acquire just as complicated a love life as any civilian I knew.

My mother told me something a few months later that I couldn't believe. But it made me go see Božena one last time. It was true. She was pregnant.

"It's not *your* child," she assured me. "It's *his* child."

"How do you know?" I wondered.

"It's possible," she said, "so he accepts it as his."

"What if it looks like me?"

"He's made up his mind. It's his."

I didn't want to blurt anything out, so I chose my words very carefully when I could find them: "I've always loved you. I still love you. Will you marry me?"

Then Božena said three terrible things to me, each of which made perfect sense:

"He and I are giving up our city apartment before our baby is born. I don't want you ever to come trying to find out about me." And: "I don't want you to marry me for the same reason I married him." The third thing she said was: "So long, Karel."

The affair with Marta dropped of its own weight when my military eligibility expired and I could afford to do a man's work. My friend Polda found me employment trucking fruits and vegetables, whenever there were any, on the full-time payroll of the State Gardens. But I needed a valid driver's license, so I took my pre-1948 one into the Traffic Bureau in the Square of Charles IV.

The clerk held the obsolete license gingerly, like an antique, and said, "Where did you get that?"

"Right here," I assured him. I knew that there was a new

form now and new standards that were less severe, but required you to attend several weeks of State driving school before you could qualify. And my new job was available right away, not several weeks later.

"The time for exchanging these was ten years ago," he said. "Where have you been?"

"Pankrác, Bory, Old Eliáš, New Eliáš, Our Lady, Camp Brotherhood, Camp Equality, Vojna, and Bytíz."

He listened respectfully and asked just one question: "You weren't sent to all those places for reckless driving, were you?"

Laughing, I said, "No, I was a State criminal." Whereupon he stamped and issued me a new license with no fee and no driving school. "You've had quite enough schooling, son," he said. "There's such a thing as being overeducated."

The job with the State Gardens was a pleasant year that gave me a chance to reacquaint myself with my native city. Then I found a better job, also driving a truck, with ŘEMPO, a large wholesale housewares cooperative. One summer Thursday in 1963, I delivered a shipment to an office and asked one of the secretaries, who had a pack of Bulgarian cigarettes lying on her desk, "Mind if I borrow one?"

"Be my guest," she said, "but please don't give it back when you've smoked it."

That made me look at her twice—and then many times thereafter, for this was Vlasta, who became my wife. From the start, I liked her style and I liked her face, which was (if you'll pardon the expression) open, frank and friendly.* Later, I even learned to live with her sharp tongue.

I asked her if she liked to swim and she said "Where?" We made a date to meet on Saturday at eleven at a spot along the Vltava that even a child could find. I drew a map to make it crystal clear. But one of our crystals must have been a factory

---

* "Open," "frank," "friendly," are words that fell into disrepute when they became the language of official Communist communiqués. When heads of State meet and the discussion is merely "open, frank, and friendly," Big Trouble is looming. When it is "warm, cordial, and comradely," it means the Big Power is being obeyed.

reject because I cooled my heels on the *right* bank of the Vltava until, toward 12:30, I thought to scan the *wrong* bank with a pair of binoculars. Across the river, I saw a nice and faintly familiar figure reading the leading Czech women's weekly, which is also called *Vlasta*.

I swam across and Vlasta pretended to be annoyed. "I want my cigarette back," she said—but she was already unpacking the picnic hamper she'd prepared.

We were married in the Old Town Hall of Prague a few months later. I moved out of my parents' apartment and into Vlasta's parents' apartment in the suburb of Odolena Voda. Unlike most Prague newlyweds, we didn't have to live with our relatives for at least the first two years; nor, despite the housing shortage, did we have to apply for a spot on the eight-year waiting list for a flat. (My criminal record might have disqualified me anyway.) Vlasta's parents had built a country cottage just a few miles out in the woods from Odolena Voda. As soon as Vlasta had confided that she was hoping to marry me, they'd begun making arrangements to put their apartment into *her* name and they themselves moved into their country place. People still managed to look after their children and pass on their property even when the State owned everything and everybody.

When Vlasta was expecting our first child, we gave *my* parents' address in the city because that made her eligible to have the baby in Podolí, the most modern hospital in Prague. And when, on August 23, 1964, we had a baby boy, I named him Karel Čapek, too. At thirty-four, amidst the anxiety and relief of fatherhood, I felt a great burst of joy: even *if* those years in prison were wasted, *which I think not*, I hadn't missed out on much or lost out on anything that mattered dearly to me. There was even an echo of Pankrác prison, a few blocks away from Podolí hospital, as I came walking on air through the vestibule of expectant fathers and they asked me, "What did you get?" But, instead of their wanting to know "years or death?" it was "boy or girl?"

Vlasta went back to work at her office three months after little Karel was born. Her mother came over every morning to bring up the baby. The Czech *babička* (grandma) has always been a major figure in the family, but never more so than under Communism: the mothers all work and the pensioned-off grandmothers do the baby-sitting. Some of them tranquilize the child by popping a *knedlík* (dumpling) into his mouth every time he opens his mouth to cry. But my mother-in-law practiced freedom of expression and young Karel was an articulate adversary of mine by the time he was three. At that age, he had sharp competition from his baby sister, Danka (short for Daniela), who was born April 30, 1967, with a silver tongue in her mouth. Both my son and I rejoiced, for different reasons, that he would not inherit my fate as an only child— nor the terrible responsibility that went with it, in my case.

Both Vlasta and parenthood introduced me to friends who'd never been in jail, but with whom I could communicate. I came to recognize that, while Polda and Pelcl and Snapshot and I had been struggling for survival in ivory towers run by Brabeces and Tom Thumbs, thousands of people like Vlasta and her friends had isolated themselves in work, family, solitude, or just some small but unmolested niche of research or craftsmanship. And many of them, despite the drawbacks of living right inside the society that oppressed them as well as us, had managed to arrive at some of the same truths we'd worked out in our relative solitude.

Marveling that *they* hadn't had to spend eleven years in jail to get there, I experienced soaring elation buffeted by letdown from the thought that I just might have wasted those years, after all. Still, it was broadening as well as comforting to have friends who understood me and yet whose Greatest Single Truth was not eleven lost years. Some of their concerns were becoming mine, too: the daily battles with shortages; the impossible prices (for a new Škoda car, four years' wages—payable in full upon application—and a five-year wait); and filtering the truth out of whatever you were told. I began to feel like one of them.

Truth was beginning to assert itself, though it was not yet strong enough to prevail. The number of prisoners released back into the system's bloodstream in the 1960s was changing the society's complexion and quickening the flow of truth. The Russians hadn't bothered to notice, for they had bled our land of its uranium and now they had what they wanted. A good part of Czechoslovakia's underpinnings and resources were now in Russia. Perhaps only those of us who'd slaved to fill the trains, going east full and coming west empty every single day, had any idea of the immensity of the loot. But *we knew*—and we and others were telling!

It began to surface in the press in the mid-sixties—even in *Rudé Právo*. Not on the front page, not on the editorial page, but in the sports and amusement pages. You started to read the paper from back to front. When Jiří Suchý, the Semafor Theatre's co-star and co-author, baptized his newborn son, Kubik, in a Catholic church, we recognized that matter-of-fact little news item as something more than promotion or show business or even religion; it was protest. (You could still get married in church, but you also *had* to have a civil ceremony.) Vlasta and I went to the Semafor, where Suchý's partner, Jiří Šlitr, spoke with a nasal whine that sounded more like Antonín Novotný than the dictator himself: "Please excuse the lighting. We have ten reflectors—nine are from the West and one is from the East. The one from the East doesn't work. Still, we like the one from the East."

The theater was filled with nice young couples laughing, cheering, and stamping their feet for more. Whenever my prison buddies (graying and balding like myself) complained about the younger generation, as they often did, I'd send them to the Semafor. And I'd remind them that there were better things for the world to revolve around than the 1950s in the camps or 1948 or the war. If the future lay with *these* kids, it boded well for us, too, so why knock them?

My employer, ŘEMPO, had a warehouse and offices in the Old Town of Prague. Across the street, the Ministry of Interior maintained a small branch office. One noon, in the mid-1960s, I was parked there in my small ŘEMPO van, windows rolled down, when I saw a familiar figure strut out of the ministry's little annex. Even seeing him up the block in dumpy, slightly baggy civilian clothes, I could recognize the squat little shape of the former commandant at Camp Equality, Tom Thumb, alias Paleček, alias Dvořák.

His route took him toward my van. I watched him in my left side view mirror and I have to admit that my heart began to pound faster the way it always had whenever Tom Thumb entered the picture back at Camp Equality. If anything, since I'd seen him last, the man seemed to have shrunk, but not the fixed smile that had been his trademark. I rejoiced momentarily when Tom Thumb vanished from my mirror (had I obliterated him through an act of will?), but now he was at my open window, peering in at me. He would, of course, always know when eyes were upon him.

His own green eyes flickered over me like a file scanner: was I friend or foe? In his case, I don't suppose it was ever a hard question to answer. The eyes' dim sparkle lost what little luster they had; the smile turned wry. But he didn't flinch. Nor did I. We stared at each other for a good minute—our faces quite close, but neither of us seeming to breathe. Neither of us broke the silence. But, when a shadow of uncertainty crossed his face, he was the one who turned aside and walked back in the direc-tinon from which he'd come. I wanted to drive away, to run away, to escape from him, from my memories of him, and from his surveillance—but I didn't budge, even when he paused to make a mental note of my license number.

Tom Thumb became a fleeting image in my mirror again and I found myself staring at the glass long after he'd vanished into his building. For days, I awaited the repercussions and re-played the scene in my head. Should I have broken the silence to talk with him about the good old times? Or should I have run him over or at least knocked him into the earth where so many of his victims now lay? No. If I'd had anything to say or do to him, it would have been to ask, more in sorrow than in passion, the greatest riddle of the ages: "Why?"

I never heard from Tom Thumb again or from anyone else about the encounter. But I told others about it—for, whenever former prisoners met, they exchanged news about the fates of their fellows *and* the careers of their captors.

Quite a few prisoners had settled in Příbram as construction workers upon their release. Their families had died or deserted them—and they had nowhere else to go; in Příbram, they had made contacts and earned the respect of the construction bosses. On Sunday visits to old prison friends in Příbram, I would sometimes go off by myself with a telescope and sit on a hill between Vojna and Bytíz. I would scan this attractive, wooded, but hostile terrain—so rugged in winter that this part of our country was called "Czechoslovak Siberia"—and wonder how the earth in which prisoners had sweated and toiled for so many long years could be left unmarked. All the camps had been dismantled by 1965. I had to see for myself that nothing was left—that our Greatest Single Truth had indeed yielded to Nature. Oh, yes! Where we'd stamped and shivered in the winter cold, grass grew. Now the corridors of barbed wire and the guard towers of wood were all gone. One saw nothing but beautiful country and I rejoiced, but the idea that nothing was left there of our suffering struck me as not quite fair.

Years later, in a work of "fiction" called *Blind Mirror,* by an ex-prisoner named Jan Beneš,* I read his "Concluding Note: The Generation of Leaves," and recognized that someone else had shared this emotion:

Nine months after loving a child is born, a little miracle, an endless age, nine months, that's nothing, nine months, that's 270 days, do you know how a convict feels who has 270 days still to serve . . .? You know nothing, he's waiting to be born, 270 days needed for the bearing of a child, my God, that's a secret, a biological secret the technical parameters of which are known to us, but can anyone explain to us the technical parameters of those nine months of nerve-calming routine, that's what I should like to know, that's what I should like to know, such a joke, 270 days, what's that to fine fellows like us, imagine 2,700 days and then what about 3,650 days or 7,305 days, imagine how many people will have been born in the meantime, and learned to walk and live and talk, and also to steal and all the rest of it, and everything that will have happened, for

* Translated into English by Jan Herzfeld; published in America, 1971, by Grossman Publishers (an Orion Press Book), New York City.

everything passes, the trees grow green, if we're lucky we can even watch them, the trees put forth leaves, and the leaves turn yellow and fall, while we cultivate bronchitis, our chief concern that there shall be something to smoke, something to acquire that's more or less forbidden, that we won't have to slave too hard, that they won't find anything for which they can punish us, for everything passes, only time once halted does not pass, only the bronchitis gets worse, and nothing has any lasting direction, everything shifts, movement, movement, movement without any aim, movement for its own sake, movement enclosed in a narrow space under lock and key, while the trees grow green, and the rats scuttle out of the latrines, and we kill them, and the rats kill one another, rats are like people, rats are omnipresent, and the trees still grow green, once, twice, ten times over, the trees never fail to grow green again, and we shall see them, and the time comes, if we're lucky, once, twice. . . .

In one year's sports coverage of the annual Peace Race, a passing allusion to Camp Bytíz's no longer being there to camouflage got past the censors—and, while it wasn't signed, we knew that one of our alumni was working as a reporter or editor. Soon, many little grievances and protests and tiptoeings-onto-the-record had spread to the front pages. All of a sudden, you could find people, even *aparatchiks*, disagreeing and even disrespecting, putting it in writing and signing it! While there were sporadic purges of editorial staffs and the party apparatus, one no longer needed to quake when some old Stalinist, out of habit, would point to you in an argument and call you a "class enemy." In earlier days, those two words could mean jail unless your Communist credentials and connections were much better than his. Now one would shrug and simply say to one's accusers, "You'll have to prove *that* to *me*."

If you put all this together, you could spot a trend that, if allowed to continue, would become a tidal wave. Prisoners in particular watched the barometers closely. We would say to each other, "I don't know how long it can last." We wondered whether the giant at the top would be driven berserk and we feared this—for we knew that we would be the first to be blamed, the first to be trampled. But perhaps the giant was tired? Or in a deep sleep? Or could it be that the giant was dead? The intellectuals and the students (quite a few camp alumni were already in their ranks or among their mentors) would poke and kick the giant a little to see. Novotný was vulnerable and better men might follow. After all, we told each other, even in Russia, a Khrushchev succeeded Stalin—for a while. But, every now and then, Novotný thrashed—and our probing toe retreated.

Our country, which was lagging behind the poorest nations of the West and even some of its Communist neighbors, could not possibly catch up economically at its two-step-forward-one-step-back rhythm. When the economic growth rate actually stagnated, Novotný turned to a professor who'd been in the same German concentration camp with him, Ota Šik. True, when Dr. Šik's medicine proved too strong for President Novotný's taste, he changed doctors and tried to disown Šik. But one of Šik's reforms, which actually took effect in 1967, changed my life. This was the reorganization of the Prague Municipal Taxi Enterprise in such a way that, after a year, its losses were not just lowered, but turned into a profit—so the rates were lowered! This was done by licensing a limited number of private cabbies to cruise the streets of Prague and even use certain municipal taxi stands, but only at nonpeak hours.

With all my antennae out, private cab-driving sounded like the first possibility of real freedom since my release from prison. As a free agent, I could work for myself within the system—legally. I invested 44,000 crowns—two years' take-home pay for me!—in a two-year-old, secondhand, Polish-made four-door Warszawa sedan.

Warszawa, as we called this new acquisition, became my third child: balky and a little bit retarded, the most difficult member of our family, yet the one around whom our future revolved. If Warszawa took sick, as she did at least twice a month, then there was no living with Father! Vlasta and her mother had to give little Karel and baby Danka that much more attention and loving, for I was sitting up with ailing Warszawa day and night—or shopping for help to doctor her.

One morning when Warszawa was enjoying an exceptional spell of good health, I took her for a fifteen-mile outing to the

town of Říčany, a small town whose Community Services Cooperative (the grab-bag collective for nationalizing all services
from the lone barber shop to the fleet of four taxis) had recently been authorized to expand to twenty-two taxis. This had
been the first part of making Šik's reforms legal; the second
part was authorizing any licensed taxi to operate anywhere in
the Republic. This was the golden key to Prague for the twenty-
two cabbies of Říčany and dozens of others who were joining
cab cooperatives that were mushrooming in other outlying
communities.

In Říčany, where there was still a vacancy, I paid the equivalent of a month's ŘEMPO wages and—with very few questions
asked—a week later, I was licensed to doll up Warszawa with
a new hat that said "Taxi" and which lit up at night. I painted
her scaly sides with the dotted lines that signified "You can
call me a cab."

I gave notice at ŘEMPO, where I'd been earning good money
as a truck driver—and had to stay on the job only another
month. (If no replacement can be found, you can be compelled to remain six months after giving notice.) Meanwhile,
I started to take Warszawa into town and drive her around for
hire at night—because, from the moment I'd joined the Říčany
cooperative, I'd committed myself to paying, in taxes to the
municipality of Říčany, a monthly sum equal to my month's
earnings at ŘEMPO. Anything I earned *above* that, I could
keep.

Every man remembers his first woman. Every taxi driver
remembers his first fare. Mine was a woman in her fifties—a
brand-new widow leaving the hospital where her husband had
just died of cancer. It almost hurt me to charge her. But when
I calculated the amount, she had the presence of mind to observe, "That's surprisingly little."

I explained my calculations according to mileage plus a
two-crown* "night differential" surcharge. Then she said,

---

* At that time (1967), the "official" value of a crown was 14 cents
(which is approximately what spending it meant to a Czech); its value
to Western tourists (who are given a 225-percent bonus when exchanging their hard currency with the State Bank) was 6 cents; and its value
on the widespread black market then was under 3 cents.

"Even when I come back—I mean, came back—by day, without any 'night differential,' it cost me a few crowns more. You're not doing me any special favor, are you, young man?"

"No, ma'am," I said. "Besides, if I charged you any more than that, you'd have every right to complain and then I'd lose my license."

She was still perplexed: "Can it be that your rate is so low because your cab isn't one of those black Volgas?"

I told her that those were city cabs and I confided that, even allowing for waiting time, I'd heard their meters were hopped up. Then I explained that I was a private cabbie and that the only taxi meters available in Czechoslovakia were allocated to the municipal services of the big cities—and even *they* didn't have enough of them! So *we* private drivers had to be on our best behavior and compute honestly.

"Private taxi drivers?" she said. "What will they think of next?"

I remarked that she probably wouldn't have much trouble with widowhood if she could take such an interest in other people at such a time. And she replied, "Well, right now, it's a blessed relief for which I've been preparing for quite a while." Then, even in the dim midnight street illumination, I could see her face age as she added, "Besides, I don't think the reality of it has hit me yet."

I wished her well and she asked me for my address. Two days later, I received in the mail a black-bordered death announcement—adorned with a hand-written request for me to drive, "at the going rate," in the funeral procession.

My shabby Warszawa looked out of place in the convoy of shiny black Volgas from the Municipal Enterprise, but I was honored when the widow insisted on riding in my car. "He's the driver who took me home when Jirka died," she told her son and her sister, "and he's an honest man."

I went in to watch the funeral service, too, at the crematorium. When I came out, my three passengers had to take one of the city cabs, whose drivers stood around grinning innocently at poor Warszawa's four slashed tires.

The municipal cabbies had declared war on the private

drivers. That I already knew. Until Ota Šik came along, a salaried job with the city cab service had been a posh plum reserved for party members, informers, ex-cops, and secret policemen spying overtime for the tips. City cabbies had lorded it over their fares and chosen their passengers in accordance with their needs. They'd had many opportunities for vice and adventure—contacts with tourists and "arrangements" with prostitutes and hotel doormen—and they still had. Which was why nobody with a criminal record, like myself, would be let in, and non-Communists, like my father, had been eased out of the Municipal Service.

Now a bunch of opportunists and even ex-convicts had not only muscled in, but were pocketing tips *and* profits themselves! What would Ota Šik think up next? Twice, Warszawa and I were forced off the road, and once we were almost sideswiped, by sleek black Moskvas and Tatras. And, more often than I cared to count, bullies in city cabs chased us away from stands we had every right to use. One of them, ordering me away, even flashed his secret-police credentials at me.

I never fought back hard, for Warszawa's sake and because, despite these troubles, we were making a good living. Driving nights and weekends, I was earning twice as much as ever— and spending much of the day getting to know my children. My passengers were, more often than not, interesting and friendly. Some of them marveled at my low rates and, when I assured them that they were the same with all us privateers, they often said, "Hereafter, I'm going to use only you people." And a lot of people began hailing us just a block or two from taxi stands where three or four city cabs were lined up. Some people even walked a block out of their way to hail us. They liked us better—not only as a symbol of freer enterprise, but also because they'd always disliked the city cab service. I knew what they meant when they talked about "running meter disease": you'd phone for a radio-dispatched city cab and, even if it arrived in five minutes, there would already be fifteen or twenty crowns on the meter (instead of the basic initial three crowns) when he drew up to your front door. If he gave any explanation at all, it was: "Well, I had to come a long way."

But the passengers knew damn well what had really happened: when he'd collected the fare from his previous passenger a block or two away, the driver simply hadn't shut off the meter.

Jaroslav Aim was finally released in 1964: one of the first into jail and one of the last out. I'd kept the contact through his mother and stepfather, whose tavern in Prague I visited from time to time. After Aim's release, I saw him several times a year. He was no longer an obsession with me, but his presence still exerted a certain charm and fascination. He already had a girl friend on his arm the first time we met as free men. She was just a housewife who'd felt his sex appeal and left home and husband and daughter for him, but he made one feel as though he'd brought along the Virgin Mary. When I teased Aim about his way with women, he didn't laugh, but said tolerantly, "You really know nothing about me and women, Karel."

The next time I visited the town where he was working as a laborer, there was a different girl living with him. And, a year later, he married yet another girl. His bride's name was Lida, but she was no swan—just a rather cowlike country girl who'd been a servant, even under Communism, and who, unlike most peasants, wasn't too bright. I felt slightly ill at ease with her, perhaps because she insisted on calling me "sir" or "Mr. Karel." But she'd clearly devoted herself to serving Aim. He, in turn, acted as though he was doing social work by marrying her. Theirs was a union I was sure would last as long as *he* wanted it to. Aim and Lida were not so much happily married as married happily-ever-after.

In her eighth or ninth month of pregnancy, Lida was about to foal when there was heavy bleeding and she lost the baby. Aim was grieving when I saw him. But I felt his sorrow was less for Lida or the lost foal than for himself. He had squandered his immortal sperm. Of course, he made it clear, he would "do it again"—and I could almost, but not quite, hear him add "for her."

They did have a baby the next time—with some bisexual

name like René, which may be why I can't remember whether it's a boy or girl. I do remember I had to ask Lida because, as usual, I wasn't getting any concrete information from Aim when I questioned him. I also remember that the baby, alas, looked more like the mother than the father.

Many people have written about what happened in Prague in 1967 and 1968. Let me start by telling you, from personal experience, how fast the times changed from one year to the next:

In late 1967, soon after I'd become one of the few semi-private entrepreneurs in Communist Czechoslovakia, somebody made an anonymous call to the police. The message was to the effect that a convicted capitalist agent, former State prisoner number 8210, was back in the free-enterprise business. A secret policeman came out to Odolena Voda one morning and almost frightened my mother-in-law to death by asking when I'd be back. She tried to intercept me all over town, but missed me all over town. Minutes after I returned home, the same secret policeman appeared and invited me to ride with him down to the police headquarters on Bartholomew Street. There, where I'd first begun to shed my hair and my teeth back in 1949, I was asked what I could do to refute their anonymous tip.

"Nothing," I said. "All I can offer you is proof that I'm legally entitled to be making a living the way I do."

They examined my papers, made a few phone calls, and grudgingly conceded that I had every right. They didn't even offer me a ride back to Odolena Voda, so I had to flag down a private cab.

In April of 1968, the same secret policeman appeared at my door.

"Another anonymous tip?" I guessed, almost cheerfully.

"Same woman, same message," he said wearily. "And don't be angry, but I'm only bothering you because my new chief and I were wondering if you have any idea who is doing this to you? If so, we'll go around and put the fear of God into her.

She's violating your human rights and we're trying to eradicate this kind of informing."

Another 1967-vs.-1968 experience: with a family and responsibilities as well as a good job, I no longer thought about escaping to the West. But, in 1967, it seemed possible to consider a vacation trip to neighboring Austria, so I applied. My application was denied because I had been in prison.

Already, in 1967, I felt free enough to write a letter pointing out: "Everybody knows now that the sentences of the State Courts at the time I was convicted were cruel and unjust, and I am surprised that such a decision could be made at this late a date." I received a reply inviting me down to police headquarters to talk about my complaint. A fat young lady listened sympathetically and then said, "But, under the law, you'll have to wait until 1970—when you've been out of prison for ten years—before you can apply to have your crime expunged from the record."

I bristled at the word "crime." But, before I could argue, the fat young lady murmured, "Don't quote me, but just keep applying no matter how many times you're told no."

It didn't matter that much to me, so I neglected to apply again. But, suddenly, in the Spring of 1968, without applying, I received the visa I'd been denied when I'd applied.

Vlasta then applied for herself and the children. Even though at least one member of a family was supposed to remain behind as a hostage to insure safe return by the others, all three of them received visas within a week. Our exit visas were valid for one trip out any time during the next year. But we were enjoying the first half of 1968 in the Czechoslovak Socialist Republic too much to want to go anywhere else for even a week. I'd always felt close—for eleven years, too close!—to whatever was in the air. But now I felt particularly lucky to be my own man, a free agent able to move around the Prague Spring, when it finally happened in January of 1968.

A cabdriver's perspective can sometimes be limited. In your country, judging by the times I've been a passenger (and therefore a listener) in a taxi, the 1964 national election was rigged and Barry Goldwater was really elected President. In Prague, I have to admit that we cabbies knew nothing about this unknown Slovak *aparatchik* named Alexander Dubček, who made off with President Novotný's other hat—first secretary of the Communist party—over the Christmas-New Year's 1967–1968 holiday hiatus.

A prisoner's philosophy is that the more things change among our jailers, the more they remain the same for us—and sometimes they grow worse. My own personal prejudice was that *any* Communist of Dubček's rank had to be presumed evil until proven otherwise, which hadn't happened yet. To my friends, I simply said, "Another bad man—this one from Slovakia." When one of our friends said, "But Novotný was so bad, it can only get better," I said, "You weren't in prison. There we learned that isn't so."

By January, however, picking up fares near the party headquarters and the special hotel for out-of-town party dignitaries, I started perceiving that quite a few people who ordinarily rode official limousines were now taking taxis.

One winter day, a fat man—whose face I'd seen once or twice in the party press—flagged me down near party headquarters. Most uncharacteristically in our "classless" society, he took the seat next to me, up front. It was obvious from the beginning he wanted to talk.

"Just drive in the direction of Krč," he told me, "and tell me what you think of Dubček."

A fairly honest answer also seemed to be the safest one: "I don't know anything about him. But, from his picture, he looks as though he could be a good man."

"Too good!" the man spluttered. "He might have made a good priest, but he shouldn't be in politics!"

The best way to draw out such a man is to pretend to agree with him—particularly when you know a bit less than he does. So I said, "I suppose there's no place for saints in this world."

That's all he needed to unleash a tirade against a man whose presence I started to feel inside my Warszawa. "The real saints of this world are people like me," my portly passenger said.

"You'd be surprised how much I've sacrificed in my life for the good of the party." He then recited an autobiography that was impressive, if one-sided, before going on to say, "Oh, I knew what was going on in the nineteen-fifties! And, if I broke a rule or two then, it was because the party told me to. I even cried once or twice back then, when it was happening. So now this man from Slovakia comes out of nowhere and *he* has tears in his eyes when he talks of the fifties and his tears are newer than mine, so he's *in* and I'm on the way *out!* What is there about that Slovak that makes men believe in him?"

I would have thrown the fat bastard out of my cab without slowing down if I wasn't afraid of him—if I hadn't been so fascinated that I wanted to hear more. So I went on "agreeing" with him—in my own fashion: "As Lenin says, you can fool all of the people some of the time and some of the people all of the time."

"Exactly!" he said. "And we're going to have a lot of changes to make, work to do, work to *undo*, when this insanity ends." A little farther on, he felt secure enough to give me his address. But he asked me to let him out a few blocks before there, "because if it gets all around the other villas that I don't have my limousine anymore, I might lose my villa, too." I could sympathize openly (while hoping and surmising he *would* lose his villa, which he soon did) to the extent that he remarked to me, "Not many people, even my colleagues, would speak out like you do. How good it is that, even in terrible times like these, there are a few of us left."

"Well," I said, "as the good book says, 'Good men still live.' "*

When I spoke it, I was just beginning to think about this re-

---

* A *Good Man Still Lives* (*Dobrý člověk ještě žije*) was the Czech title of Romain Rolland's 1923 novel, *Colas Breugnon*, which achieved immense popularity in Czechoslovakia between two world wars and, said with plural implications, became the Czech expression of thanksgiving. Because the expression has the status of a prayer, the Czech-language translation of the modern Karel Čapek's memoir—to be published by the émigré house of 68 Publishers Toronto—will be specially entitled "I Am the Other Karel Čapek."

markable Comrade Dubček. Any man who made such enemies so soon couldn't be all bad.

When we reached our destination, my fat passenger tipped me handsomely, shook my hand, and said resonantly, "Yes, good men still live. And it's a pleasure to meet a man who has the courage of his convictions."

That was the cue I was waiting for. "Oh, I beg your pardon," I said evenly, "but I have only one conviction and it's a matter of public record. It was for breaking one or two little rules in the late nineteen-forties. And you'd be surprised how much of my life I sacrificed for the good of your party! Eleven fucking years!"

I slammed the door and drove away fast—before he could stop blinking and start recording. I still feared *them!* Besides, I didn't want him to see how I was sobbing.

Many times *after* August of 1968, people would step into my cab and say that Dubček was naïve and he moved too fast. I would argue that he couldn't have stopped the tidal wave any more than he could have helped riding it and leading it. For it was a moral movement of such urgency that the most moral man near the top rose to it. But, in the seven months between the fat man and the invasion, nobody had harsh words to say in my cab about Dubček. Some had doubts that the man was as good as he seemed, but they all wanted to believe that such a good man did indeed live. And, now that he was tangible, we were all finding a little bit of him in each of us.

I listened closely to Dubček. The first time was on the radio. In the beginning, I feared the worst—for he spoke in harsh, halting Slovak *with a slight Russian accent!* So little was known about him that only a few days later did I learn that he'd spent his boyhood in Russia (from 1925, when he was three, until 1938, when he was sixteen) where his father had gone to help build an agricultural cooperative in the world's first socialist state. But, maybe, because of the way Dubček spoke, one paid attention to his every word—and suddenly I stopped noticing his language. For this was the first time I'd ever heard a Communist leader talking about what mattered, about reality.

Dubček was not easy to listen to, but he was *worth* listening to.

It didn't seem to matter to Dubček that he was the man who was saying something. He wanted you to pay attention to *what* he was saying.

After seeing this homely, informal, and yet innately noble politician on TV, I talked him over with Vlasta and paid him the supreme compliment: "This man makes so much sense that I can't believe he was never in jail himself."

I was cruising near the Prague Castle on Friday, March 22, 1968—the day Novotný finally doffed his other hat by abdicating the presidency—and I heard the shout of tumultuous joy that pealed out from his own chancery. Just the first second of it—for then every motorist in earshot started tooting his own horn. Novotný's last act before resigning, we learned later, was to pardon the imprisoned writer Jan Beneš, who wrote so eloquently that "everything passes, the trees grow green and put forth leaves, the leaves turn yellow and fall, one thing leads to another, yet nothing happens, we are hurrying toward the society of the future, which will be Communism, a pittance of grain and a few rags, so that man has to go with his buttocks bare, and one thing leads to another, somewhere there's a horizon. . . ."*

Eight days later, I avoided the Castle because it was bad for traffic and hence bad for business on the Saturday when General Ludvík Svoboda was installed as the seventh president of the Czechoslovak Republic. I knew that people who were there would want to stroll and breathe the free air of the Prague Spring, not stew in a hemmed-in taxi. So I stayed home and watched the ceremonies on television.

Svoboda was the kind of white-haired old soldier any country would be proud to picture on its postage stamps, but I remembered his unheroic, unmilitary, unmanly stand in 1948, when, as the nonparty minister of defense, he subverted the Army to insure the Communist coup. But, since he and I were now twenty years older and perhaps wiser, I was willing to give him a second chance—though I personally favored an-

---

* *Blind Mirror.* Previously cited herein.

other contender who'd been a hero in 1945 and a villain in 1948: Josef Smrkovský, leader of both the Prague Uprising and the Prague People's Militia. His four years in prison for the wrong reasons didn't help the crew-cut, crinkled Smrkovský with me as much as his inability to talk anything but turkey on TV and to the press: "If I were in the Soviet Union's shoes, I would worry about developments here."

From the end of March until August, you could breathe freedom in the air. Every day brought something new—sometimes encouraging, sometimes worrisome, but always interesting, always affording some shred of hope, some promise. There was so much to be witnessed, so much to be read in the press, so much to be learned from the newscasts.

Working nights—when the tips and rates were better and the traffic lighter—I would come home at the end of the morning rush hour; sleep a little; play with the kids and eat a late lunch; read the press, which now took so much more time to read; and take a short nap around 6:00 P.M. (Except once a week, when the witty and scathing *Literární Listy* came in to pry open our minds with the wry essence of all we'd seen and heard; to stimulate thinking and laughter that made napping impossible.) At seven o'clock, there was the nightly TV newscast. Nobody missed that—and the streets of Prague were deserted, except outside closed stores that projected TV in their display windows. "The Seven O'Clock News" on our one channel was billed in the advance listings as half an hour long, but now it was lasting until eight or even later. Theaters and concerts postponed their 7:00 or 7:30 P.M. starting times to "half an hour after the TV news ends." Then these downtown entertainments would either be performed without intermissions or else a TV set would be brought in so that the audiences could catch the ten o'clock news.

I usually went to work right after the seven o'clock news; took my "midnight supper" at 10 P.M. in a tavern that had TV; and spent the rest of my night on the road discussing the latest events with my fares.

At first, thanks to the past history of the Municipal Taxi Service, passengers, particularly students, were a trifle wary of talking politics in a cab. But I didn't try to break down their resistance. They couldn't keep from talking for long. It took only a few seconds of conversation before it came out that I was a private cabbie *and* an ex-prisoner. Immediately, they wanted my opinion as a philosopher-on-wheels—named Karel Čapek, no less!—who'd lived on the other side of our country's face.

Ota Šik's frequent appearances on TV in the Dubček era had not only gained Šik fame and his ideas favor, but they had confirmed what my riders had always suspected: that even the worst economy run according to the worst philosophy—and ineptly at that!—could yet begin to function better in the hands of sensible management. Riding a private cab, driven by an ex-convict, with lower rates seemed to supply a living, instant token of what they had just heard on TV.

Even though they turned to me because I seemed exceptional to them, what thrilled me throughout the Prague Spring —and beyond—was that *they were all on my side!* For once in my life, I felt like a fish in the water.

I learned something else from those dialogues inside Warszawa—that, even after twenty years of silence, free speech comes as *naturally* to man as fish take to water. And it was not just people thinking alike that sometimes made an evening of a dozen different conversations feel to me like one continuing conversation. One passenger would pose a question and the next would supply a bit of the answer.

People even drank differently. Back in 1967, drunken passengers were sulky, morose, and quietly mean or belligerent. In 1968, they were friendly, amusing, and loud. Happy topers make splendid tippers. And the Saturday-night howling, when the taverns closed, was no more. If secret policemen and ex-secret policemen drank harder in these new times, they did so in secret—and tormented only their kin.

One day, in the Spring of 1968, *Rudé Právo* published a letter-to-the-editor. It began: "I am a cripple—and may I take this occasion, when so many brickbats are being cast at our dedicated policemen, to tell you about one kind patrolman who helps me across Revolutionary Boulevard every morning on my way to court?"

The writer was obviously a lawyer or judge. He went on in a devious, obsequious Stalinist way: at a time when the police were under most-justified and long-overdue attack from above, below, and even within, the writer was singing their praises for something about which nobody could argue with a cripple.

I knew who had written the letter, even before I saw the signature, but what threw me was the title beneath his name. Judge Prášek was still a judge! That little speck of dust—who'd condemned me to "fourteen years at hard labor plus one day's solitary confinement, with neither bedding nor light, during each month of your imprisonment"—was still dispensing "justice"! In another court and another time, perhaps, but, in my mind, I had left him for dead.

I slammed the paper down hard, first with rage at such a walking miscarriage of justice and then with sudden joy that, four or five months into the Prague Spring, even such an unpurged lizard felt free to crawl out of its hole and wield its forked tongue, if not to shed its scales or grow a new tail.

Driving through the night, I used to stop at the *hydeparks* (an "Englishlike word" I couldn't have taught my prison pupils because it only entered the Czech language in 1968) that had sprung up in Old Town Square, Wenceslas Square, and the plaza beside the House of Children department store. The *hydeparks* lasted as late as 2.00 A.M., so they were good places to pick up fares in the owl hours. But I was content just to park my cab and walk around and listen in—not so much agreeing or disagreeing with what was being said, but soaking it up as though at an outdoor promenade concert of free speech. Often, at one *hydepark* or another, I met fellow ex-prisoners doing the same—just listening, just happy it was happening—and looking over our shoulders, too. But any policemen on hand were just listening, too, or smiling or sometimes arguing (just as citizens, not as authorities), but never inhibiting. "It's like it was at the beginning of 1948," one uniformed cop remarked to me, "except this time I think something good is happening." And I said, with just a rueful edge to my words, "Yes, it's as if those last twenty years never existed."

One day, a tiny item appeared in the press: a group of former prisoners would meet on Tuesday evening on the Slavonic Island (Žofín) in the Vltava—just behind our riverfront Mánes Café hangout—in the large hall where the folk dancers perform for tourists in the summer.

It didn't occur to me that a one-sentence item could herald the biggest event in the Prague Spring for me. But I should have learned by then not to judge news by space. My own one sentence—to "fourteen years at hard labor plus one day's solitary confinement per month"—had rated not a word in the press at any time, then or now.

Whichever of the boys had arranged it, I figured they must have overestimated the size of their audience. Well, I would help fill the empty chairs by taking along my wife and son—show them off to any of my prison buddies who might turn up out of the blue. Dressed in their Sunday best, Vlasta and little Karel, not yet four, rode in style on the back seat of Warszawa while I chauffeured them downtown.

As we drove along the Smetana Embankment toward where (at the First of May Bridge) it becomes the Gottwald Embankment, I noticed that the pedestrians were not just the usual fashionably dressed operagoers strolling toward the National Theater, but also a more purposeful, well-dressed (though a little more dressed-up than dressy) wedge of people hurrying through their midst. The wedgers clearly *weren't* going to the opera. They were people like us going to make a little night music of their own.

Most of them had wives and many of them had children with them, too. We all, who'd had the worst of it, wanted to show that we'd made the best of it and the most of it. Even from behind, you could tell who in the crowd had been arrested and who had not. Some had canes, some were limping, and quite a few were sick. But anyone in that privileged crowd of operagoers should have wanted to rub shoulders with us. And, indeed, as the ex-prisoners politely opened their own corridor of traffic in the throng, a number of unhurried operagoers did pause to look at us, as though some Very Important People on a mission of great urgency were cutting a swath through their casual pleasure-seeking.

As Warszawa inched forward, I looked again—and it suddenly occurred to me that there were more of *us* on the Embankment than there were of *them*. Faces in the crowd until lately, *we were now the crowd!*

Without hunting for a better parking space, we bade Warszawa good evening as soon as we could. All three of us Čapeks wanted to join those people of ours—so unique, so clean-cut, yet each different from one another. It was a summit. United we had stood or fallen as prisoners. But this was the first time, as free men, that we'd been allowed to unite as a body.

The operagoers parted from us, almost reluctantly, by turning left and crossing over to the National Theater. The prisoners and our families proceeded along the Gottwald Embankment for a few steps, walking hard as if to trample the grave of that hated name, before turning right and crossing a small rainbow footbridge that put us among our own.

Even before we entered the meeting hall, we were all remembering each other and all liking each other. Everybody knew everybody else—even if they'd never met or didn't remember from where. "Weren't you with me in Leopoldov?" a man asked me. "No, I was never in Leopoldov," I said, "but I was at Pankrác, Bory, Eliáš, Brotherhood—"

"Bory!" he interrupted. "You were on sisal hemp with me. Remember that informer—what was his name?"

"Dumitrescu!" I said, and we both spat. "And I remember *you* from the day Mr. Brabec made us do exercises in the yard! You did two extra push-ups *after* you were unconscious."

Little Karel looked up at this round-shouldered superman with wide eyes. The man smiled down at him: "Your father was a fine yardbird, too." Others congratulated me on "your lovely wife, and be thankful your young jailbird here looks more like her."

All around us, the roll call of shared prisons went on: "You must have been at Rovnost when I was, but we didn't meet till

Bytíz . . . "What happened to you after we both left Prokop
and I went back to Jáchymov?" It was almost as though we'd
come straight from the camps to this hall. The years in between had been good to some of us, but it was the bad years
that brought us together.

We filled the ground floor and the balcony and all the small
meeting rooms—there were thousands of us!—and those who
couldn't find a place simply mingled happily in the hallways
and aisles of that historic old building, now officially a neighborhood cultural center. I met Heteš, the butcher from the
Jaundice Brigade who hadn't thought he could learn English,
and I wonder what his wife thought when I greeted him with
"How's your *hemeroidy?*" and he responded with another of
those useful Czech words, "*Fajn!*" (pronounced "Fine!"). Father Houžvička was there in civilian clothes. "Still conducting
a streetcar?" I asked him. "I'm a motorman now," he told me.
"I got my promotion and a raise after we got Dubček. They've
even notified me I can go back to the priesthood now—but I
don't think they realize I've got a wife and kid." Even Jaroslav
Aim had come to town by himself for the meeting, and he
reproached me silently for bringing my child and keeping him
out late.

Those of us who'd brought our wives kept forgetting to introduce them to each other. But Vlasta Čapková and Slávka
Hetešová looked at each other, smiled, and exchanged their
first names—and then they were friends, too, and still are.

There were speeches from the platform, where one chair was
left vacant in honor of those of us who didn't survive, and our
organization was given a name that night: K-231, a *Klub* bearing the statute number of the law under which we were persecuted ("231. Crimes Against the State"), the brand name of
the blanket of injustice that had covered our lives in the jails,
camps, and mines. Our motto was "Never Let It Happen
Again." Our objectives were legal rehabilitation, compensation, and firm guarantees of individual liberties. We fired off a
telegram to Dubček expressing OUR ESTEEM FOR THE WAY IN
WHICH YOU ARE RESTORING THE DIGNITY OF HUMAN LIFE TO OUR
PEOPLE, for we knew that Dubček had not only wept at our

fates, but had asked aloud, "How was it possible for Communists to behave this way?" We even drafted a letter to Josef Smrkovský, now the speaker of our Parliament, apologizing for the way a few of us anti-Communists had beaten him when he'd had the ironic misfortune of landing among us. We even invited Speaker Smrkovský to join K-231. Though he never did, he was always our friend and often our voice in the ruling councils.

The most impassioned speech was by Dr. Jan Šmíd, a true survivor, a physician who'd been condemned to death twice— once by the Nazis and once by the Brabeces at Bory for leading an abortive uprising there. "For twenty years, they were hunting the Nazi, Martin Bormann, in the jungles of Paraguay," Dr. Šmíd told us, "while all the time he was sitting in the Ministry of Interior in Prague."*

Some of the speeches were interesting, if hectic, as people shouted information from the floor to bolster a speaker's ideas, and crusades were launched and gained momentum before our eyes and ears. Out of that meeting, for example, came one of the great video moments of the Prague Spring a couple of weeks later: a K-231 founder named Ota Rambousek (now a New Yorker) confronted the former second-in-command from Leopoldov. As the camera showed us a split screen of close-ups —the face of the glib "penologist" and the scars that Rambousek acquired *at his hands*—the official shed his façade and, before the eyes and ears of an appalled nation, reverted to habit by threatening and trying to intimidate Rambousek.

That night on Slavonic Island, quite a few speeches were dull, too. When they were, prisoners contented themselves just to look upon each other, be with each other again, and yet remain free to go home to different beds from the double and triple bunks where we'd shared so many nights of our lives, three or four hours at a time.

---

* For another account of that K–231 meeting by one who was on the platform that night, see Chapters 29 and 30 of *Solution Gamma*, the memoir of a K–231 founder and its general secretary, Jaroslav Brodsky, which is available in an English translation by Káča Poláčková, published in 1971 by Gamma Print, P. S. "M," Box 2, Toronto.

After a while, little Karel fell asleep in Vlasta's arms. But, after he woke up the next day, whenever people asked him what he wanted to be when he grew up, he'd answer, "A prisoner!" Prisoners, to him, were some kind of fraternal society where good men came together and, with only a little quiet boasting, showed how they had bettered the walled-in world outside the walls wherein they'd first met.

I have sung and danced to songs about "a night of love," but if ever there was one, this was it. That night on Slavonic Island, children laughed and cried and slept, young men cried, and old men with cancer written across their bodies laughed so uncharacteristically that one feared their suddenly dancing, crinkling eyes would tear through the wrinkles that had hardened around them. Vlasta put it to me this way: "I've never been prouder of my husband's past." After the meeting, we spilled out into the chilly beer garden behind the hall. But there was so much human electricity on that island that night that we basked in our own warmth. When you say "Prague Spring" to me, my mind goes back to that evening on that island—and my memory hasn't let go of it yet. As with the *hydeparks* and with Dubček himself, the essence of that evening was that it happened.

Part 6

To Die in Prague

Other happenings were gathering speed, too. As wrongs were righted and censorship lifted, there were East German denunciations of Smrkovský as a "favorite of West German reactionaries and revanchists" and Dubček as "the head of a stinking fish" that was polluting the Red Sea. There were Soviet denunciations of Dubček as a "counterrevolutionary" and even (God save us!) a "pure democrat." When the investigation of Jan Masaryk's death was reopened twenty years too late, the Russian press even lashed out at his old man, saying that T. G. Masaryk was "a bourgeois nationalist who financed a plot to kill Lenin in 1918." And there were gratuitous proclamations by Soviet generals that the Red Army stood ready to come to the aid of *loyal* Czechoslovak Communists.

More than sabers rattled with troop movements near our borders upon Russia, Poland, Hungary, and East Germany and with Warsaw Pact maneuvers on our soil, after which the Red Army stayed and stayed. There were unprecedented summit meetings: Dubček went to Dresden for "a comradely talk" with the leaders of Russia, Poland, East Germany, Hungary, and Bulgaria; to Carlsbad to chat with Soviet premier Kosygin, who dropped in there suddenly to take the waters; to the Kremlin to explain himself to Soviet first secretary Brezhnev; and, finally, we thought, with the entire Czechoslovak Presidium for a tense four-day confrontation with the entire Soviet Politburo in the Slovakian border town of Čierna-on-the-Tisa. The showdown in Čierna ended on August 1, 1968—and it was followed two days later by the signing in Bratislava of a treaty wherein the Čierna negotiations were ratified by the participants plus Russia's four Warsaw Pact stooge nations. Most important to us, however, was our Ministry of Defense's official communiqué: "The last Soviet Army units which had taken part in the staff exercises from June 20th to 30th left Czechoslovak territory on August 3."

Dubček had bought us some time, we thought—and, in this breathing spell that proved to be a lull, we found time not just to hang upon events, but to wonder what Mother Russia was going to do. Those who thought rationally, with civilian logic, said the Kremlin was in no position to intervene. Trampling over Czechoslovakia would turn the rest of the world—including many Communist parties and even a few Communist nations—against Russia. She would also lose the crocodile virtue that she displayed toward America's involvement in Vietnam.

Those of us who applied prison logic, however, suspected that the Russians didn't care what others thought. They did whatever they wanted, and then brazened or bluffed or rationalized it out once the coffins were sealed or the coffers were bare. Should they ever fear they were losing their grip on something they had firmly in hand—be it uranium or a people or a nation—they would not let it go. We knew this. We feared this. But, in the Prague Spring, one could hope to be wrong.

Tito of Yugoslavia and Ceausescu of Rumania, who had stood by Dubček in his crisis for their own reasons, came to Prague separately that August and were given heroes' welcomes. On Friday, August 16, 1968, I cruised through the Firehouse Square hoping to catch a glimpse of Ceausescu's motorcade when he and Dubček left the Castle, where they had paid a call on President Svoboda. But—business before patriotism—I saw a tall foreigner striding toward me like a prospective customer. I halted, reaching back to open the door. But you beat me to it, lowered yourself into Warszawa's backseat, and I had met my Boswell.

Our story has come full circle, but our friendship has just begun. One hundred thirteen hours later, at dawn in that same

*Firehouse Square, I will be a hostage on a traffic island sur-
rounded by Russian tankmen dressed blacker than the night
we thought was departing. Kafka will live, but I will nearly
die, when ten lost Red Army tanks—detailed to capture the
castle—won't find Prague's soaring symbol of sovereignty on
their indecipherable maps. Then, after a few bad minutes, I
will be set free and relatively unmolested for another two and
a half years, during which time my family's life in occupied
Czechoslovakia will be a continuous game of Russian roulette.*

Seven hours before that happened to you—around 10:30 on
Tuesday night, August 20, 1968—I was driving my cab near
there when I heard an airplane and then another overhead. As
one who'd picked up many good tippers out at Ruzyně Airport
(tourists who'd say apologetically, "Excuse me, all I have is
German marks"!), I knew the flight schedules pretty thoroughly and was surprised to hear planes arriving that late in
the night. Well, I thought, there must be bad weather somewhere else and the flights are being diverted here. Or maybe
Czechoslovak Airlines is running later than usual. When I
heard a third plane, I leaned out to look. All three aircraft
had made a high-pitched sound I wasn't used to hearing. And
they came in such quick sequence that the sound of the first
two still hung in the air as I watched the third plane drop down
onto Ruzyně. Despite the high whine, it was a propeller plane
and a big one, with four engines. I was used to the sound of
Tupolevs and Ilyushins, so I guessed that this was some other
make of plane—for cargo, maybe. I was not so skilled at aircraft identification that I could have spotted Antonov prop-jet
transports bearing troops and tanks.

Close to midnight, I took a customer to the Vinohrady (Wine
Castle) district of Prague and then drove back toward town
along Vinohradská—a main artery that, during a good part of
my eleven-year absence from the open road, had been named
Stalin Boulevard.

The early morning hours were generally so free of other
autos and the curbs so uncluttered that one could always relax
and keep just one eye on the road, the other on the sidewalks
and crossings for signs of life and customers. That's why I was

jolted when, near the headquarters of Radio Prague, I had to stop short for a traffic jam. Six other private taxis had stopped to double-park and even triple-park along the four-lane boulevard.

Guessing there had been an accident, I stopped and got out to offer assistance. But there was no damage to be seen—just six cabbies and a dozen other passersby standing in front of the Radio Building. I asked one of the drivers what was the matter. In an incredulous voice, he told me news he could not yet believe: "They say the Russians are coming!"

I couldn't quite believe him myself—though I started to when I looked at that crowd of men in the grip of something stronger than themselves. One driver told me that a man from the Radio had nodded and shrugged when they'd seen him hurrying through the lobby.

Usually, one could walk right into the Radio Building without being challenged by anyone but a porter or night watchman. Now, however, a middle-aged city policeman was carefully threading a rusted chain through several looped stands to keep us out. "Do you think that will repel the Russians?" I asked him.

"What else is there to do?" he asked back in a sad voice that made me know for sure. Nevertheless, I asked. "They've taken the airport already," he replied, turning back to threading his loops.

I rejoined the other drivers, who, by now, numbered two dozen, including a couple of municipal cabbies. What could we do? What could anybody do?

"Nobody knows about it," one of us said. "Let's at least try to wake the people up and make them listen to the Radio."

"But there's nothing about it on the Radio," someone else said.

"There will be! There will be! And why die in your sleep? They may bomb us."

And I said, "There's at least one cab here for each district of Prague. So let's take a district apiece and wake it up with our horns and our lights."

We each took a district where we had family or relatives, but we pledged not to spend more than five minutes with them while waking up the rest of the community. Knowing our neighborhoods, we wouldn't miss any main drags or many side streets. Somebody spoke up for the area that included Odolena Voda, so I asked him to make sure my wife got the word. (We had a phone, but Odolena Voda was a long-distance call from Prague that had to be placed through an operator who went home at midnight.)

I took Vyšehrad because my parents were there. It felt naughty and slightly obscene to be shattering the night silence with automobile sounds. Warszawa, having a Slavic horn, never went beep or honk. Her happy sound was a toot that sounded like *Hohoho!* Her noise of urgency was more of a hoot: *Hooo-hooo-hooo*. But, in the early hours of Wednesday, August 21, 1968, she gave a wheeze, almost a sigh, of *Hohhhh* that quickly became a shrill Arab wail of *Hooooohhh*. In the night, as we gathered speed, she sounded like another car not too far away.

Making a terrible noise in the night and blinking my lights at other motorists, I was sometimes avoided like a drunken driver, but more often peered at with owlish curiosity. Whereupon I would stop and shout, "The Russians are coming! The Russians are here! Spread the word!" Then, without waiting to discuss the matter, I would drive off into the night with a *Hohhhh* and a succession of mournful *Hooooohhhs*. It was drizzling and, in the Square of Charles IV, I thought I was having windshield trouble until a man on the street shouted at me: "Why are you honking? Why are you crying?"

By the time I reached my parents, I had covered most of Vyšehrad and already other cars were making noise into the night. My parents answered my pounding on the door after a few minutes. "Now what have you done?" my mother wanted to know. "Are you in trouble, Son?" my father asked.

"We're all in trouble," I told them. "The Russians have come!"

"They'll put you back in prison!" my mother said, beginning to tremble. This was the first time that morning I'd thought about my own fate. I said, "Perhaps." My mother started to sob. And she said, "This time they'll kill you."

"Maybe they'll kill us all," my father said, taking command.

"So you get dressed," he told my mother. Turning to me, he said, "And you get back to your own family. I'll look after your mother. Thanks for letting us know." Then he shut the door in my face.

Hooooohhh! Hooooohhh! through the night went Warszawa and I. Blowing her horn was my way of crying; it cleared the tears from my eyes so I could drive. *Hooooohhh! Hooooohhh!* through Wenceslas Square, where Warszawa panted for a moment and I heard an even shriller voice calling, *"Taxi! Taxi!"*

An old lady was flagging me down with an umbrella. She climbed in primly and said: "I need to go to Smíchov Station."

The trains to Germany stopped at Smíchov, so I asked her, "Are you running away from the Russians?"

"What Russians?" she said. "I'm running away from this noisy city to my country place where I can get a good night's sleep."

So I told her the news and she said, "Good! Maybe *they'll* quiet this city down. It's becoming impossible."

Both Warszawa and I were speechless all the way to Smíchov Station. There, railwaymen and a few passengers were talking with great animation. The lady paid, but didn't tip. I didn't bother to follow her in and find out whether trains were running at all. I made my getaway before anyone else could climb in.

All the way home, I saw small clusters of lost, stoop-shouldered people looking like supporters of a losing team after a football game. Driving along the Vltava, on the Captain Jaroš Embankment, I could see that all the lights were burning in the Central Committee Building directly across the river. I had the car radio on and I heard the Presidium's proclamation of an invasion: "To all the people of the Czechoslovak Socialist Republic: Yesterday, August twentieth, nineteen hundred and sixty-eight, at about twenty-three hundred hours, the armies of the Soviet Union, the Polish People's Republic, the German Democratic Republic, the Hungarian People's Republic, and the Bulgarian People's Republic crossed the State borders of the Czechoslovak Socialist Republic. This took place without the knowledge of the president of the —" Then the radio went dead. I kicked Warszawa with fury, but it was not my steed's fault! The plug had been yanked by the minister of telecommunications, a die-hard Novotnýite who had been demoted from minister of culture, but still retained enough pull to betray his country at a crucial moment.

Others would have heard the aborted announcement, too, so I stopped honking my horn and drove cautiously as I neared an aircraft factory a couple of miles before my home. It had a runway for test flights and occasional small military aircraft, so I knew it would be one of the Red Army's first targets. But the night shift had already blockaded the runway by parking a couple of planes and a limousine on it and strewing old engines around it, too. A helicopter, however, was buzzing ominously overhead.

Warszawa and I did the last two miles in little more than a minute. The Red Army would be in Odolena Voda soon and all of Prague, I knew. So I wanted to be with Vlasta, see Vlasta, hide my woman and protect my children from the Russian soldiers as best I could—or die defending them and me. Mostly, though, I just wanted to spend the next few hours with my family before the invaders came after them or me.

The lights were on in our house. Vlasta was up. Her first words to me were an angry "I know! I know!," but I knew she wasn't angry at *me*. The children were sleeping sweetly and soundly. How a man's fate can change! When I'd left for work a few hours earlier, I'd gazed at both of their faces in innocent, earnest repose. I'd bent over to kiss them without disturbing their sleep and gone off knowing that all was in order while I was on the job. Now they were still asleep, but nothing in my world or theirs was any longer in order and I was still looking upon them as though for the last time.

The Radio came back on the air toward dawn—and it was never silent after that. *"Be with us, we are with you"* was the slogan it coined and lived up to on August 21, 1968—with distress signals so strong and in so many languages that they reached people everywhere but in Russia:

> This is Czechoslovakia calling to the world while the tanks are crushing our cities and killing our children. We ask you to raise your voices, please, workers of the world. Protest against this illegal occupation. Call for the imme-

diate withdrawal of foreign troops. There is no counter-revolution in our land. Our voice is now too weak. But we call to all to support the sovereignty of Czechoslovakia.

Instead of just one TV channel, there were—at one point—twelve channels broadcasting across Czechoslovakia. Towns that had never received Czechoslovak TV before (but where people, as in the West, had acquired TV sets anyway) suddenly erupted with it—and some of the transmissions were so strong that they hit the Swiss Alps and were relayed to the rest of the world from there. Eleven of the twelve channels called themselves "legal television," although their transmitters were hunted high and low by the Red Army (which, at one point, shot up a refrigerator thinking it was a transmitter). The twelfth was our original Channel One, whose studios the Russians had occupied; we now called it "collaborationist television." Our newspapers were publishing several clandestine editions a day. Weeklies were now publishing daily, and so were several monthlies, including the women's magazine *Květy* (*Flowers*). How was this possible with their headquarters ransacked and occupied? Chalk it up not only to Czech ingenuity, but to the same genius for hoarding spare parts that had enabled us to hear the BBC even after the Nazis had taken away our "Little Churchill" coils.

"We have no weapons, but our contempt is stronger than tanks," the Radio said. "You know where you live. There's no need for the rascals to know, too. Switch around street signs. Take house numbers off doors. Remove name plates from public buildings. . . . The mailman will find you, but evildoers won't."

I got out my tools, but by the time I reached the front door of our four-family apartment house, one of the other tenants—an elderly widower known in the neighborhood as "the old Stalinist"—had removed our house number. He waved his screwdriver at me and said, "Wish I had a gun instead of this."

If only the Army had taken command the way our Radio had, I think we might have beaten the Russians. But, in its whole half-century history, the Czechoslovak Army (not just under General Svoboda) had been used exclusively against its own people. Although it had been cut off the air, the Presidium's proclamation that we were the victims of an invasion had been read to the troops. It contained a sentence that "because the defense of our State borders is now impossible . . . our army, the security forces, and the People's Militia were not given orders to defend the country." Without an army, who could counsel physical resistance or spend the lives of our people? Particularly against such odds in such a *Blitzkrieg*—by the time we'd heard about it, it had already happened.

The children slept late. Vlasta and I listened to the Radio some more—and then I reacted just like a prisoner. I took off my shirt and told my wife, "Well, I can't change anything. The last time I tried, it cost me eleven years. So I might as well get some sleep and be fit for the day to come." But I kept my trousers on in case I had to defend my home in a hurry.

When I woke up, it was noon. The children were playing inside the house. Vlasta was monitoring the radio, except it was now Radio Free Pilsen ("home of the world-famous Pilsener beer") and Radio Free České Budějovice (the German name for České Budějovice was Budweis, "home of the original Budweiser beer") because Radio Prague had fallen to the Russians in a battle that killed five Czechs and wounded at least fifty more. Radio Free Pilsen was broadcasting a message from local elementary-schoolers, meeting in a playground, to the Soviet occupation commander: "We are children. We want to grow up free. You also have children. Please go home and look after your own children. They are very much like us. Don't leave them alone without their fathers."

People from the neighborhood dropped around—to pay condolence calls on their friends—and seemed surprised to find me still around. They advised me to flee. I saw no sense in that yet. But, to make them happy and see for myself what was happening in the city, I decided to be on the move—at least as far as my parents' house in Vyšehrad. After I'd had a quick lunch of leftovers, Warszawa and I set out for Prague in early afternoon.

The aircraft plant near my home was now guarded by soldiers. I started to throw one of the "defenders" a cheery salute when something about him made me start and Warszawa almost stall. Crew-cut, blond, and very neat, even in his baggy field uniform, he looked more like a very sharp nineteenth-century soldier or World War I doughboy than a sloppy modern soldier—in other words, the difference between a Russsian and a Czech. Yes, the factory was occupied.

The gas station down the road was open for business, but the attendant apologized for only being able to feed Warszawa half a tankful. He also advised me to stick to the Left Bank of the Vltava as long as I could.

The Plain of Letná—where the world's largest statue of Stalin had stood during my absence from public life until a rather embarrassed Novotný ordered him dynamited by night —was now a bivouac ground for the Red Army and a landing field for Soviet helicopters. Passing below it, I was on the Left Bank's riverfront drive and could see the wisdom of my warning to avoid the Right Bank. There, where party headquarters and Charles University (among other key targets) stood, the Embankment was lined with tanks and soldiers—and aswarm with Czechs arguing with them, gesticulating at them, and even chalking words on their tanks. The *hydeparks* had moved right into the midst of the enemies who'd come to kill our freedom of expression. Occasionally, a shot would ring out —and a *hydepark* would scatter, but not dissolve. Sometimes, though, its population was one less, for the shot wasn't always just a warning fired into the air.

I stayed on the Left Bank until the last bridge before Vyšehrad. Halfway across it, two Russian soldiers were flagging motorists down with red handkerchiefs. In case anyone ignored the signal, there was an armored personnel car with fourteen men and at least fourteen weapons.

The two Russian foot sentries stared at me blankly. I looked at them with recognition. Again, as at the K-231 meeting, it was as if twenty-three years hadn't happened. They were no older than and no different from the Russian troopers who'd come—and gone!—in Vlasov's Men's wake in 1945; in fact, I could swear I remembered those two from the first days of liberation from the Nazis. But, no, these were the sons of their fathers. Still looking tired and a bit dazed, they had come from another time and another world to put an end to ours. The reality of it was too shocking to think about with words. I hated them! I *wanted* to resist. I *did* cry.

They watched me impassively. I must not have been the first to weep.

After a long minute of detached inspection, almost mystic in its silence, they let me move on. From there, although tanks and other armor flanked the Square of Charles IV, I made it to my parents without incident. My mother was calm by now and my father absorbed in the radio. After listening for a while, I went back to Warszawa—and there, in her backseat, was a passenger reading an underground edition of *Literární Listy* that said, "Should we never meet again, we want you all to love each other, protect each other, and hope for truth. Hold fast until liberty can be guaranteed by those to whom you've given your trust. See you again in better times."

My patient passenger said, "I hope you don't mind, but I haven't been able to get a cab by phone and I'd like to go home."

Thus did I go back to work for the next three hours—and, on and off, for the next few days. Many times, the Russians stopped Warszawa, but only twice did they search her. They hadn't yet been told all the horrid truth about Ota Šik (who'd been in Yugoslavia when the Russians came and went directly from there to a professorship in Switzerland) and private taxis, so they presumed that Warszawa and I were public servants— just like their tanks and themselves. They were less interested in a worker like me than they were in the moguls who could afford to ride in cabs. My passengers were always searched and their underground periodicals confiscated. One passenger was taken away for protesting after a Russian sentry, on the First of May Bridge, removed the man's jacket, took two underground newspapers out of its inner lining, tossed them into the river, and kept the jacket for himself. And, of course, searches for clandestine propaganda were wonderful excuses to make off with transistor radios, pens, and wristwatches, too.

Private autos had a rougher time than public taxis because anyone driving his own car was suspect to soldiers from a land where hardly anyone owned his own. The low grade of affluence to which their nation had bled us struck *them* as the height of prosperity—undoubtedly C.I.A.-financed.

I saw the driver of a Škoda MB-1000, just ahead of me at a roadblock, get a rifle butt in the face for being fresh. The sentry opened what appeared to be the rear trunk and, with a big AHA! look on his face, asked the motorist accusingly, "What do you call *that?*"

"The engine," the man replied—and, for giving an honest answer, he lost at least a couple of teeth.

The only peril to Warszawa and me came when we drove down streets that had Soviet armor on them. Without signaling and without swerving, tanks would simply ram or crash or demolish whatever was in their path. Sometimes, I'd turn onto a street and a dozen soldiers atop a personnel carrier would point their weapons at me in much the way that policemen point fingers at you. I'd simply back out and try another street.

On the first night of Soviet occupation, it was hard to drive home because Russian armor was still pouring into our little land. The highway that leads from East Germany through Odolena Voda to Prague was clogged with tanks and trucks. When I did reach home after two hours, Vlasta had heard that Dubček and Smrkovský, along with the prime minister and two Presidium members, had been flown off to Moscow in chains—and she'd decided I was next on the list, so she'd packed a few sugar cubes and bread and toilet articles and a change of underwear and a flashlight as a flight pack for her husband. But I told her the traffic was too thick for Warszawa and me to try to escape—so I did what your Senator Eugene McCarthy thought your President Lyndon Johnson should have done instead of protest to the Russians about the invasion of Czechoslovakia: I slept on it.

(Smrkovský, incidentally, had left like a true prisoner. On his way out of the Central Committee—remembering that, in four years of jails, what tea he'd been given had never been sweetened—he'd pocketed three lumps of sugar from a dish and remarked, "I'll need these where I'm going.")

The next day, Thursday, we awoke to find Russian troops bivouacking in the woods behind our house, so I didn't go into the city. They left us alone—but we apparently didn't leave them alone. On Friday morning, Vlasta shook me awake and her face was so white that I sat up fast. She hadn't been letting the kids out to play, but little Karel—whose fourth birthday it was—had sneaked out. I put on my shirt and went looking for him. I found my birthday boy at the edge of the woods, shouting words he'd heard at a Russian soldier who was wearing an undershirt and trying to shave by the reflection in his mess kit. The words my son was speaking were *"Rusáci prasáci!"* ("Russian pigs!").

The Russian soldier was having trouble enough shaving with a rifle slung over his shoulder. And he was pointing the weapon at my son almost playfully—but, in Prague, one small boy and one mother and one infant in a pram had already been machine-gunned because of just one "Ivan Go Home" sign the boy had been chalking on a wall.

I gave the soldier a weak, conciliatory shrug and an obsequious smile. And I called angrily to little Karel, who came running. He and I walked slowly toward home, father and son with an arm around each other, but I didn't begin to breathe until we'd turned the next corner.

"Those are real guns," I told my son.

"Well, they're real swine," he told me. Vlasta kept him under closer surveillance from then on—which left me free, later that morning, to take Warszawa into Prague. There, the *hydeparks* were still in bloom, with everyone trying to tell the Russians the truth. For their pains, some Czechs got shot, some got argued with, some got ordered away at gunpoint, some got ignored, and some got listened to. The Russian soldiers who kept their ears open reminded me of the Russian mining engineer at Eliáš who hadn't known we were prisoners—and who'd been "sent home" when he found out. The same was happening to these troops, who'd been told by their generals that they'd be welcomed as "liberators" and instead discovered that they'd enslaved us. A few, just a few, committed suicide; a few, even fewer, balked at what they were doing and were shot on the spot for disobeying orders; and many, very many, were so demoralized that, on Friday, tougher replacements were brought into Prague and a couple of the more susceptible divisions (mostly Ukrainians) were withdrawn.

On the streets, I yielded right-of-way to shiny, vintage Russian tanks—which, even more so than the men, were the same as twenty-three years earlier—and to Czech ambulances bearing badly wounded civilians. We were an innocent people, but what was happening to us was not so innocent. Even if our nation had no weapons, and even though we weren't fighting back with physical resistance, blood was still being spilled.

I was driving Warszawa through Strahov Park on Friday when a doctor and nurse, both in white, stopped me and asked me to drive over to their hospital and pick up a discharged patient. She was a sprightly grandma, even with her shoulder and back encased in plaster. She gave me an address down below in the Malá Strana (Lesser Quarter). That's where she lived and that's where, on Wednesday night, she might have died. On that first night of total occupation, the Red Army had commenced "night firing exercises"—red tracer bullets followed by live shells—without warning. As the colorful tracers spat their way over Malá Strana, the grandmother had stuck her head out of her attic window in the hope that they were loud sparklers celebrating some Russian defeat or retreat. When she'd realized what was happening, she'd turned to go back in. Just then, a bullet had lodged in her back.

Because no ambulance could come out in the curfew that the Red Army had decreed, she'd lain on the floor of her apartment all night, bleeding. The next morning, she'd been taken to the hospital, where her wound, fortunately, proved minor.

She showed me the bullet that had been removed from her back. It was small, brassy, and almost like a cheap, ornate button for a woman's dress. "I'm going to keep it to remember them by," she told me. "And those rascals will get it a hundred times over."

"Well, you stay away from them," I told her when I'd helped her into the house and refused to let her pay me. ("This goes on the National Health," I told her.) "It'll take another hundred of these to put me under," she said—and I believed her.

Much of my taxi business in the next week was to and from Embassies (where my passengers sought visas) and police headquarters (where they sought passports). The police were particularly cooperative. Almost anyone who applied was granted some kind of authorization. Once, when I took a man in, the policeman at the desk asked if I needed anything. I showed him my exit permit and he certified that it was still valid. "While you're here," he added, "and since you haven't used it, let me extend its validity to a year from today." Which he did with three rubber stamps.

It gave me a little more time to make up my mind, but I could hardly think of going. For the unity we felt in those days right after the invasion made it the best of times. It was an even better time than the Prague Spring, when dissent and reform had at last sprouted and flowered. Now, with the Prague Spring in shambles and our dream in defeat, we knew where we stood and we knew that we all stood together.

Dubček, Smrkovský, and the three other leaders had been taken to a lonely mountaintop in the Ukraine to await execution as soon as an acceptably docile "Workers and Peasants Government of Communist Czechoslovakia" could decree their doom. But the Russians had been unable to recruit even a token force of quislings willing to emerge from the shadows long enough to "justify" such a semblance of legitimacy. On Saturday, the five semicondemned men had been removed to the Kremlin and—along with President Svoboda, who'd taken an entourage from Prague to Moscow—they were "negotiating" with Brezhnev. Our nation had stood so morally strong that it now seemed possible we were doing the impossible: defying a war of occupation by peaceful means and setting yet another example to a watching world.

In this, we underestimated what the Russians were doing to our heroes and our morals in the Kremlin. "If we can't find the puppets," Brezhnev had said, "then we'll have to put strings on the leaders." We also overestimated how attentively and com-prehendingly the rest of the world was watching our agony and our elation.

This time around in the annals of repression, the Russians needed puppets more than balky slaves. And let it never be said that they hadn't progressed with the times. For their loose-leaf book of Marxist-Leninist ideology, they had taken a page from Fidel Castro, who'd shown that the quickest and most economical way (in the short run, that is) to dispose of opposition is to export it. Castro exported the Cuban middle class. Russia was just beginning to export and even deport its Jews. And our Prime Minister Oldřich Černík, upon his return from Russia—where he'd gone in chains with one foot already in the grave—had, even before disclosing the "settlement" that had been "negotiated," sounded a private warning that "the best minds should get out of the country while the getting is good." Although the Russians had come, half a million strong, claiming that the fourteen million of us needed help sealing ourselves off from rightist infiltration from the West, our borders with Germany and Austria remained virtually unmolested by the Red Army.

While I didn't yet feel any urgency, I could understand the haste with which people popped into my cab and said, "Take me up to the Austrian Legation quick!" And, a week after the invasion, Zdeněk, an old buddy from the Jaundice Brigade, "dropped around" to see me. Nobody "dropped" all the way out to Odolena Voda without having something spe-cific in mind, so I wasn't surprised when Zdeněk told Vlasta and me, "I'm about to make a big decision. I've heard the speeches Dubček and Smrkovský have made. The words don't say anything, but the grief in their voices says everything to me. And I don't like the noises Husák is making." (Deputy Premier Gustáv Husák—a Slovak Communist who'd spent six of the Novotný years in prison as a "bourgeois nationalist"— had returned from the Moscow negotiations preaching "realism.")

I didn't try to influence Zdeněk in any way. Zdeněk was the twin who'd stayed manly in prison while his well-connected brother, on the outside, was going homosexual and then trans-vestite. Now Zdeněk had a wife, a son, a passport, and all the right visas to Austria and then Canada—just for himself.

"My wife won't hear about leaving," he explained. "Ruth and I love each other very much. But she says that, if I go, I go alone. So I'm going to take a calculated risk. Ruth can't be pushed to apply for a passport. But if I go, I think she'll start chafing to go soon—and we can hope there'll still be time. If not, well—don't tell her this, but—I'll be legally abroad, so I'll come back legally, too."

Two days later, Zdeněk set out for the Austrian border in a "hired" cab called Warszawa with Karel Čapek at the wheel. I wasn't going abroad, but I wanted to reconnoiter the frontier for my own future reference. Our friend Polda, who'd been chauffeuring his Arab diplomat back and forth, recommended a new crossing that had opened just before the invasion and wasn't even on the Russians' outdated maps. Polda added that the few Czech officials at this crossing were so sympathetic that, if they asked whether you had any underground news-papers, it was because they wanted to read them, not confiscate them. At Polda's suggestion, I unscrewed one of Warszawa's side doors, stuck some *Literární Listy*s and *Rudé Právo*s in-side it, and then screwed it back on for the journey.

The invasion, after nine days, had "normalized" into an occupation, which was growing less and less visible in Prague as the Russians tightened their hold on the leaders. But Soviet tank power still abounded in the countryside—ready to roar back into the capital on a minute's notice. The southbound highway out of Prague was awash with armor hogging and grinding up the road. I became a master of defensive driving that day. Whenever tanks came at us, I'd pull over to make way. Otherwise, they just would have swept Warszawa off the road, as I saw them do to other cars. It was even more dan-gerous when the tanks were going in the same direction as Warszawa. Try to pass one and you might find yourself crushed between it and a tank coming the other way. To make matters worse, the tankers deliberately toyed with us—and twice we were unnecessarily crowded off the road by them.

It took us six hours to make the usual three-hour, 120-mile trip to the border—partly because of tank traffic on the road, but mostly because the people in the provinces had heeded the Radio's call to turn road signs around and thus mislead the invaders. I felt just a little of the frustration the Russians must have experienced when, fifteen minutes after passing through the medieval South Bohemian town of Třeboň— which adjoins one of the largest fish ponds in the world—we found ourselves *entering* Třeboň. Finally, rather than keep going around in fishponds, we asked a local lad to ride with us and show us the way to the next town. He said he'd "ride back with the next person who looks lost, unless it's a Russian."

Several times, we were stopped by Russian roadblocks. The sentries went through Zdeněk's one suitcase and my glove compartment and trunk. When they asked where we were going, Zdeněk replied that he was going to the next town.

About eight miles from the border, we picked up a basically good-looking, though distraught and bedraggled, young girl who spoke only German. From the soft, almost humble, way she spoke, I'd have guessed she was Austrian or East German, not West German. From the plain style of her rather conservative miniskirt, I eliminated Austria as her possible nationality, too. So Zdeněk and I had trouble believing her when she said she was a West German. And we were even more troubled when she went on, obviously practicing a routine on us, to say that she'd been visiting in Prague, but had lost her passport and wallet during the invasion.

She really spelled trouble for Zdeněk. His "calculated risk" with his wife Ruth might go a-gley if she found out he'd left the country with a pretty German girl. But the more immediate risk was arriving at the frontier, even with one's own papers in perfect order, accompanied by somebody with no papers at all and only a dubious tale to tell. Nevertheless, being ex-prisoners and gentlemen, all we could do was shrug at each other and keep moving forward.

At the first barricade, which was as far as Warszawa and I could go, I delivered Zdeněk and the underground newspapers to the guard. He was delighted. He called his officer and two Slovak sentries, who were being dragged on patrol by a big husky dog, and the Customs man behind the next barricade. After they'd divided up the journals, I tried to capitalize on their goodwill and tell the girl's story a little more convincingly in Czech.

The officer in charge was a swarthy Jewish bureaucrat in uniform. He shook his head and said, not unkindly, "I can't let her go without any papers. Papers that don't look kosher: yes —because papers are still papers. But no papers: no."

The girl began to fight back the tears and we all looked at her sympathetically. The officer murmured to me in Czech, "You may not know this, but we're getting five or six cases like this a day. They came here before the invasion because they thought that, in the Prague Spring, it would be easy to get to the West from here. But we were very tough on them even then—much tougher than we were on our own people—because any East Germans or Poles who escaped through Czechoslovakia would have given the Russians an excuse to intervene." He rolled his eyes mournfully at his own last few words.

Now the girl's tears burst loose—and, with them, the truth. Yes, she was East German. Her parents had escaped to the West earlier in the year, but they'd left her behind to finish her studies and start out in West Germany with a diploma. Instead, because of her parents' escape, she hadn't been allowed to complete her degree. She had gone through Czechoslovakia to try to rejoin her parents. Her education had been shattered. Now were the Czechs, of all people, going to wreck her family, too?

The officer, the Customs man, and I all understood her tirade in German.The two young Slovak soldiers and their police dog didn't understand the words, but they grasped the emotion. All the officials, even the dog, shook their heads sadly. When the girl saw what their answer was, she swooned. I caught her and, with Zedněk's help, laid her out on the back seat of Warszawa.

"Better get her out of here," the officer said sadly, "before she makes trouble for you and trouble for us. I'm supposed to arrest people like her. We have a good thing going here for the Czech people, so let the Germans look after themselves." From the bitter way he said "Germans," not "East Germans," I could guess he'd lost his kin to the Nazis.

"Just as an academic question," I persisted, "what are the chances for anyone trying to cross the frontier illegally?"

"Not a chance," he said. "In the no-man's-land over there, there are mines that even *we* don't know about. I don't think her family wants her dead on arrival or even minus one or two of those pretty legs."

There was nothing more to do, then, except to say a fast farewell to Zdeněk. In prison, our private greeting had been a variation on the bittersweet song hit "See You Again in Better Times": "See you in Montreal in better times." In the last days of August, 1968, I said good-bye to Zdeněk with: "See you in Montreal now that better times are here." Then I watched my old concentration-camp buddy pass on foot through the barricades, control points, zigzags, and barbed-wire corridor across a cleanly raked and heavily mined no-man's-land with guard towers standing balefully overhead. As Zdeněk rounded a bend and disappeared in the direction of the lone Austrian control point, it occurred to me that freedom resembled nothing so much as a prison camp. But, of course, Zdeněk was on his way out and our whole nation was on its way back in.

(Zdeněk wound up not in Montreal, but in Vancouver. And his marital gamble worked. His wife and son joined him less than two months after we parted.)

The exhausted East German girl slept most of the way to Prague. Then, on the outskirts, she began to clean herself up, primp a bit, and hitch up her miniskirt. "You going to be all right?" I asked her. I was not too anxious to bring this particular stray home to Vlasta.

"I guess so," she said. "That was my third attempt and I'll just keep on trying."

"Good luck," I said. "Can I take you anyplace in particular?"

"The Alcron Hotel," she suggested. "There are all kinds of

Western journalists and TV teams there. Maybe one of them will marry me and take me out with him."

Driving through the night in Soviet-occupied Prague, I saw the Central Group of Soviet Troops Temporarily Stationed on Czechoslovak Soil—as they were now called—stuffing mailboxes with their terrible Czech-language hate sheet: *Zprávy* (*News*), printed in East Germany. If they saw me, they would chase me away by pointing their weapons at me—temporarily, for I would always withdraw.

They looked ashamed—and angry—at having to tiptoe through our land planting their ideas like thieves in the night. Not that they didn't brazenly appear downtown in broad daylight to press their paper upon people. But *Zprávy*, with its armed newsboys working out of armored carriers, created such a traffic and litter problem that its sponsors preferred middle-of-the-night home delivery. I rejoiced at this moral victory of ours—until I remembered that our buildings are locked up at night. To get into the lobbies, where the mailboxes were, the Red Army must have obtained passkeys to every house door in Prague!

Starting that September, five mornings a week, I would wind up my work by joining the American Family Levy for their breakfast coffee and taking Monica, four-going-on-five, and Erika, three-going-on-four, to the French kindergarten on the same street as the Alcron Hotel. For this, I was paid 70 cents a trip—in Tuzex crowns, the scrip money that entitled me to buy in the special Tuzex stores where scarce goods could be had for Western currencies only. (It was legitimate for the Levys to pay me this way because possession of Tuzex crowns signified that they'd already exchanged their dollars with the State Bank. If they paid me in dollars, I could have been arrested.) Although this was the end of my working day, I didn't consider this work—to spend half an hour or more of it speaking English with such delightful Americans.

"Karel Čapek," my wife, Valerie Levy, tells me after you've worked for us a month, "has a better vocabulary of English

words than I have." Coming from Val, a New York-born pro-
fessional linguist, this is indeed a tribute.

"I have a confession to make," her husband the writer ad-
mits. *"Every now and then, when I grope for the right word
and he gropes for the right word, the word he comes up with is
—well—preciser."*

"More than that," my wife says. "It's a very private English."

*"An O. Henry English, a Jack London English," I suggest
helpfully.*

"No," Val concludes. "A Karel Čapek English."

The American Family Levy was a refreshing antidote to the
Russian women who started appearing in the shops of Prague,
buying up shoes of all sizes, and the Russian civilians ("our
nurses," we called them) arriving at the railroad stations and
disappearing behind the scenes at ministries and police
stations.

One incident that autumn helped *me* decide where our future lay. About two months after the invasion, I'd delivered
your daughters to school when a pair of dainty young English-
men with a movie camera intercepted me outside the Alcron.
"My dear boy," one of them began right away in English, "have
you the faintest notion of where we could have ourselves a
Russian soldier?"

"To film, we mean," the other one interjected, giggling.

"He knows that! You see, we're flying back to London this
noon—we're English, you see—and if we don't have a Russian
to show them, our parents are simply *not* going to believe we
were in your perfectly gorgeous city and they'll think we were
fooling around in Amsterdam again."

I shouldn't have said, "Yes, I know a place," but I had trouble
saying no to people who spoke such fruity British English. It
was music to my ears—or, at least the sound of a different
drummer, after more than a month of listening to the Noo
Yawk Levys. I craved a little variety of exposure. So perhaps
I should blame *you* for the trouble that followed.

There was a little Soviet garrison on a side street in Smíchov.

I invented a good verbal excuse for going past it and then drove down the block—very slowly. Behind me, I heard the camera humming, but I kept my eye on the two Red Army sentries. Filming anything or anyone belonging to the Central Group of Soviet Troops Temporarily Stationed on Czechoslovak Soil constituted military espionage—and, where Western foreigners were involved, it would go hardest on their Czech "collaborator." Still, theirs was not a particularly unusual tourist request; it just happened to be the first time I'd obliged it.

The Russian sentries spotted us as we neared the corner. One of them squinted after us, trying to read my license number. It was the other who worried me more at the time. He unslung his rifle and took aim at us.

I stepped on the gas ever so slightly to beat a yellow light before it turned red and turned the corner.

"Good show!" one of my passengers chirped.

"I even filmed him trying to shoot us!" the other gushed. "Oh what will Mother say?!!!"

"Can we go back for retakes?" the first wondered.

My head didn't stop pounding and I didn't find my English until we had turned several corners and crossed the Vltava without being followed. Then I drove them straight back to the Alcron, where they tipped me frugally and thanked me lavishly: "You've simply *made* our trip." . . . "And you speak such divine American!"

I went home, took a little nap, and forgot about their little lark by the time I woke up to play with the kids. Toward evening, I was taking a bath when Vlasta barged in and said, "There's a brown-leather man outside prowling around Warszawa."

I dried and dressed myself quickly, just in time to answer the knock on the door. He was a young Czech secret policeman who came right to the point: "I need to have a closer look at your car. Have you a flashlight I could borrow?"

"There's one in the glove compartment," I told him. While I already recognized that he was a big improvement over the 1950s or even the 1960s (when you *and* your car would be whisked off to wherever flashlights and interrogators were), this wasn't enough to relieve me. As we walked outside together, I asked, "Is something the matter?"

"The fraternal Army took your license number," he said, watching me closely.

"I know what 'fraternal Army' means," I said, "but I don't know what this is all about."

He offered no explanation until he had examined Warszawa's fenders, bumpers, tires, and undercarriage. Then he stood up and said, "Nothing here. But I'm afraid I still have to take you with me to the district station. The fraternal Army says you ran down one of their soldiers on the street in Smíchov and you broke his knee."

I whistled and said, "May I talk to my wife before I go?"

He said, "Of course"—which was a new wrinkle, too. I told Vlasta to contact a lawyer I'd met at the K-231 meeting. Even though K-231 had been decreed defunct on August 22, 1968, I was sure he could still help me as one man working on behalf of another. By the time Vlasta had found and reached the lawyer's home phone number two hours later—only to be told by his subtenants that he'd gone to Sweden on August 25 "for an indefinite stay"—I had told my story at the Prague East District police station and been driven home with apologies. The story I'd told them had been substantially correct—the only variations being that the two dear boys "had told me which street to go to" and "I didn't notice their movie camera until we were on that street," The Prague East police chief, who was both frank and sympathetic, told me, "There's nothing to disprove *your* story and there's nothing to prove *their* story and we'll tell them so."

I was so confident that I suggested, "Why don't you ask them to produce the soldier with the broken knee?"

"That would be inviting trouble," the chief said coolly. "They'd gladly break his knee themselves just to prove their point. Why, they may even have done it already. They're ex-post-facto experts, the Russians. They're still searching high low for someone who'll say he invited them here on August twenty-first—and they'll keep at it until they get what they want."

The Russians kept coming back at the Prague police in my "case," too. The East District chief advised me to take War-szawa in for a day's examination at the Traffic Bureau labora-tories in the Square of Charles IV "*before* the Russians ask us to make you get one. Then we can say it's already done." The Traffic Bureau gave Warszawa a clean bill of health—at least, as far as injury-accidents were concerned. By the time my case was resolved, my friend the police chief had disappeared from Prague East headquarters and the official I had to deal with down at the Traffic Bureau kept me waiting for an hour. "Please excuse the delay, Mr. Čapek," his receptionist apol-ogized, "but, if it's any comfort, the meeting he's in is about *you.*"

"That's no comfort at all," I remarked.

When the door finally opened, out strode two Red Army majors in greatcoats straight out of Gogol and with faces direct from the battle of Stalingrad. They glared at me as they took three giant steps right out the door. If looks could kill, I had just received a death sentence. But the kindly Czech official who appeared behind them ushered me into his office and said, "Whew! It was close for you! Let's close this case while I'm still on the job." After he'd stamped the word "Closed" on a bulging dossier of depositions, lab findings, and requests in Cyrillic re the Čapek Affair, I asked him if he knew the where-abouts of the ex-Prague East police chief, so I could thank him. "You'll find him downstairs," I was told. "We're keeping him on the payroll as a porter for a few more weeks so he can qualify for his pension."

Downstairs, my purged protector accepted my condolences; brushed off my apologies by saying I wasn't the only one for whom he'd stood up to the Russians; and congratulated me because "whatever you did or didn't do, it rated two majors."

"Last time," I said, "it got me eleven years."

"I wouldn't worry any more about this time—for now," he said. "But I wouldn't forget about it, either. Our brothers from the East are past masters of the salami technique. Whatever they want, they'll whittle away at both ends until the meat they're after drops of its own weight—right into their open mouths. Look how they're doing it to our heroes."

In April of 1969, the Soviet minister of defense, Marshal Andrei Grechko, came to town and pried Dubček loose from the party first secretaryship and Smrkovský from the Parliament speakership. Husák replaced Dubček; Dubček replaced Smrkovský. Smrkovský was also dropped from the Party Presidium. This salami slicing (*you* call it "musical chairs") would lead, within fourteen months, to the removal of both from the Central Committee and their expulsion from the Communist party. Smrkovský went the short, fast route toward becoming a nonperson. Dubček took the long, slow route—making his tormentors slice off every pound of flesh while the lip service they paid him turned to vitriol and slander. In between removal and expulsion, he spent a couple of months as Czechoslovak ambassador to Turkey—and undoubtedly disappointed the Russians, who meant the job to be a one-way ticket into defection, when he came home to face the music. When Dubček refused to recant or self-criticize, the new dictator, Husák, said of him that "in the relatively short time he headed it, he brought our party to a disintegration such as it had never known." President Svoboda, seventy-four—whose finest hour came in 1968, but not in 1969—branded Dubček "inconsistent and lacking the principles characteristic of Leninism." *Rudé Právo* found Dubček "unprincipled, compromising, cowardly . . . weak and two-faced." *Rudé Právo* ought to know.

Both those good men, Dubček and Smrkovský, were living on borrowed time from August 21, 1968, but hadn't even gone to jail since their initial ordeal and might yet die natural deaths.* Karel Čapek, after eleven years in jail and a frightening traffic brush with the Central Group of Soviet Troops Stationed on Czechoslovak Soil (the word "Temporary" faded fast), couldn't afford to stay around and wait for the outcome.

---

* Smrkovský died of cancer in early 1974.

It was in the spring of 1969 that I first broached the subject of leaving as a family to Vlasta. "It's not *just* because I'm afraid," I told her, "but it's for the sake of our sanity and our children. When our son starts school next year, he's going to bring home lies and I'm going to correct them and he'll say in school, 'But my daddy says . . . !' I'll be making trouble for him and he'll make trouble for us."

Vlasta wouldn't hear of leaving. She was mimeographing clandestine copies of the suppressed speech that Dr. František Kriegel (one of the Presidium members who'd been taken to Russia in chains with Dubček, Smrkovský, and Černík) made at the May, 1969, Central Committee meeting that removed him from power and expelled him from the Party. Kriegel had declined to sign the agreement in Moscow or ratify the "Treaty for the Temporary Stationing of Soviet Troops on the Territory of the Czechoslovak Socialist Republic." One of the "realists" who denounced him had made a reference to "the so-called August events" and Kriegel, in his swan song, asked, "Is someone trying to say that August, 1968, was no event at all?" And he went on to say, "The treaty was not signed with a pen, but with the muzzles of cannons and machine guns."

Swayed by the eloquence of Kriegel's "naïveté" at a time when even good men held their tongues, Vlasta was optimistic. "We're going to win!" she insisted. "Besides, I can't leave my parents forever. I can't leave the place where I was born. I'm the type who lives and dies in one place."

Vlasta was right. Our homeland was still the place for such women—but not for the likes of me.

"I'm Czech," Vlasta went on. "I'm from here and this is where I belong. Karel, there's always been misery. Some years are bad and others are worse. But we've always made it somehow."

"Together?" I said. And in that word Vlasta sensed many meanings—all involving parting from her parents, from her homeland, but she could never let herself conceive of parting from her children while they're young or from her husband till death do us part. In despair, Vlasta fell back on the Bible, saying, " 'Whither thou goest I will go' "—and, as she spoke,

we both remembered that Zdeněk's wife, who'd hesitated before following him, was named Ruth.

That was when I gave Vlasta my word that, no matter how
far and how long I took her away, she would die in Prague.
Next to my marriage vow, it's the most solemn promise I've
ever made.

"We will show you Faust's House, Alan."
"When we all go back to Prague together, Vlasta?"
"I do not want to die in this other place."

They took the candles away from the grave of Jan Palach,
the boy who set fire to himself in January of 1969 as a protest
against censorship and the dissemination of *Zprávy*. They
wouldn't even let us put flowers on the statue of St.-Wenceslas-
on-horseback, but instead of using barbed wire to seal off our
patron saint, they landscaped him with an impenetrable garden
of shrubs, hedges, and lush, prickly flowers tended by watchful
gardeners in brown-leather jackets.

When Jaroslav Aim came to town that June, he didn't want
to talk about prison or K-231 or politics. "I've had enough of
that," he said. So I told him we were thinking about a trip to
Vienna and, somewhat relieved at the switch in subjects, he
gave me the name of "a perfectly Austrian aunt I have there."

Aim and I spent our day together roaming through Prague.
At a shoemaker's shop that morning, he left some boots to be
repaired and asked the young girl who made out the receipt,
"When will they be ready?"

"In three days," she told him.

The minute we'd entered the store, I'd seen and he'd seen
that she'd admired his looks. (Throughout prison, he'd looked
like a college boy. Now, in his forties, he resembled a graduate
student of twenty-six or twenty-seven.) So, knowing he had
her in his hand, Aim turned on the sex appeal: "Do you think
you could use a few of your charms on the shoemaker and
persuade him to get it done tonight? I'm leaving on an early
train tomorrow."

She promised she would. On Aim's receipt, she wrote both the shoe shop's and her own home phone numbers. "If you haven't called for your shoes," she told him, to my amazement, "I'll take them home with me and you can pick them up there. Do you have a place to stay?"

"No," he said, although I'd invited him out to Odolena Voda and he'd accepted. "Do you know of a hotel?"

"Well," she said, "call me about the shoes and perhaps I can help you out."

After a long good-bye, Aim remarked to me on the street, "We don't get service like this out in the provinces."

And all I could say was a teasing "Ladykiller!"

He said (as he'd said more than once before), "There's a lot you don't know about me and women, Karel."

A little later in our wanderings, Aim asked me if I knew of "a small quiet coffeehouse where a man could have a quiet talk with a woman and there's no liquor served?"

"Ah!" I exclaimed. "You *do* have plans for the shoe-shop girl!"

Aim said nothing, but looked hurt. I pointed out that almost any coffeehouse in downtown Prague would serve wine, too, but he might like the leisurely, genteel atmosphere of the Hotel Golden Goose's coffeehouse on Wenceslas Square. It was there that we wound up our day together. The place obviously met with Aim's approval. After a while, he excused himself and went to the pay phone, where I saw him consulting his shoe-repair ticket.

When he came back, I remarked, "That shoe stub had a hot number on it." For this, I received yet another hurt look. From there on out, Aim was unresponsive to my conversation. He seemed eager for me to leave. Out of courtesy, I renewed my offer for him to sleep over at Odolena Voda. But I was not surprised when he declined, saying he wanted to "stay somewhere nearer the station to catch the first train out." So I said good-bye.

On Wenceslas Square, in yet another of life's fleeting O. Henry moments, I passed the shoe-shop girl—a package in her hands—hurrying toward the Hotel Golden Goose. I saw her, but she didn't see me because she didn't have eyes for me.

On the twenty-first of August, 1969, the first anniversary of the invasion, I was in Wenceslas Square—though I left Warszawa at home for her safety's sake. I saw the Czechoslovak Army used once more against its own people; this time, the tanks weren't Russian. I saw helmeted riot police chasing and clubbing and tear-gasing and water-cannonading people like me who just wanted to mourn the Prague Spring together. Behind the bullet-pocked (from August 21, 1968) National Museum atop Wenceslas Square, I saw police issuing grenades and stink bombs to their provocateurs. The Russians had found the "realists" to "normalize" our idealism.

In the wake of August 21, 1969's police riot, "Emergency Laws" suspending all civil rights were decreed in the name of the three highest State officials: President Svoboda, Prime Minister Černík (a "realist," but nonetheless on the way out), and Parliament Speaker Dubček!

It didn't matter that Dubček's name had been affixed without his knowledge or consent. The edict activated my decision to escape. My family and I had exit visas that would expire in a week. The frontier was still open—but not for long. So many people—particularly medical and technical talent—had fled after the invasion that President Svoboda had declared an amnesty until September 15. Anyone who'd left the Republic could come back without being prosecuted for leaving illegally; of course, he *could* be tried for the "crimes against the State" that had impelled him to flee. One could surmise that, soon after the fifteenth of September, the frontier would be sealed. (It was, on October 9, 1969.) Thus, when I told Vlasta that the time had come, there was anguish in her eyes—but no argument from her mouth.

We packed everything we could that wouldn't rupture Warszawa or arouse suspicion. Winter clothes and a beloved feather mattress of Vlasta's (since Bory, nothing with feathers enchanted *me!*) had to be left behind because they could not explain their way into a short summer tourist trip to Austria.

We told the children only that we were "taking a little trip to Vienna for three weeks." They couldn't yet comprehend the difference between "three weeks" and "permanently," if not "forever." Three weeks, after all, was 2½ percent of my daughter's life up to then.

On Sunday morning, August 24, 1969, with Warszawa loaded to the gills, we wheezed around to our parents—and broke the news to them that we were leaving at noon. My mother, who'd been pleading with me to "get out while you have your skin," took it the hardest. She sobbed and threw her arms around me trying to restrain me from going. My father said gruffly, "Good!" Then he added, "The important thing, Karel, is to go together or not at all."* Vlasta wept when we told her folks, but they helped convince her my decision was right. We were unhappy to be fleeing our Motherland, our Fatherland. But, although we didn't know when or if we'd ever see them again, at least we knew we weren't fleeing our mothers and fathers.

We took the same route I'd taken with Zdeněk. The countryside was cool and glistening, but still and serene with no tanks this year. We didn't get lost in Třeboň because all the missing road signs had been replaced with spanking new ones in "normalized" Czechoslovakia. Still, we paused there to picnic by the lake, take some pictures with my camera, and photograph the scene forever with our eyes. You look at your country differently when you're leaving it for a good long time, if not forever. Vlasta saw it through a film of tears. Later, in Austria, well-meaning people would say to me, "It's better here, no?" And I'd say no. Still later, in America, they'd say, "Sure must of been bad over there!" Again, I'd say no. For— still recalling that picnic in Třeboň, with the children romping around the lake just the way they might on any other summer

---

* Some two hundred Czech and Slovak couples fled the country and left their children behind on the misguided assumption that the Red Cross would or could reunite them. For details of the tragedies of these divided families, see one of the two most concerned U.S. periodicals, *Good Housekeeping*, Oct., 1972 ("When Children Are Held as Hostages") or *Catholic Digest*, April, 1973 ("Child Hostages").

Sunday outing—I could only add, "Everything was fine, but I just couldn't afford to live there."

The men guarding the frontier crossing were still Czechs and Slovaks, with no Russians in sight, but there was not a single face there from my last year's visit with Zdeněk and the East German girl. Nevertheless, these men were competent and affable, too—even when they took the film out of my camera.

"We're doing you a favor," the Customs officer told me. "If it's just family pictures, as you say, then it's developed free of charge and waiting for you when you come back home. And if it should be military targets or installations you've photographed, then you'll know what we have in our hands even before *we* do—and you'll know whether to come home or not. Have a good trip."

He didn't give me the chance to ask, "What if they're family pictures, but we're not coming home?"—and I knew better than to dare. So Warszawa rattled her way across the corridor and Vlasta shuddered at all the fortifications while the children went *"Bang! Bang!"* with their fingers. The landscape was all too familiar, but I suddenly realized it was the first time I'd ever crossed such a desert in my own car. I patted Warszawa lovingly on her dashboard.

Around the curve where Zdeněk had disappeared on his way to Canada, there was a little hut with two men in it, playing cards. I waited while one of them put on a hat, straggled out, saluted, and said, "Austrian Pass Control." I showed him our passports and visas. He glanced at them casually, handed them back, and saluted. Then we drove straight ahead to the Austrian city of Linz. The road we came in on was called the Pragerstrasse.

Part 7

Good Men Still Live— But Where?

On Sunday night in the baroque main square of Linz—where Adolf Hitler attended commercial high school—the natives were letting go of the weekend with one final promenade. Thanks to severe bombing in the last days of the war, followed by a Four Power occupation that lasted until 1955—ten years during which hardly anything moved forward, but anything worth taking was plundered by the Russians—Austria had been, until very recently, the poorest country in Western Europe. The people were not, as a whole, much better off financially than the Czechs. But Vlasta's first observation jibed with mine. She said, "The people look so rich!"

Naturally, the people were wearing their Sunday best. But *their* Sunday best had fabrics *we* could never hope to see. Every Austrian could afford one quality dirndl or loden suit. All that Ota Šik had wanted for our people was that, around 1972, "by fundamental changes in the system . . . we will achieve the [1968] level of Austria, which is one of the least economically advanced nations of Western Europe." He hadn't even promised this. He had just said there was a chance—and he had warned that "if there is any further delay, the country's situation and its population's living conditions will grow much worse." The night of August 20–21, 1968, had shattered Šik's vision for us. Now he was in Switzerland and we were in Austria.

We dipped into my hard-currency treasury of $700 (amassed

from some Deutschemark tips plus some last-minute exchanging of Vlasta's and my savings on the Prague black market) for
a quartet of *Linzertorten*, the almond-and-apricot local pastry.
"*Mit Schlag?*" the waiter asked. I said "*Natürlich!*" and added
that we'd like to splurge on two coffees and two milks. When
our order came, the whipped cream tasted strange and so did
the children's milk. When Vlasta said, "Too rich!," she and I
smiled. In Prague, since 1950 or so, the milk and the *Schlag*
had always arrived at least a wee bit sour. Because we'd become
used to this and our children knew nothing else, the taste of
fresh milk and cream struck us as exotic and even not quite
right. "Well, we must learn to live with it," I said—and we
plunged back into our feast.

We spent our first night of freedom in a motel room that
was overheated by plumbing as well as by our bodies. In the
morning, I played with the dial of the radio in our room—and
Radio Prague came in loud and clear. The new minister of
education—a Lysenko geneticist and militant atheist who,
when he was a professor, used to conduct his exams on Sundays
—was saying that "the entry of Soviet troops in August of 1968
was necessary. It was not aggression, it was not perfidy, it was
not occupation, it was not . . ."

"Turn that off!" said little Karel. "It's stupid." And, for once,
we didn't flinch at what was high treason there in Czechoslovakia, but merely accurate here in the West.

We weren't yet refugees. I wanted to cast the die, to declare
myself, to defect. But to whom could we defect? To the motel
clerk? Should I have thrown my arm around that card-playing
"Austrian Pass Control" officer and ruined his Sunday-afternoon
poker game? I wouldn't have blamed him for shoving us back
through the corridor into the prison we'd fled. There didn't
seem to be anybody to defect to—and Vlasta wanted us to wait
a week and enjoy a little time in the West as the tourists we'd
pretended to be. She was hoping, too, that a week of vacation
would relax me enough to want to return while we legally
could.

We drove *east*, for much of Austria (the word "Österreich"
means "Eastern Empire") lies east of Prague, including the

capital, Vienna. For two hours, we cruised along a sleek and smooth Autobahn, the likes of which Warszawa and I had never driven. We had no trouble finding our way around Vienna. It looked like a formalized, flattened-out Prague with much better road markings. And, much as they deny it, there is so much Czech blood in the Viennese that we didn't feel as though this was, in truth, our first time in Vienna.

We looked up Jaroslav Aim's "perfectly Austrian aunt." She welcomed us and—when I confided in her that we were defecting—invited us to stay as long as we wanted in her perfect little house in the garden district near the Schönbrunn Palace, the Max Reinhardt Seminar, and (this worried me a little) the Czechoslovak Embassy. We moved in right away—but we told our hostess we wouldn't stay more than two or three weeks.

"My dears," she said, "you are welcome to stay longer if going to America takes longer. In Vienna, everything takes time. That's why there is so much of it here."

"In one week," Vlasta assured her, "we'll be ready to go back to Prague."

It was a week later, when the arguments were really raging, that we remembered the American Family Levy was scheduled to visit Vienna from Prague for a pre-back-to-school weekend of shopping and recreation. We knew you'd be staying at the Pension Elite on Wipplingerstrasse, as usual.

"Let's go say hello to the Levys," Vlasta said.

"Or good-bye," I countered. But I wanted to see you, even though I felt a bit afraid to break the news to you that you were about to lose your kiddies' chauffeur.

The four Čapeks appear in our pension one afternoon while my wife is napping. Karel comes right to the point: "You, Alan, are going to make the most important decision in our lives."

I have only to look at Vlasta's imploring eyes to know what the question will be, so I play for time: "I couldn't possibly with four children running around a tiny pension."

We leave Valerie a note that she should shop by herself when she wakes up. Then the seven of us cram into Warszawa and ride out to the Prater, that amusement park which is one of the joys of Vienna. Aboard the Riesenrad—*the slow-moving giant Ferris wheel that was famous even before Orson Welles, Harry Lime, Anton Karas, and* The Third Man—*Vlasta strains to see Czechoslovakia in the distance while her husband tells me how his son's being brainwashed by the new minister of education would "make a mess of the boy's life and maybe ours, too."*

Aboard the Liliputbahn—*a half-hour miniature railway ride with grade crossings at which real uniformed flagmen halt real Vienna traffic—I tell the Čapeks that "no man can make this decision for any other." I, in particular, cannot. "Suppose you go back on my say-so and then, as is very likely, you're not allowed to go out again and meanwhile I'm kicked out? I'll have you on my conscience and you'll be cursing my name in Odolena Voda."*

"Or in Bory," Karel adds succinctly.

On roller coasters and midget airplanes, in swan boats and fairy lands, I tell the Čapeks about the lots of Czech émigrés I've known in America. I tell particularly of George Voskovec, who made a go of it as an actor in New York and Hollywood after 1948, while his partner in the famous prewar Prague comedy team of "V&W," Jan Werich, stayed in Prague and survived as a satirist, comedian, and sly public hero—even after President Novotný thanked Werich for "giving me so many good laughs in my lifetime" and Werich replied, "I should thank you, Mr. President, I should thank you." But I tell the Čapeks, too, of how mutual friends say (though V&W won't acknowledge it) that "if their lives could be reversed, George would be a happier man in Prague and Jan might be happier in New York."

I will not make up their minds for the Čapeks and—wishing them luck, whichever they choose—ask them to let us know when they've decided. The American Family Levy is back in Prague when the letter comes with an Austrian postage stamp and no return address:

I thought it many times over and over again and the result is, I'm sorry to say, that you can see where this letter is from. I would like to express all my thanks to you and

Valerie for so much you did for us. Otherwise, we're all in a good state of health and not in such a very good state of mind, but looking forward to finding at least a little bit better place to live in.

The day after we saw you, we'd gone downtown to Caritas, the Catholic welfare organization, where a young nun who looked very nice and sweet, more girlish than spinsterish, interviewed us. She seemed to be living, however, about five yards off the ground. Too many of her questions had to do with our religious background and too few with us. When, with little Karel and Danka making a rumpus right before her eyes, she asked, "Do you have any children?" Vlasta puckered. But I finished out the interview, though, with very little confidence that we'd ever hear from her—which we never did. I had even less desire to have *her* arranging our future.

The American Fund for Czechoslovak Refugees and the Tolstoy Foundation, which we tried next, both shared the same premises on the Franz Josef Embankment. While I chose between their nameplates (I liked the word "Tolstoy" better than I liked the word "Refugees"), a petite and stylish lady in white hat, white gloves, black boots, and long, bright red coat arrived at work and unlocked the door of the Tolstoy Foundation, which proved to be a one-woman shop.

"What can I do for you?" she asked in perfect Czech.

"I'm not a *Russian* refugee," I apologized in English. "I'm just a refugee from the Russians."

"At a time like this," she said in perfect English, "we help whomever we can." She led me into her office and shut the door in the face of Vlasta and the children.

The name on her desk was "Dr. Barbara Lee Podoski" and I remarked, "There used to be a famous tailor's salon in Prague called Podoski's. Are you related to them?"

She replied, "I'm married to a Polish-American, but I'm one of your people. I was born in Brno and I left in nineteen thirty-eight."

Even if Mrs. Podoski is related neither by blood nor marriage to the Podoski tailoring family, she is certainly the most perfectly put-together person I've ever met. Many people nowadays are works of art, but almost every one of us is still being formed—by oneself, by one's attitudes, by experiences —right unto the grave. Not Mrs. Podoski! She was only in her fifties, but completely formed. Blond hair, impeccably coiffed. Eyes focused yet guarded by thick, tinted, purple-rimmed spectacles on a face that is otherwise totally open and believing. A young girl's figure—very tiny. But a deep, masculine growl to warn the world of men that this delicate vase could not be broken. And, I could guess, a life behind her whose story I'd like to hear if she ever had the time. She certainly didn't at that time. In September of 1969, she had her silken white hands full.

Dr. Barbara, the law graduate from Brno who left not just because there might have been a distant Jewish relative in the family, but because she knew, after Munich, that when Hitler came, there would be no law to practice. Sergeant-Major Barbara, who joined the Women's Army Corps to speed up her U.S. citizenship and Hitler's end when his war followed her across the Atlantic—and who wound up her military career as a W.A.C. fighting the war in North Africa and Italy, sometimes behind the enemy lines. Mother Barbara, who—after one bad union that produced her one beautiful daughter, Marina Lee—met her second husband, Josef Podoski, at the Library of Congress, where they both went to work after the war. Librarian Barbara, who retired in 1968 on a disability pension because she was slowly, incurably going blind. She'd left Washington—on the day the city was burning in the wake of Martin Luther King's assassination—to attend a thirtieth reunion of her law-school class in Brno. After a few hours of the Dubček Spring, she'd convinced Josef (himself retired) they should pull up stakes in Washington so that she, at least, could end her days of sight in her reborn homeland—storing up such wondrous visions every day as few 20–20 eyes have been privileged to see in their lifetimes. The homeward migration was slow and cumbersome, but Barbara was as far as Vienna on August 21, 1968, preparing to go the last seventy-five miles when the Russian tanks beat her to Brno. The Tolstoy Foundation, with which she'd had literary contacts, asked her to

*open a field office in Vienna—and the refugee Class of 1968
never had a better friend than Dr. Barbara Lee Podoski, '38.*

*How do I know Barbara's story so well? We are old friends,
though I didn't meet her until seventeen months after you did,
Karel. It is early 1971, and all four Levys have just been deported from Prague under guard on the overnight local to Brno
and Břeclav (where our secret police escort disembarks) and
Vienna—eleven hours to do 200 miles; no sleepers and, for the
first six hours, no heat. On the third Friday of 1971, chilled and
forlorn, we arrive at the Pension Elite once more—but this
time as refugees badly in need of warmth and sleep. On Sunday, tired of sleeping and mentally unwilling to let go of
Prague just yet, I leave a cheery note for my family ("Out to
Mass. Back for lunch with G-d's help!") and wander out along
Wipplingerstrasse to a tiny side street bearing the miraculous
name of Thrust-to-Heaven (Stoss-im-Himmel). At the other end
of Thrust-to-Heaven stands my favorite Viennese church, St.
Maria am Gestade (Our Blessed Lady of the Riverside), with
its lacy cupola and narrow, slightly crooked, Romanesque nave
inside, and, outside, a wide stone staircase leading down to the
next street, the sunken Tiefer Graben (Deep Ditch), where an
arm of the Danube once flowed. Medieval fishing boats and
river boats ferrying salt used to tie up at the foot of these steps
while the boatmen climbed up to worship at this church they
made their own. In the nineteenth century, Vienna's ebbing-
and-flowing tide of Czechs adopted it as their "official church,"
too— and I have remembered that every Sunday's 8:00 A.M.
Mass is held in Czech.*

*Today's is a requiem for the student Jan Palach's martyrdom
by fire two years ago. Amidst the smell of incense and the sound
of Czech, I am dizzy from being nowhere in this world and yet,
for only an hour, alas, exactly where I want to be. And I cry
for Jan Palach and I cry for me and my wife and our uprooted
children and I cry for all the people we've left behind, with or
without saying good-bye, and I cry all the more for you and
Vlasta and Danka and Karel, who've had to leave a beloved
country that was never mine, but was always supposed to be
your own. I make no noise, but when the Mass is over, Barbara*

Podoski is standing over me and saying in English, "You can't be one of us Americans because you care so much."

I knew none of this, Alan, all the time I knew the lady, but I *will* tell you something I knew then: my wife *hates* Mrs. Podoski.

"Hate Barbara???!!!" I exclaim in shock. "Vlasta, that's impossible!"
"I hate that woman. She shut the door in my face. She attacked my child. I hate her!"

Let me tell you what happened between these two good women because it acted out for me a little slice of how the world works.

Mrs. Podoski started filling out papers on me. "Why do you want to leave?" she asked. The sound of children fighting drowned out part of my reply. Mrs. Podoski marched to the door, opened it on the waiting room she shared with the American Fund for Czechoslovak Refugees, and growled, "I can't do my work with all that noise." I was relieved to catch a glimpse of other children besides my own out there—though I think my ears had recognized Karel's blubber and Danka's yelp.

"Why do you want to go to the U.S.?" Mrs. Podoski asked. A familiar howl prevented my answer. Mrs. Podoski was at the door while the vibration was still quivering in my flesh. There was Danka, whose forehead had just been bumped by her big brother's forehead. There was Karel, whose head was hurting even more than his victim's. And there was Vlasta, bending over to comfort both kids.

"Stop that!" Mrs. Podoski commanded in Czech.

"I can't," said Vlasta. "Besides, you can't expect a two-year-old to be quiet all the time."

"Nevertheless," said Mrs. Podoski, "you can't expect me to do my work with such noise. So, if your children make any more noise, you'll all have to leave the office while I interview Mr. Čapek."

Vlasta straightened up. "We'll leave!" she said. "We'll go! We'll get out of here! I don't want to stay one more minute in this place. I can still go back to Prague and spare you a whole lot of paperwork."

Danka stopped crying and said, "Let's go to Prague and kiss Grandma."

"Both grandmas," little Karel corrected. "I want to go, too."

Mrs. Podoski softened. She even showed us a photo of her newborn granddaughter in Washington. But the damage had been done between her and Vlasta. And, if two good women a generation apart—but with similar beliefs and the same need to die at home—can make enemies so fast, how can good men still live between them? Not just in this situation, but in all situations. I've sometimes marveled at two-timing philanderers. But I've never envied them.

Mrs. Podoski dispatched us to the Traiskirchen refugee camp, where we could expect a few hours of processing (security clearances, blood and urine tests, immigration interviews, etc.) and maybe four or five months of waiting. I asked if we could live in Vienna (where I might find work) during the time we weren't needed for processing. But Mrs. Podoski explained that the refugee organizations were so understaffed and underfinanced that they couldn't afford to track down each family every time they needed to go to a lab or an interview. It was easier to reach them by posting rosters in the camp. The Traiskirchen facility had been made available by neutral Austria, which had been uncompromisingly generous and hospitable to political refugees ever since the Hungarian revolution of 1956. Official Austria was unfailingly kind; the people— as do people everywhere—varied, though we'd had no bad experiences until we left Barbara Podoski's office.

Walking toward the Schottenring, where Warszawa was parked, we were feeling almost sorry to be leaving Vienna so soon—and talking about what to buy as a gift for our hostess, Aim's aunt. We were still on the Franz Josef Embankment when a voice suddenly interrupted us in German-accented Czech with: "So here you are again, *Tschusch.*"

Tschusch (or *Čuč* in Czech) is a Viennese pejorative for a poor Slavic immigrant. I said, "Are you talking to me, lady?" "I certainly am, *Čuč*. I've had my troubles and you've had yours. But I keep mine to myself. Someone ought to punch your noses, all four of you."

She was speaking Czech in a heavy Sudetenland dialect, so I knew we'd never settle our grievances on the spot. All I said was: "If someone's got to punch our noses, why don't you call out the Hitler Youth? Anyway, you've got the wrong parties. None of us is named *Čuč*."

And we walked away—a little less sad about leaving Vienna.*

That afternoon, we checked into the *Flüchtlingslager* (refugee camp) in the town of Traiskirchen, just south of Vienna, near the spa of Baden. The *Flüchtlingslager* was an uninviting Hapsburg Gothic military caserne: brick, massive, and gloomy, a little like a prison camp and a lot like a jail. Now we were officially refugees at the mercy of the Austrian authorities. A beige dossier had been opened on us and I was issued *"Flüchtlings* Legitimation Number 6441." Then I was parted from my family for two days in an "Isolation Barracks," while Vlasta and the kids went off to a "Family Isolation Barracks" to live with other "widows" and children whose men were in solitary confinement.

It was just that—in a polite Austrian civilian way rather than a brutal Communist hellhole way. Although there was no Mr. Brabec, I did have to knock on the door of my neat little room for a guard to let me go out to the hall toilet. And I was interrogated, in a routine manner, by Austrian authorities who were establishing that I was who I said I was; that I was not wanted for any nonpolitical crime that I knew of; that I was not a secret-police infiltrator coming to coerce refugees out of

---

* To its credit, Official Vienna recently put up posters scolding the Viennese for such bad manners as the Sudeten lady displayed. A small Austrian boy looks up at towering *Gastarbeiter* (migrant worker) and says, "My name is Kolaric. Your name is Kolaric. How come they call you *Tschusch*?" The Viennese got the message with a vengeance. Nowadays, they would address Čapek or any other Slav as "Hey, Kolaric!"

asylum; that I'd been offered and had waived the right to speak with a representative of the Czechoslovak Embassy in Vienna; and that I wanted to go to America of my own free will.

The rest of my forty hours in isolation allowed me time to meditate on how, for a refugee who might have gone directly from the Iron Curtain to Traiskirchen, freedom would start up just like tyranny—with guards, quarantine, break-up of families, and interrogations.

When I was reunited with the other Čapeks, we were assigned to a barracks that was one giant room with forty double-decker bunks. The kids gladly took upper berths. They even felt sorry for their parents and promised to exchange with us subpeople some other night. I declined the offer, telling them, "Thanks, but no thanks. I had my share of upper bunks in prison."

Danka gazed around from her high perch and proclaimed, "I am going to like it here in prison."

And little Karel said, "Now I know why all those K-two hundred thirty-one people were so happy."

But Vlasta, after the children had gone to bed at eight o'clock, told me what *she* thought: "This is one nasty place, Karel. I don't like the West. It's all so inhuman."

"Well," I comforted her, "at least we're among our own." Almost all of our seventy roommates were Czechoslovaks.

The next morning, we began to learn how nasty and inhuman our own people could become in the West. In the morning, as usual, the two Čapek children awoke a little before seven and started playing quietly in their upper bunks. At 7:30, their playing increased in volume. "Tell them to shut up!" a woman called out.

I told the kids to "quiet down," which they did until eight. Then they started up again as Vlasta and I began to get up. A man grumbled at us: "What's the big hurry? Nothing happens here before eleven." But 8:00 A.M. was late enough for us, so we tiptoed out to breakfast.

When we returned, after exploring the camp and learning that, as a matter of unexplained policy, I wouldn't be allowed out into town for a fortnight (but the rest of my family could go out on Sundays), it was nearly eleven. A baleful-looking delegation in housecoats and undershirts was awaiting us. It was headed by the woman who'd told us to shut up our kids. She was a young Moravian divorcée with two kids of her own —an attractive blonde, but no Brigitte Bardot; puffy and pouty, like the young Shelley Winters. She was also a talented demagogue. This I recognized from her first question: "How does it happen that you have such noisy kids?"

"I think they're perfectly normal, healthy kids," I replied.

"Ours sleep until eleven, just like we did—until today!"

"Well, I have average kids, but you must have exceptional kids," I said. "I'm sorry if ours woke you up, though."

"They better not do it again!"

"We'll do our best, but that's the best we can do."

That night, we watched what this exceptional mother who was no B.B. (Vlasta called her the "Queen Bee") did with *her* two kids. What she and the other mothers did was keep them up until 11:00 P.M. or even midnight. Every time their children, even two-year-olds like Danka, dropped off, they'd be awakened. That was how they slept till 11:00 A.M.

In Traiskirchen, the technocrats of child-rearing had taken power. It was clear to Vlasta and me that Queen Bee was the first secretary of the Technocrat party—and that we didn't want to join.

They all watched disapprovingly as we let Danka and Karel drop off between 8:00 and 9:00 P.M. But they held their fire until 7:45 the next morn, when Danka's first cackle drew a barrage of "Shut ups!" and, from the Queen Bee, an anguished *"What kind of people are you?"*

Prisoners learn never to personalize a problem, but to confront the issue rather than the personality of the adversary (openly, that is). Most demagogues and Communists, in particular, prefer to do it the other way. So I shifted the ground as best I could. "We're the kind of people," I replied, "who put children's health ahead of adults' convenience."

Vlasta chimed in: "It's natural and healthy for a child to fall asleep around eight and get up around seven. And, in a place like this, a good mother tries to keep life as normal and healthy as possible for her kids."

Queen Bee glared at Vlasta and asked, "Are you calling me a bad mother?"

And I pointed out, "Vlasta didn't say it; you did."

The remark wasn't wasted on her, but the others—first the men and then the women—were starting to agree with us. A few even argued with the Queen Bee. We let the debate go at that, for all we wanted was the right to live our lives in a way we deemed appropriate and moral. But I remarked to Vlasta that "the atmosphere here is less cooperative than it was in prison."

We might have stayed on in that barracks and had further confrontations with Queen Bee's reign if we hadn't found out that there were family barracks, too, with four-bedded private rooms. Seniority at Traiskirchen and family needs were the only eligibility requirements. Within a week, we'd qualified to move there—and we did so.

Even without a husband, Queen Bee was much more eligible than we were; she and her kids had been in Traiskirchen for three months. Some families chose to remain in the mass barracks because the family barracks were more primitive, shingled, older housing. But I think others, like Queen Bee, stayed because there was more power to be had among the masses. How quickly all the problems of society were repeating themselves in miniature—how the tensions were magnified!

Our letters and postcards to Prague had arrived. On our second Sunday at Traiskirchen, my friend Polda from the Jaundice Brigade came visiting. He arrived at the main gate in the Arab diplomat's limousine he was chauffeuring. His boss, visiting Vienna, had given him the Mercedes and the day off.

Polda wasn't allowed in and I wasn't allowed out. (Neither was Warszawa, but we had Mercedes.) Vlasta got passes for herself and the kids. Then, while she and Polda engaged the gate guard in conversation about cars, I climbed the wall and climbed into Mercedes' backseat.

We spent a balmy September Sunday in the Stadtpark of

Vienna. The children fed the ducks and swans while the three adults drank coffee at an outdoor table. Polda had brought letters from our folks. He even had the photos that Czechoslovak Customs had printed for me. Now Vlasta was answering her mail and writing other letters for Polda to take back. Polda and I chatted about old times, my decision to leave, and the times ahead. As we drove back to Traiskirchen toward nightfall, Polda said, "Maybe this is the last time I see you."

"Or else we'll meet in another country in another jail," I said.

Freedom thus far had been a series of boxes—the motel room in Linz; Aim's aunt's house in Vienna; the different kinds of barracks in Traiskirchen—from which you could sometimes move (to the next box) without waiting to be transferred. I reflected on this after Polda let me out of his limousine in Traiskirchen, a block before the *Flüchtlingslager*, so that I could safely climb the wall and escape back into confinement.

Not for long, though. Hustling our way upward, ever upward, even within the limited options of the refugee camp, I'd learned that the Austrians were opening a bunch of Alpine "family camps" for refugees in summer resorts now that the tourist season was over. (This was to prolong the summer employment season for hotel help.) It hinted of good food, good air, and good nature, as well as opportunities to work in the rural areas where much of the manpower was migrating to the cities. I volunteered as soon as I heard about the "family camps."

The last phase of our migration through Austria, then, was an idyllic autumn in the Austrian Alps—where, in late September, we rode our faithful, but not-quite-trusty, steed Warszawa to a tourist home in the *Sound of Music* territory between Linz and Salzburg. There, amidst a cascade of heavenly lakes—the Attersee, the Wolfgangsee, and the Mondsee (Moon Lake)—Vlasta and the children thrived and bloomed like edelweiss. On a diet of long walks and hearty meals, all four of us rekindled a zest for living that our uncertain summer had stilled, but not killed.

I took a job in a nearby factory, where some 150 workers and fifty refugees were manufacturing, of all things, helmets for the Austrian Army and for export to the military machines of Switzerland and Norway! As one who used to be privileged to wear UNRRA miner's helmets, they struck me as being of inferior quality—but I comforted myself with the hope that we were equipping the armies of small nations that, unlike Czechoslovakia, might never have occasion to need this equipment.

(Now that I'm in America, it strikes me as funny how political everyday living and working has always seemed in Europe—even the casual job of a man in transit, let alone the morals of a citizen of a "socialist republic." In the New World, on the other hand, no "ordinary man" I've met seems to feel that political developments—be they wars in Indochina or scandals in Washington or even local elections—are affecting his way of life.)

On our last weekend in Austria, we made an outing to Salzburg. On our way home, Warszawa gave a convulsive shudder, made a sound that was definitely a death rattle, and stopped dead. Yes, it was indeed a death in the family. Warszawa was beyond repair or resuscitation. The wrecker who came to tow her away offered to do so without charge and pay me two hundred schillings (then $8) additional for whatever organs still worked and could be salvaged in case anybody ever needed another Warszawa repaired. There was no other repository of Warszawa spare parts in all of Austria, he told me.

Waiting for a bus that would take us back to our resort, we watched poor Warszawa's remains go bouncing down the road in the lively, almost lifelike, embrace of the wrecker's arm. And we all mourned my doomed third child who had brought us into and through the Prague Spring, a livelihood, and an escape when August's Winter became unbearable. Warszawa had lived and died a vital member of the Čapek family. Now, as our flight to the New World loomed, the old law of survival of the fittest had asserted itself. The unfittest Čapek, who would have been left behind anyway, had dropped dead.

Warszawa Čapková (1965–1969), may you rust in peace in your Alpine junkyard!

The children looked forward to their first plane trip, though Karel asked, "Will Grandma be at the plane?" On the day before your Thanksgiving holiday in November of 1969, the thirty refugees in our resort were delivered by bus to Vienna's Schwechat Airport. There, we joined up with ninety others coming from Traiskirchen. Barbara Podoski was there with our dossiers and forms all made out for U.S. Immigration. Somehow, she had wangled us an official "sponsor" in Edison, New Jersey, but plane tickets to Chicago, where several Jaundice Brigaders had certified we could stay with them. Our fares had been paid by the American Fund for Czechoslovak Refugees. I signed an agreement that I would eventually repay the fund, at my convenience and without interest, the $600 our travel was costing. It is a debt that I've just begun to pay off.

As she saw us off on a chartered Alitalia DC-8 jet, Barbara Podoski pointed out that "you're going nonstop to New York, which is a better deal than the tourists get. The commercial flights aren't nonstops."

We took four window seats on a plane full of folks like us, most of them speaking Czech. The plane sailed into the sky. At 25,000 feet, the children asked me to tell them "when we start to fly." I told them they'd been flying for half an hour. They played pilot and co-pilot for an hour or two and fell asleep. I took two pictures of fleecy white clouds from my window and slept, too.

The cabin crew served us two good Italian meals, not too spicy, and the nonalcoholic drinks were free. Three hours before New York, however, I felt compelled to invest a quarter in a bottle of Italian beer; I had never been so thirsty in my life and the Arctic wastelands beneath us kept reminding me of one giant ice bucket.

Other passengers were feeling the same call and the Italian steward was almost apologetic about having to take our money. "We have 120 people aboard," he said, "and we stocked enough provisions for 160, but we've run out of soft drinks. I think it's because most of you people haven't flown before and the air conditioning makes you thirsty." I gulped the bad *birra* as though it were the elixir of life.

We circled John F. Kennedy Airport for an hour at dusk—so close to America, but not yet there. While we were circling, the lights of New York came on all at once—and the skyline lit up like a picture postal of Manhattan-by-Night, though we still couldn't find the Statue of Liberty or the Empire State Building, and somebody said that what we were looking at was Queens or Jamaica. The crew begged us to get back in our seats and fasten our belts. Ten minutes later, we landed.

The first sight that met our eyes when we set foot on American soil was a mound of garbage bigger than a jumbo jet. Men with flashlights led us around it to a couple of shuttle buses, which took us to a special shed (not so clean, either), where nobody checked our papers. But a Czech-speaking refugee organization man was there to tell us we were booked on United Air Lines to Chicago. "You have only three hours to make the connection," he said, "so please hurry!"

This mystified me, but by the time we'd claimed our luggage, cleared Customs, and taken a red-white-and-blue United car from Kennedy to LaGuardia Airport, we just barely made our flight. In our haste, I left my umbrella behind in the red-white-and-blue car. When I realized this as we hurried through the LaGuardia labyrinth, I decided not to hold up the parade by trying to retrieve it.

Vlasta and I arrived at Chicago's O'Hare Airport toward midnight on Thanksgiving Eve, 1969, with two sleeping children in our arms. An old, but hitherto never close, friend from the Jaundice Brigade, Tonda, was waiting for us with his wife, Jola, who'd been a prisoner, too. They'd escaped through Yugoslavia in 1967, almost a year before the Prague Spring, and had thus established themselves early in the "Bohemian" colony of Cicero—where "Bohemian" means Czechs and various other Slavs, not hippies or beatniks. He was working as a machinist at the Danly Machine Tool factory in Cicero and she was working as a department-store sales clerk. They had a new car, a color TV, and a spare bedroom—which we were exposed to in rapid succession as Tonda whisked us through the ghostly-lit clover leafs of O'Hare and the ghastly ghettos of Chicago to the sanctuary of his home, where he switched on the TV the minute we entered. While Jola blew up a couple of air mattresses for the kids and Vlasta conked out in our bedroom, Tonda poured us a couple of beers. I couldn't tell whether he wanted to talk or watch TV.

It turned out he wanted to do both—and this was my introduction to conversation, American style.

I'll tell you how I reacted to it. I fell asleep on Tonda's living room sofa. So Vlasta and I slept apart on our first morning in America.

I awoke toward noon on Thanksgiving Day. Jola and Tonda must have taken the kids out. Vlasta was still sleeping and nobody else was around. I tiptoed to the porch of the two-family house in which the Tondas lived. I'd seen enough movies to expect to find a twelve-pound newspaper and a gallon bottle of milk, but if there were any, they'd already been taken inside.

My first daylight view of America, then, was a row of flimsy, papery-looking, red-brick houses—all alike. While they didn't arouse me aesthetically, they were oddly comforting because they reminded me of the maternity clinic where I'd been born in Prague. I had started my life there—or so I'd been told—and now, after all my travels, I'd found my way to a flimsy, paper-brick womb in the New World.

I pulled down the shades so that Vlasta wouldn't awaken to the same view. Then I climbed into bed with her so she might not know I'd slept out. I knew that Cicero wouldn't look like her birthplace to her—because Vlasta had been born at home in the days before midwives were nationalized and abolished.

When Vlasta arose, I braced myself—but pretended to be half-asleep. She, too, tiptoed to the porch, peered out at the flat, flat flatness, and retreated. As she jumped back into bed, she said, "I want to go home."

On Cermak Road, the grand boulevard of Cicero, with its used-car lots and potholed pavements, I'd talk to my wife

animatedly and vivaciously, even foolishly or flirtatiously, just
to distract her from what was before her eyes. But Vlasta saw.
And she said, "I want to go home."

Riding the Chicago Transit Authority's "el" through the
black belt of ramshackle slums that separate Cicero from Chicago, I found myself sitting sideways to block the view from
Vlasta. Compassion told me that, even in the uranium mines
of Czechoslovak Siberia, I hadn't touched bottom. But Vlasta
saw—and her eyes filled with tears as she asked me, "Can this
happen to us?"

"I've been told," I said, hating myself for even speaking such
reassurance, "that if you're white in America, you'll never starve
to death." It didn't help my conscience any to learn later—
from reading rather than experience—that even this "ugly
truth" wasn't so.

Within a week of our arrival, I had a job and we had an
apartment. The job came on the first try: at Danly's—where
Tonda had already put in a word for me—as a $3.96-an-hour
mechanic assembling one small machine part on the night
shift. (Actually, my pay was $3.60 an hour, plus a 10 percent
"night bonus.") The apartment came to us on the third try.
"How long do we have to wait for an apartment?" had been
Vlasta's first question of Tonda and Jola—and she'd wondered
why they'd laughed. On the Monday after Thanksgiving, they
sent us to a Czech-born real-estate agent (a class of 1948 refugee) who was waiving his fee of one month's rent for people
like us. He gave us some names and addresses. The third one
we visited had three names on the mailbox for the downstairs
apartment. When I saw that one of them was "Josephine
Čapek," I knew, sight unseen, that the upstairs apartment was
for us.

Mrs. Čapek proved to be the mother of our landlady, Mrs.
Mary Schulz. She and the Schulzes live right below us—and
we hit it off with Mrs. Schulz from the start, when we took off
our shoes and put on our portable slippers, the folding "house
shoes" we'd brought with us from Prague, just to walk through
the five-room apartment we were inspecting. "I like having

Czech tenants upstairs for several reasons," Mrs. Schulz told us, "but one of them is that the apartment lasts longer with them in it."

The apartment came furnished with everything, including a black-and-white TV set that we still shut off when we want to talk, and the rent has gone up only once in our four-and-a-half years here. That was from $125 to $135 a month in 1971, when I bought a green 1968 Pontiac Bonneville sedan and the Schulzes let me share their two-car garage.

We moved in on the Thursday after Thanksgiving, 1969. I told Vlasta, "Next time you say you want to go home, remember, this is it."

Vlasta Čapek says now, "When I first saw Cicero by daylight, I was ready to pack my bags, except I hadn't yet unpacked them. Now I have to admit that I'm not only used to the place, but I can even see improvements. Every time they take away a used-car lot on Cermak Road and put up a highrise, well, I can only cheer. The streets are cleaner in 1974 than they were in 1969, while I have the idea that the rest of the world is getting dirtier. In summer, when everywhere is supposed to grow greener, Cicero actually does. I can buy rohlíky [little bread horns] and housky [Czech breakfast rolls] freshly baked on Cermak Road and I can make my own knedlíky and zelí [dumplings and sauerkraut] far better than with what I had to work with in Prague. Cicero's not a bad place to live, but it's not where I want to end my days."

I don't know how long we'll live here, my Vlasta, but I promise you we won't die here.

I can't generalize about America, but what struck me about Cicero from the very start was its capacity to rebuild and regenerate itself. When one class of émigrés moves outward and upward to the suburbs, there's always, alas, another class of émigrés moving in. But Cicero is not dead, not left to die. To a Prague eye, it may look godforsaken, but it's not manforsaken. We're surrounded on every side but the West by those desolate black or racially mixed slums, less than a mile from our door. But we're a people who, back where we come from, made housing of slum caliber into livable homes that were even pleasant places to visit. Cicero remains a safe and enjoyable place to stroll—as it was in my early days on the night shift at Danly's, where I could walk to work, even at midnight.

Once we had an address and I had a job, I wrote the good news, discreetly, to all our relatives and friends in Czechoslovakia who I thought would care.

Yes, I got a "Dear Alan" letter from you that asked a question I'll always remember: "I have to put up with the job of an assembler in the tool-and-die set factory of Mr. Danly in Cicero—which is not so bad for the beginning, but how many beginnings can a man afford?"

The same basic letter—with "look after the ladies for me" added—to Jaroslav Aim elicited no response. Thus, I scribbled a personal greeting at the bottom of a Christmas card we sent him—and signed it "Can you write? Karel." On January 20, 1970, I received this answer:

Dear Karel:

You wrote to us, wishing us everything good for Christmas and the New Year. Well, then I have to answer you. Thank you and your wife—and we are wishing the best to you. I didn't answer your previous letter. I had received it, but I'd hoped you could gather why I didn't answer. Apparently, you didn't.

Yes, you were right. I was very taken aback by your departure and if I didn't matter enough for you to say a personal good-bye, I certainly didn't care to bother you with a letter from me. But now that I've received your greeting card, I think it suitable and obligatory to answer you at this time.

You don't realize many things, Karel. From the way you went without saying good-bye, you obviously don't think much of me. Well, be that as it may, it's your own business.

You seem to have come to the conclusion that I've succumbed to women. You make too much of my passing glances at them. If you could see inside me, Karel, you would end up smiling at your own misjudgment. But I've never considered it necessary to explain myself to you.

If I myself don't understand something about someone I know, rather than let my imagination run wild, I ask him directly—

But I did, Jaro! So many times—in Bytíz, in Vojna, in the country, in the city. And you never gave me a straight answer.

—or else I trust him to the point of knowing that he must have his reasons for his kind of behavior. If you had really known my situation, you would have tried to help me with my request without jumping to conclusions.

Here, Aim was alluding, I think, to his request for a café to take a woman to—which I had met by suggesting the Golden Goose. His letter went on:

In spite of all this, I am writing to you anyway. That last time in Prague, I expressed some of my disappointment in my friends without naming names. It still goes on.

I am very sorry that I have to write this to you, but there is no other way. I am not angry with you in all respects. No, I am thankful to you for many things and I am not forgetting them. Perhaps it's no credit to me, but my anger does not last. And even friendships that don't last are still fondly remembered. But this is not the time for friendship. In the end, it is every man for himself. I thought this would be clear to certain people, but I was once again disappointed. Friendships don't dwindle so much as people, inside themselves, dwindle away from each other.

Friendship is a process, Jaro! It was something we lived on in the places where you spent sixteen bad years and I eleven. It bloomed in Bytíz, it blossomed in Vojna, it withered in Prague, and it died in Cicero. The fragile web was broken by the time Aim concluded:

Besides, I cannot understand why you are writing to me. If you can do anything for me, Karel, please be so kind as not to write to me anymore. This is all I am asking of you. With best to you and your wife and kids, I wish you contentment—and so does my wife Lida.

To which Lida had appended: "Mr. Karel—I have read this letter." Meaning, I suppose, "It goes for me, too."

Since Aim had shown his letter to *his* wife, I showed it to my wife.

Vlasta read it with puzzlement. "I must be forgetting my Czech," she said, "because I don't understand this letter at all."

"Well," I said, "it's a real 'get lost!' letter."

"Yes, but he seems to be picking a fight with you." Vlasta reread the letter and added, astutely, I think, "It reads like a letter he hopes someone will open and read along the way."

I shook my head sadly and said, "Inside barbed wire, he was a better man than any other. But outside —?"

"Saints have to survive, too," said Vlasta, who knew all about Aim's escapade with the shoe-shop girl and had seen enough of him to give him her own rating of holier-than-thou.

And so I concluded my obsession with Jaroslav Aim by observing, "Oh, boy, what civilian life can do to a man!" Then I thought to myself, "I wonder what it's doing to the Czechoslovak people." And when I thought those words—*"the Czechoslovak people"* for the first time, instead of *"my people"*—I felt less like an alien where I am now, but more like an émigré.

I have to admit that I haven't made *new* friends easily in America. Maybe American factory hands have a different cultural index from Czech laborers or maybe it has to do with the partial staffing, in recent generations, of Prague factories with defrocked professors, journalists, and executives. But I beg to report that I have trouble conversing with my fellow workers.

God knows I've tried! My English is fluent and I happen to be a talker. I can talk about automobiles for an hour—and it's fun. I can talk about women for an hour or two—and it gives me pleasure, too. But just throwing phrases around on the same subject all evening is a sport in which I can hardly hold my own. And, of course, Americans have their own codes of talking—mostly having to do with regional origins and status—which I haven't yet penetrated. My fellow workers also talk a lot about work, which I mostly want to forget about after hours. I mean: it's not the high point of *my* day and I don't think it's the high point of *their* day, either.

You may object that I'm talking only about a very specialized

milieu of workers at Danly's. But I'm not. I've been meeting
Americans in all walks of life ever since I got here. Democracy
is almost as effective as cab-driving in exposing you to a variety
of people—and making them lend you an ear. I've met cemetery managers and undertakers (more about them in a minute) and I've even met the actress Jane Fonda. I went to an
antiwar rally just to see what she was like and I wound up
talking with her. Oh, boy, was *that* ever like being back in
Czechoslovakia around the beginning of 1948!

Your own interest in my life has already taken me into a
literary salon and an expense account lunch or two—and the
Sunday afternoon we spent sitting on the floor sipping mar-
tinis with Nelson Algren will always remind me of your warning that "all generalizations about Americans are false." With
that disclaimer, let me go on to say that, here, conversation can
be intense or it can be superficial, but—even with the TV turned
off—it usually turns out to be distracted. You tell someone
something that's meaningful to you and, the very next day, he
asks you something that indicates he never heard what you
said or else he's forgotten it. Or: Someone tells you something
one day that's meaningful to him and then, a day later, he tells
you the same thing all over again. Just in general, I keep having the same conversations with the same people—not just
conversations I had eight weeks ago, but conversations I had
the night before! It cheapens the value of what matters to them
and what matters to me if we can't build upon them. *How
many beginnings can a man afford?*

One of the charms of Cicero is that we could resume the
threads of *old* friendships, particularly those formed in prison.
Heteš, the butcher to whom I'd taught English my way, is here
—and our wives, who met at the K-231 meeting, practically
keep a direct line open by phone when they're not together in
person. Mirek Zástěra, who taught me in Bory how to add
weight to feathers by watering them, was already a media
heavyweight when I arrived here—as editor of *Denní Hlasatel*
(*Daily Herald*), America's only Czech-language daily newspaper. Now he conducts the weekly "Czechoslovak Radio

Kaleidoscope" ethnic program on WSBC. And I had never met Jan Beneš, the novelist whose prison "fiction" reflects so much of my life, *before* I came to Cicero, even though I'd *known* him from the moment I picked up his prose. Here, we're good friends. In fact, when Mirek was between jobs and Beneš was having trouble making ends meet from his writing, before he won an $11,000 P.E.N.—Rockefeller Foundation grant, I found them temporary jobs at Danly's.

Thirty of us have formed a local K-231—we call it Former Political Prisoners of Communist Czechoslovakia. We wrangled at first about whether it was to be a protest group or a social club or a welfare society or what. We finally agreed that, from our little corner of Chicago, the best we could do would be to exchange information about fellow alumni in distress in Canada, Western Europe, or even Australia—and find them opportunities in Cicero or elsewhere in the U.S.; write to them with offers of jobs or hospitality; and even assist financially in their travels (which the refugee organizations won't do after the initial relocation). In our first year, we managed to find work in the States for two men stranded in Canada—and just our offer to help another of our fellows came, he wrote, "in the nick of time. I was on the verge of suicide." When a man who has survived the prisons of Czechoslovakia says that, he isn't talking figuratively.

To put ourselves on the map and finance our mission, we held a Former Political Prisoners picnic in Desplaines Park. People without criminal records were welcome too—and more than two hundred people, prisoners and nonprisoners, Czechs and Americans, showed up. For them, the high points were butcher Heteš's pork chops and stuffed veal birds as well as Pilsener beer at premium prices. But, for me, the high point had come a few days earlier, when I was delegated to apply for the picnic permit from the Chicago authorities. I was asked three questions:

"What is the basis of membership in your group?"

"We're all ex-convicts wanting to hold a picnic."

"What kind of crimes did you commit?"

"Political."

Now came the tough question: "For or against Mayor Daley?"

I mulled that one for a moment and decided that, whatever we may have done in Czechoslovakia, it was more *for* the mayor of Chicago than *against* him. So I said, "For." Permission was granted.

Meanwhile, back in Prague, a page-two item in *Rudé Právo* for Friday, March 26, 1971:

TODAY ON TELEVISION:
EXPOSURE OF A SPY

PRAGUE, March 25 (ČTK)—Czechoslovak Television introduces today, March 26, at 7:30 P.M., a public-affairs program entitled "A Well-Kept Household," acquainting TV viewers with the anti-State activities of American Alan Levy on the soil of the Czechoslovak Socialist Republic between the years 1967 and 1969.

In this series, documents, writings, and photographic materials on film show the association of A. Levy with the American espionage service, then especially with the American Special Forces, known under the name of Green Berets. In this series, some new facts are revealed concerning the activities of this unit in Czechoslovakia in the year 1968. Assembled in the program are proofs of the contacts of A. Levy with Czechoslovak citizens, especially cultural workers, and of the great movement of foreign operatives in the Czechoslovak Socialist Republic in the year 1968.

Remembering how much I'd talked about you and your well-kept household, my mother tuned in. She'd never met you and wanted to see what you looked like. As you know, you'd been filmed during your last days in Prague—though the TV *didn't* show the famous jig your wife danced in the Foreign Ministry's parking lot when she realized she was being photographed from a green Škoda.* The commentary, as you also know, said you'd been accredited as a foreign correspondent,

* See "How to Get Kicked Out of Prague," The New York *Times Magazine*, May 16, 1971, pp. 28–29, 99–104.

but "finally he admitted who he really was and admitted he never came here to write. He was exposed and there was no point in denying it." Then, with a one-two punch that floored at least one viewer, they "documented" your link with American Intelligence—by showing first a letter from you addressed to me and then a police archives card with my crimnal record and two photos on it: a full face and a side profile of the eighteen-year-old Karel Čapek taken right after my arrest in 1949.

I don't know whether they said where I was now, because my mother fainted and my father was too busy reviving her to listen. Once before, right around the time those pictures were taken, she and he had thought I was safely in the West (they'd had mail from me from Germany, hadn't they?) only to find out that I was right there in Pankrác awaiting trial for treason. After my mother awoke from that 1971 telecast, many reassurances crossed the Atlantic, but she didn't quite believe we were here until she somehow wangled a visa to visit us in December of 1972.

I still have the letter, Karel, which you sent us in 1971, as soon as you had our address in Vienna. It was signed "Charles Stork, C.I.C. (ret.)—that old rotten yarn again!":

Dear Alan:
Ever since our last reunion in Vienna, I've been wondering how long you'd be able to endure in Prague and secretly hoping you could do it somehow. I dare say that, so long as you stayed there, I was nursing some uncertain hope that this time around it might not be so bad.
If I go once again over the beautiful months of 1967–68–69, I feel I'm very thankful for them. It was a MIRAC-ULOUS WONDERFUL TIME. I feel I have to use big letters, for what words could describe something that cost you and me so much?
We are living sort of dull lives here—exposed to daily wear-and-tear by two aggressive junior Čapeks; otherwise, doing nicely and feeling deeply with many of my kind who wander through the vast polluted American plain looking vainly for some small Bohemia and the spirit of the Prague Spring.

I had come to America, not only because I spoke the language and liked the four Americans I knew well, but also out of curiosity about what made America so great. I remembered your remarking that, in 1968 in Prague, you hadn't felt like an American abroad, but like a New Yorker transported in time back to the Hudson Valley two hundred years earlier for the American dream's beginnings.

Actually, I haven't yet found your country great so much as big. But I'm keeping an open mind. I suppose there are those who would say that since, with overtime and bonuses, Karel Čapek earned $10,000 in his first year in the melting pot, mine is a success story that could happen only in America. If my vision of America were more Horatio Alger's and less O. Henry's—or Karel Čapek's—I might have accepted that. And then where would I have been when I was laid off a few weeks later as the recession of 1970–1971 came closer to home?

That was, in fact, my second minor disaster. On the night shift at Danly's, I'd met a young Czech artist in exile: a stone-cutter-turned-welder named Ladislav Hurka. He was tall, blond, and brawny—a strong South Bohemian who could cut any stone with just hammer and chisel. Hurka had never had the privilege of prison schooling, but he had left Czechoslovakia a year before I had because he could no longer practice the particular art that had been passed on to him by five generations of Hurkas.

Hurka's special skill was to carve faces and images directly onto gravestones or plaques. Working from a photo with his diamond-pointed needles, he reminded me more of a dentist than a sculptor or tattoo artist. But, whatever you wanted to label his talent, he was a genius at it. Each monument took a good two and a half days' hard work, which no dictatorship of the proletariat could afford to allow an able young man to spend on mere adornment of the dead. Old pensioners still practiced the art, privately and furtively, but Hurka could not —so he left.

In America, there was no outlet for his genius, either. Instead, he was at Danly's, telling me that "if I were a salesman and if I spoke better English, I could make a go of it here."

Since I possessed those two particular abilities, we formed a partnership and I even had a calling card printed up that read:

KAREL ČAPEK
Artistical Monumental Engravings

Representing L. M. HURKA

By the time the cards were ready, Hurka and I had toured Chicago's cemeteries. Some monuments had photos of the deceased baked into stone. The most artistic carvings we could find were crudely cut mechanical flowers or family crests that had been sandblasted onto gravestones from prefabricated rubber sheets. In all of Greater Chicago's graveyards, we found only five specimens of Hurka's art that had been worked directly on the stone. Three of them were at least twenty-five years old. The other two had been made to order in Czechoslovakia—one of them by Hurka's dad.

The cemetery officials we talked with had long admired these odd stone faces in their crowd. They would have welcomed more. When we showed them two samples I'd had Hurka make up, called "Einstein" and "Einhorn"—the first a likeness of the late scientist; the other a rendition of an imagined unicorn—they took our names and numbers and promised to recommend us highly. But cemetery managers are at the end of the road, not at the point of sales.

Although we'd set our price quite reasonably, for such a once-in-a-lifetime occasion, at $120 to $150 per three-day job (plus the cost of the stone, ranging from $60 to $140), we were given a runaround when we went to the gravestone quarries, dealers, and undertakers with our "Einstein" and "Einhorn" samples and calling cards:

"Sorry, it doesn't fit into our pattern of mechanization."

Or: "I've heard of Einstein and I think I've heard of Čapek, but I've never heard of L. M. Hurka."

Or, most maddeningly: "There was an old German fella in

here who used to do this sorta stuff and I kinda promised him that if I ever got an order, I'd call him, not some other guys. . . . No, I lost his name and phone number. You see, it was twenty-thirty years ago."

What we found mostly was a deaf ear and a blind eye, although a suburban Sears, Roebuck displayed our two stones for a month. No orders, no sales. An aggressive florist displayed photos of "Einstein" and "Einhorn." He made three sales at $100 each, less a 25-percent commission for his services. Later, he told us, "You boys could have had a lot more business if you'd have let me sell it for $99.95." It hadn't occurred to us and he hadn't suggested it.

The recession, however, was gaining momentum and there were few among the living (or the living-above-income) who were willing to spend on such frills for their dear departed. And among those who departed was my partner Hurka—for the state of Washington, where he found a job in the aircraft industry after he was laid off by Danly's, too.

After Hurka & Čapek Artistical Monumental Engravings had gone out of business, four more widows called me up with orders. Amen.

Laid off by Danly's myself, I was out of work for just two days before latching onto a $3.90-an-hour daytime job as a torch-cutter trainee at Ryerson Steel, ten miles from home. Hurka had taught me torch-cutting during dull moments together at Danly's. It took me only two days more to learn how to shield my eyes and steer clear of the radioactive precision-checking devices that reminded me of my days in the uranium mines. With this education behind me, I was put to work cutting prefabricated parts for the uglification of Chicago's skyline. A little bit of Karel Čapek's made-in-Czechoslovakia precision craftsmanship is in the 110-story, 1,450-foot Sears Tower —the world's tallest building; this week, anyway—and a couple of other glass needles poking into the Lake Shore smog. But, after a few months of my commuting to Ryerson Steel, the capitalist system pulled itself up by the bootstraps for a while and I came back to Danly's in triumph—as a $4.50-an-hour maintenance man. It's the job I do now.

I am one of the two men on each shift responsible for taking care of the fire hoses, sprinkler systems, and extinguishers all over the Danly plant. The work is simple and not demanding, though I work at it like a zealot because I love my fellow man more than enough to willingly save his life if a little preventive maintenance is all it takes. Besides, maintenance work is what I was cut out for. My job at Danly's is very similar to some of the *better* assignments I had in the mines, not to mention my boiler-room work in Vojna. So, whether this be freedom or just free enterprise, rest assured that I qualified for it in the Communist jails of my own land. I am a professional prisoner.

And I am a survivor. I have survived six and a quarter years of Nazi occupation; twenty-one and a half years of Communism—eleven and a quarter of them in prison and a year and a day of them under Soviet occupation; and even a year or two of Nixon recession. And, through all of those ordeals—from construction sites in Příbram to construction work at Ryerson; from double shifts at Prokop to night shifts at Danly's—there has never been a single day that didn't give me at least one little smile.

I made it. I survived physically. I survived mentally. I survived morally. I survived without having to surrender my self. In fact, I *found* my self during those formative years in prison. I know more about myself and my capabilities and my limitations than does anyone I know who was on the outside during those bad years. And I bettered myself in prison. I taught myself English and I arrived in America with my self-esteem intact and the question, properly phrased, on my lips: *"How many beginnings can a man afford?"*

I'm just turning forty-four but I think that—after nearly forty years in Central Europe plus more than four in Cicero, Illinois —I can begin to answer that question for myself now. If a man builds on *all* his experience and lets life happen to him, he can afford to gamble and can afford an infinite number of new starts. For, if he learns from himself, then it is never just a beginning. And it is never

THE END . . . .

Current conditions in Czechoslovak labour camps and prisons

(Reprinted from Autumn, 1973, issue No. 5 of Pravda Vítězi!*— "Truth Will Prevail" published in London by the Committee to Defend Czechoslovak Socialists.)*

So-called Prisoners' Councils have been established. (Similar Councils were introduced in Nazi concentration camps). Members were selected by the prison authorities. Most were prisoners who were willing to collaborate with the warders and the STB (secret police), to inform on other prisoners and spy on them according to instructions given at regular briefings.

Many are criminals of the worst type. One example is Sozenica, who brutally murdered his wife, cut her up and put her into a suitcase which he delivered to her mother. He is now head of the Prisoners' Council at the Tesla Works at the Bory (Pilsen) prison. As a reward for informing, he is allowed to go into the town with his visitors at any time, and once every six months he gets one or two weeks' holiday.

Another is a killer who murdered his wife and dissolved her in acid in the bath. At Bory he has a privileged job: he repairs television sets. He is not only free to go where he likes within the prison walls, but he often goes into the town without a

313

warder on the pretext of buying spare parts for television sets. In return he informs on his fellow prisoners.

All informers enjoy privileges, both as regards work and pay: they receive special bonuses, they supervise the work of others, are free to move about the camp, and watch television at any time, may have visitors at any time and may receive an unlimited number of parcels.

The repressive measures taken against other prisoners do not apply to them.

Political prisoners are cruelly exploited. They have to fulfil incredibly high work norms and are paid absurdly low wages (some as little as 400 Crowns a month, even when they have fulfilled their target by 100 per cent). Political prisoners receive 9 per cent in pocket money; the rest goes to the prison management for their 'board'.

In all prisons pensioners are also required to work, and their pensions are retained by the State. They too have to fulfill work norms by 100 per cent. The disabled also are forced to work; in the case of one-armed prisoners, the norm is reduced by 50 per cent.

Warders (called 're-educators' today) treat prisoners, particularly political prisoners, with the arrogance of masters and slaves, although many ought to be behind bars themselves. Some steal commodities intended for sale. The warders in Mirov prison steal whole kilogrammes of tin foil for cooking purposes which is made there to be sold.

In Pankrac (Prague) prison warders steal furniture and plumbing and electrical equipment. In Leopoldov (Slovakia) prison they steal electrical equipment from the workshop of the EZ (railway electrification) works. In Bory (Pilsen) prison warders steal food from the prisoners' rations or allow the cooks to do so. As a result, the prisoners receive little or no sugar in their coffee and meals with little or no fat content and negligible portions of meat.

Political prisoners at Bory and Mirov are still denied the rights of political prisoners. They are segregated in top security wings with a particularly repressive system comparable to that applied to 3rd Category prisoners, although the courts classified them in the 1st Category (first offenders) at Bory and 2nd Category at Mirov.

Prison doctors and nurses treat sick prisoners not as patients but as prisoners, as though they themselves were warders. For example, they remove the thermometer before it has had time to record the prisoner's temperature, with the result that prisoners often work with a fever. The medical staff are loathe to prescribe drugs for prisoners. The chief prison doctor at Bory is Dr. Sadilek.

Lawyers may not speak to prisoners unless a warder is present. Political prisoners have fewer rights than common criminals, to whom warders usually behave in quite a friendly manner. At Bory prison Captain Karel Tvrklik, chief warder of Block 5, where the political prisoners are segregated, and the prison governor Major Jezek, are responsible for these conditions.

Theoretically, prisoners may send complaints to the Czech Minister of Justice and other central authorities, but all the complaints are forwarded by these bodies (if the prison authorities send them off at all) to the administration of Czech 'reform and re-education institutes' (prisons) which is staffed by warders who have been promoted to these high posts. All complaints are therefore doomed to be rejected, and severe reprisals are taken against their authors.

(Reprinted with permission)